Graceful Speech

GRACEFUL SPEECH

An Invitation to Preaching

Lucy Lind Hogan

Westminster John Knox Press
LOUISVILLE • LONDON

Scripture quotations from the New Revised Standard Version of the Bible are copyright © 1989 by the Division of Christian Education of the National Council of the Churches of Christ in the U.S.A. and are used by permission.

Book design by Sharon Adams
Cover design by Lisa Buckley

First edition
Published by Westminster John Knox Press
Louisville, Kentucky

This book is printed on acid-free paper that meets the American National Standards Institute Z39.48 standard. ♾

PRINTED IN THE UNITED STATES OF AMERICA

06 07 08 09 10 11 12 13 14 15 — 10 9 8 7 6 5 4 3 2 1

Library of Congress Cataloging-in-Publication Data is on file at the Library of Congress, Washington, D.C.

ISBN-13: 978-0-664-22877-4
ISBN-10: 0-664-22877-1

For
Kevin, Paul, and John

Contents

Acknowledgments   ix

Introduction   xi

Part One: Becoming a Preacher

Chapter One	Graceful Speech: Christian Communication	3
Chapter Two	A Great Cloud of Witnesses	15
Chapter Three	You the Preacher: Growing into the Preaching Life	31
Chapter Four	The Virtuous Preacher: Even in "Terrible, Horrible, No Good, Very Bad" Weeks	51

Part Two: Crafting the Sermon

Chapter Five	Fish of Every Kind: Getting to Know Our Listeners	69
Chapter Six	Where to Begin: Empty Pitchers and Living Water	87
Chapter Seven	Detectives of the Divine	107
Chapter Eight	The Sermon Journey	121

Part Three: Communicating the Gospel

Chapter Nine	Putting It Together	137
Chapter Ten	Seasons and Festivals: Preaching Special Occasions	157
Chapter Eleven	Open My Lips	173
Chapter Twelve	Communicating the Gospel: Looking Forward	191

Epilogue	Workers in the Field	205

Works Cited   207

Acknowledgments

As you will discover in this book, I frequently turn to the metaphor of dance when describing preaching. In the writing of this book I have had many dancing partners without whom this book never could have been completed. I can not thank them enough for their contribution as dancing partners—helping me to listen to new beats, to learn new steps, and to get the rhythm correct.

I would like to thank the members of the Academy of Homiletics and the *Societas Homiletica*, who have been wonderful conversation partners and have helped me to remember that we never preach or teach alone. I also appreciate the opportunity afforded by the Wabash Center's Consultation on Preaching, the chairs of the consultation, Thomas Long and Nora Tisdale, and all my colleagues in that important discussion, whose insights helped shape the structure of this work.

Thank you to the students, faculty, staff, and administration of Wesley Theological Seminary for offering me a year of sabbatical that allowed the time for this undertaking. In particular I would like to thank my colleagues in preaching, Laurence Hull Stookey, William B. McClain, and Anders R. Lunt, for long years of wonderful collaboration, for helping me to become a better teacher, and for stepping in during my absence. I also need to thank the fall 2003 Introduction to Preaching class for their help and comments as I put this book together.

Several people have gone above and beyond the call of duty, reading portions of the manuscript, getting me back on track, and offering encouraging words when they were needed: Susan Halse, James Wallace, and Susan Hedahl.

But especially I must thank my family, my sons Paul and John and my husband Kevin, who listened and listened, read, and read, and read this book and helped me beyond measure.

Introduction

Each and every day, each and every hour, maybe each and every minute, some-where in God's globe, the people whom God created and into whom God breathed the breath of life, gather to hear the good news of God's saving love for them. They sing and shout praises to God and learn how to live in the fel-lowship that gives them a glimpse of the heavenly community that awaits them. And each and every day, every hour, perhaps every minute, whether we call it preaching, a homily, teaching, or proclamation, someone stands before a community declaring the good news.

When I tell people what I do, I am often met with a puzzled look, followed by the question, "Can you teach people how to preach?" To which I joyfully respond, "Of course!"

Preaching is, to quote Thomas Edison, an intriguing mixture of inspiration and perspiration. Preachers are called by God and inspired by the Holy Spirit. But preaching is also a practice and art that can be studied and learned. Preach-ers are able to improve and grow in their preaching by listening to God and listening to skilled preachers and teachers. And so I offer this book to you, adding it to the marvelous collection of preaching textbooks that date back to the early history of the church, with the goal of strengthening the preaching of the church.

As I began this project, I asked preachers what they thought should be included in a preaching textbook. What had they learned in their preaching classrooms that they used every day? What did they wish that they had learned in their preaching classes, but didn't? What did they want to tell those who were just learning how to preach? Many of their comments and suggestions are woven into this book. I would like to single out one comment, however.

When I asked a friend what he wanted new preachers to know, his response was quick and certain: "Tell them that people are listening to what they say!" And I would agree. He is correct; people do listen.

As I write this introduction I am celebrating the twenty-fourth anniversary of my ordination as a deacon in the Episcopal Church. At my ordination I was given a Bible and reminded that the book was "the sign of your authority to proclaim God's Word." But while I was in seminary I had begun to learn that people do listen. During the spring of my first year of field work, the Third Sunday of Lent, I was given the opportunity to preach at the principal service. You can imagine how thrilled I was when I looked at the readings assigned for that day, only to discover that they included Jesus' warning that, "unless you repent, you will all perish," just as those who had been killed by Pilate or by the collapsing tower of Siloam. I worked carefully, preparing my sermon. I was ready, but as I finished preaching and looked out at the faces in the congregation, I realized that preaching was much more than my hard work and my study. Their silence told me something had happened that was far beyond my beginner's ability. I had done my best, but God had taken my message to a depth I would never have thought possible.

I learned that the people were listening. They were hungry to hear the word of God. And I knew that what I had learned in my preaching classes had helped to make that moment possible. It is my goal in writing this book that you will learn how important you are in the preaching equation. I hope that you will begin a process of reflection and study that will help you to become the best preacher God would have you to be.

To this task I bring many years of experience in the Episcopal Church. I bring the experience of being both welcomed and rejected as a servant of God. When I entered seminary in 1976, the Episcopal Church voted to ordain women as priests. But while the first regularly ordained women were ordained in 1979, acceptance is taking a great deal longer. Over the years I have had the privilege of getting to know and preach before many congregations. They have taught me what it means to be a preacher. You will find my sacramental background woven through this book.

I bring experience as a teacher. Since 1987 I have taught preaching at Wesley Theological Seminary in Washington, D.C. I write, therefore, out of an experience of teaching at a school that, although it is a United Methodist seminary, has a wonderfully diverse student body. I teach students of all racial and ethnic backgrounds, of a wide denominational background, students who will be serving both inner-city parishes and small, rural churches. You will find my ecumenical experience also woven through this book.

And finally, you will find that this book reflects my background as a rhetorical scholar. I did my PhD work in rhetoric and communications and have sought to bring that scholarly conversation to bear on my homiletical investigation.

In the chapters that follow I invite you into an exploration of what it means to be a preacher, who God is calling us to be, and how we can be the best preacher possible. The first part of the book, chapters 1–4, is devoted to the issues that provide a foundation for us as preachers. Chapter 1 examines a theological understanding that I believe informs who we are and what we do. Chapter 2 takes a historical approach to questions that continue to be crucial in the preaching enterprise. Chapters 3 and 4 examine your role and identity as a preacher.

In the second part of the book we turn our attention to the development of the sermon. Chapter 5 explores the identity and role of the listener in the preaching moment. Chapter 6 explores the preacher's approach to Bible study. Chapter 7 examines the other resources available to preachers in the preparation of their sermon. Chapter 8 discusses the form and arrangement of the sermon.

The final section of the book invites you to examine more effective ways to turn a written text into a *sermon*, the oral event of communicating the gospel. Chapter 9 focuses on language and illustration. In Chapter 10, we look at preaching for special occasions. Chapter 11 is devoted to the delivery and performance of the sermon. And in the final chapter I ask you to dream with me: Where is preaching going, and where should preaching be going in the future?

You have been given a wonderful gift in your call to preach. It is my hope that this book will help you as you learn to live into that gift.

Silver Spring, Maryland
The Feast of Ss. Peter and Paul

PART 1

Becoming a Preacher

1

Graceful Speech:
Christian Communication

All spoke well of [Jesus]
and were amazed at the gracious words that came from his mouth.
Luke 4:22

The moment comes when our eyes are opened,
and we see and realize that grace is infinite.
Grace, my friends, demands nothing from us
but that we shall await it with confidence
and acknowledge it with gratitude.
Isak Dinesen, Babette's Feast

My heart overflows with a goodly theme; . . .
my tongue is like the pen of a ready scribe. . . .
grace is poured upon your lips;
therefore God has blessed you forever.
Psalm 45:1–2

When people encounter the living God, they can't keep silent. The Scriptures are filled with the stories of those who met the living God, those whose eyes were opened and who realized that God's infinite grace poured over them. Likewise, the Scriptures are also filled with the words spoken by those grateful people and the songs they sang following those awe-filled moments.

Moses could not remain silent after turning aside and standing before the bush that burned but was not consumed. Filled with the grace of God, he stood in Pharaoh's court demanding the freedom of his people. Miriam saw the gracious love of God in the wind that drove back the sea, freeing the children of

3

Israel. She gathered the women about her and with timbrels they sang, "Sing to the LORD, for he has triumphed gloriously; horse and rider he has thrown into the sea" (Exod. 15:21). With grace poured out on his lips by the burning coal, Isaiah shouted, "Here am I; send me!" (Isa. 6:8). And in response to the heavenly messenger's invitation, Mary proclaimed that the living God, who called her blessed, would continue to overthrow the powers of the earth. God, she declared, will "[bring] down the powerful from their thrones, and [lift] up the lowly" (Luke 1:52).

Through burning bushes, winds, live coals, and angels, God has communicated with the people whom God has created. God has demonstrated the love that God has for them, and called them to be and do things they never thought possible. In return, God's people, through the very grace of God who has called them, have lifted their voices in unending praise and thanks to God. "The Mighty One," Mary sang, "has done great things for me, and holy is his name." And Paul declared: "Indeed, this is our boast, the testimony of our conscience: we have behaved in the world with frankness and godly sincerity; not by earthly wisdom but by the grace of God" (2 Cor. 1:12).

The great good news is that God continues to love us and do great things for us; God continues to pour grace upon our lips, calling women and men to sing songs of praise, speak words of justice, challenge, confront, and announce to a world, seduced by the siren's call of sin and death, this good news of God's love. Like Mary and Paul and all the saints who have gone before us, women and men continue to be filled with the grace of God enabling them to praise God and declare the good news that God is still turning that world upside down, scattering those who depend only on themselves, and lifting up those who have fallen.

DOXOLOGY: NAMING GRACE

Praise, doxology, Jürgen Moltmann argues, is the appropriate response to God's over-flowing love and self-donation: "Real theology, which means the knowledge of God, finds expression in thanks, praise and adoration. And it is what finds expression in doxology that is the real theology. There is no experience of salvation without the expression of that experience in thanks, praise and joy" (Moltmann, 152). Praising God keeps us focused on the God who created us and continues to fill our lives and our world with saving love. So, we speak of God's great saving acts, recalling what God has done in the past and helping the people of God to learn to recognize where and how God is acting today. As Mary Catherine describes it, preaching is all about "naming grace," pointing to the "power and presence of God" (Hilkert, 45).

We become, for one another, therefore, the burning bushes, the wind, and the messengers, called by God to announce to the world God's great acts and to bring the good news of God's overflowing love and grace. God has poured grace into our lives and has opened our lips so that we might praise God's holy name and speak to one another words of love and comfort. Likewise, it is the grace of God working in the hearts and minds of our listeners that enables them to hear this great good news.

We communicate the story of our God who spoke to us in creation, in the incarnation, and in the breath of the Holy Spirit because we are made in the image of God, whom we have come to declare is characterized by communication in loving relationship. Preaching is one dimension of that broader communication. To understand Christian communication and preaching, let us turn our attention to the Trinity, the relational God who communicates God's own self to us.

THE ROUND TABLE OF THE TRINITY

St. Patrick may have used the clover, but Andrei Rublev, the preeminent iconographer in medieval Russia, used the table to paint for us an image of the mystery of the Trinity. In one of the most famous icons of the Trinity, Rublev drew on the story of Abraham and Sarah entertaining the angels (Gen. 18) to portray within our world the relationship among the divine persons. Seated around an earthly table, Abraham's tent has become the temple of Jerusalem and oaks of Mamre the tree of life. Abraham invited the strangers to rest under the tree, and so in Rublev's icon we see the three angelic figures enjoying Abraham's gracious hospitality. They are seated around the table on which Abraham has placed a chalice. Each figure looks at or gestures toward one of the other figures, creating an open, circular image of the *perichoresis*, the divine dance that is God. The icon, Catherine LaCugna observes, "expresses the fundamental insight of the doctrine of the Trinity, namely, that God is not far from us but lives among us in a communion of persons" (LaCugna, "God in Communion," 84).

Recently, homiletical scholars have returned to this Trinitarian table as an image of preaching. Lucy Rose wrote about preaching in the round-table church, and John McClure described the "Round-table Pulpit." We speak, shout, praise, sing, and preach because we have been created in the image of this God in communion, whose grace fills the earth and whose breath and voice bring all life into being. "In the beginning when God created the heavens and the earth, the earth was a formless void and darkness covered the face of the deep, while a wind from God swept over the face of the waters. Then God said; "let there be light"; and there was light" (Gen. 1:1–3). The writer

of Genesis tells us that it was the very breath of God that moved over the water
of chaos, separating the land from the water, the dark from the light. God
spoke and trees, flowers, fish, birds, and humans came into being. We communicate with God and with one another because of God's self-communication
within God's self and self-communication to us.

In the doctrine of the Trinity we come to know who and what God is like.
As Catherine LaCugna observes, "The ultimate aim of the doctrine of the
Trinity is not to produce a theory of God's self-relatedness. . . . The doctrine
of the Trinity is an attempt to say something not only about God, or only about
the recipient of the divine self-communication, but about the encounter
between God and humankind and indeed with everything that exists"
(LaCugna, *God for Us*, 320).

PENTECOST TO TRINITY

At the close of the time of the New Testament, the early Christians had experienced God as *Abba*, as Christ, and as Holy Spirit. Luke tells us that after the
startling events of Pentecost, those who "believed" gathered together "praising God and having the goodwill of all the people" (Acts 2:47). They told of
what God had done in Jesus, how, though he had died, God had raised him,
and how they had been sent out to continue to tell this good news. But what
did it all mean? Who was this Jesus that they had known and followed? What
was the relationship between Jesus and the one that he called "*Abba*"? How did
the death and resurrection of Jesus bring about our salvation? While it took
centuries for the early church to begin to make sense of what was meant by
what we call the Trinity, by the fourth century the Trinitarian understanding
of God as one nature and three persons had come to be the orthodox position.

At the Council of Nicaea in 325 the church rejected Arianism and declared
that Jesus Christ was God, that he was begotten, not made, of one substance
with the Father. Jesus was not an intermediary or "demigod," but was in fact
God, who had come into the world. To speak of Jesus, who he was, what he
said and did, was to speak of the transcendent God. To know Jesus was to know
God. And this speaking, this reflection was made possible by the ongoing
grace of God, the Holy Spirit poured out into the world. Therefore, the doctrine of the Trinity declares that we know God because God makes God's self
known to us through God's saving acts in the world, but especially in the life,
death, and resurrection of Jesus the Christ, through the power of the Holy
Spirit. The doctrine of the Trinity tells us both about the *immanent* Trinity—
God's eternal being and inner life—and the *economic* Trinity, salvation history,
and God's relationship with us.

RECOVERING THE FULLNESS OF THE TRINITY

Over the centuries more attention was paid to the immanent Trinity, to God's nature, and less to the economic Trinity. Consequently, the doctrine of the Trinity came to be viewed as an abstract theological concept that had little or nothing to do with the daily, practical life of the Christian. We neglected the image of the table set in our midst.

At the urging of many major twentieth-century theologians—Karl Barth, Karl Rahner, Wolfhart Pannenberg, Jürgen Moltmann—the church turned a corrective eye toward the doctrine of the Trinity in order to renew and recover this understanding that is central to our identity and belief as Christians. The Trinity is not, they argued, an abstract, outdated, and outmoded thought. Rather, it is the way that we are able to speak about who God is, how God acts in our world, and how God is in relationship to us, to the world. Catherine LaCugna observes that the doctrine of the Trinity is

> the affirmation of God's intimate communion with us through Jesus Christ in the Holy Spirit. As such it is an eminently practical doctrine with far-reaching consequences for Christian life. . . . In Jesus Christ, the ineffable and invisible God saves us from sin and death; by the power of the Holy Spirit, God continues to be altogether present to us, seeking everlasting communion with all creatures. (LaCugna, *God for Us*, ix)

In other words, David Cunningham observes, "the doctrine of the Trinity postulates an integral connection between God's own character and God's relationship to the world" (Cunningham, 57). This character and this relationship shape who we are and what we do as preachers.

What does it mean to say that God is one nature and three persons? What are some of the characteristics of God with which we have been reacquainted by a revitalized theology of the Trinity? How do these characteristics shed light on our role as grace-filled, and therefore graceful, communicators? There are many, but three are central: relationality, mutuality, and participation.

Relationality

Many of us live in cultures that celebrate and prize autonomy and independence. Whether we ground that understanding in Descartes's *"Cogito ergo sum,"* or Frank Sinatra's "I did it my way," our sense of personal freedom and self-reliance takes priority over all relationships—with God and with our family, friends, and neighbors. Paul spoke of the church as the body, and each of us as a separate but necessary part. He understood that if I were an eye within the body of the church, I might be necessary, but without the hand or foot or others I could not function. Today we prefer to think of ourselves as full, complete human beings who join with other full, complete human beings. The church is viewed as a collection of separate, finite individuals who come together by choice, rather than a community that comes together out of necessity because we need one other. Do we understand that we *need* to be in relationship in order to be whole and complete? Rather than "doing it our way," what if we are to do it *God's way*?

To speak of God as three persons in one communal relationship is to speak of difference. The Father is different from the Son, and they are each different from the Spirit. Each is a distinct, unique "other." And yet, they are in a relationship of oneness. In this relationship, Elizabeth Johnson notes, "Relationality is the principle that at once constitutes each trinitarian person as unique and distinguishes one from another" (Johnson, 216).

In the Eastern Church's understanding of the Trinity, being in relationship was the "supreme characteristic of God" (LaCugna, "God in Communion," 91). In the *immanent* Trinity, therefore, the Father was understood to be a full and complete "person," but only when understood to be in community, in relation to the Son and to the Spirit; "the three divine persons mutually inhere in one another, draw life from one another, 'are' what they are by relation to one another" (LaCugna, *God for Us*, 270–71). If we think back to Rublev's icon of the Trinity, there are three divine beings sitting about the table, but to remove one would not leave an empty space at the table; it would remove the entire being.

Rublev drew on the image of the table, but early Greek Fathers referred to this relationality as the *perichoresis* of the Trinity. Close to the Greek word for dancing in a circle, this word presents us with an image of Father, Son, and Spirit in a dynamic, transcendent, self-giving, self-receiving "divine dance."

As preachers, we are engaged in the same kind of dance. As Martin Buber put it, "In the beginning is the relation" (Buber, 18). Our lives as preachers are informed by the reality that we are not individuals who choose to be in relationships, but rather we preach the Word in a milieu in which relationships with God and other persons—even when they are estranged—are in the foreground.

Mutuality

What is the character of the relationship among these three different divine persons? It is not just enough to say that they are in relationship. As David Cunningham observes, there are very different degrees and qualities of relationships (Cunningham, 165). Some are deep and long lasting, others superficial, and some are abusive. To say that individuals are in relationship does not tell us enough. The doctrine of the Trinity declares that the divine persons are in a relationship of radical equality and mutuality.

A principal argument in the development of the doctrine of the Trinity revolved around the relationship between God the Father and God the Son. As we noted earlier, Arius (whose ideas were eventually declared heretical) taught that the Father was superior to the Son. But, as Cunningham goes on to note, "One of the central claims of classical trinitarianism is that the Three are radically equal to one another; none is in a position of superiority over the others" (Cunningham, 111).

It is difficult for us, I believe, to imagine what that looks like and what it means to live in such a relationship. By applying the terms Father and Son to the different persons of the Trinity, we imply a hierarchical relationship. I certainly knew, when I was growing up, that I was *not* in a relationship of "radical equality" when my mother or father asked me to do something that I didn't want to do—mow the lawn or clean my room. We value autonomy and individual freedom, yet we also live in a world that compares and contrasts our autonomy to that of those autonomous others. Some are our superiors, others are our inferiors. Consequently, our thinking is challenged when it comes to the Trinity.

In spite of the fact that we speak about the Trinity in terms of the parental-filial relationship or numerically of the first, second, and third persons of the Trinity, theirs is a relationship of coequality. The persons of the Trinity join in the divine dance where all are equal; no one person leads and no one follows. Elizabeth Johnson observes, "They are coequal in divinity, greatness, and love. . . . There is no subordination, no before, or after, no first, second, and third, no dominant and marginalized. . . . The trinitarian symbol intimates a community of equals" where difference flourishes and does not exclude or threaten the relationship (Johnson, 219).

This image of a discipleship of equals also makes a difference for preachers and pastors who understand their responsibilities as speakers and hearers within the community of faith. Relationality and mutuality recognize that the authentic differences among persons, their sometimes enriching and challenging otherness, are part of the communicative structure within which preachers are called to engage in their task.

Participation

Another way of envisioning the relationality of the Trinity is the concept of participation. The persons of the Trinity "participate" with one another in a profound way. It is not just the idea of taking part in or working alongside someone. Rather, as David Cunningham suggests, "I am interested in those instances in which we take part, not in some*thing*, but in some*one*—an *other*. . . dwelling in, and being indwelt by, one another" (Cunningham, 166). Each person of the Trinity dwells in and is indwelt by the other persons of the Trinity. It is a deep relationship of communion and fellowship that characterizes not only the *immanent* Trinity, God's self, but the *economic* Trinity, our relationship with God, as well. God invites humanity to join in the dance.

Rather than dancing, perhaps we should use the image of juggling when envisioning the participation in and with the Trinity—the juggling of radically different things. How do we combine things that are different so that they are all equal and are able to exist in unity? How can we speak of a God who is omnipotent, transcendent, eternal, and at the same time, Emmanuel, God with us? "The Beyond and the Intimate," Ted Peters notes, is a challenge at the center of our relationship with God. He asks how we are to hold together "God's eternity and the world's temporality. To know God as only the eternal one beyond time is not enough. We need to know God also as intimate," as God with us (Peters, 19).

We know that intimate God in the life, death, and resurrection of Jesus Christ. We know that God in the Spirit who dwells with us, even until the end of time. We know that we have been invited by the living and loving God to participate in this relationship of mutual equality. The incarnation of the Word demonstrates that God dwells not only within God, but within us. "It would be hard to imagine a more thoroughgoing instance of mutual participating between humanity and God. . . . [And] the significance of the incarnation is precisely its revelation of a more intimate relationship between God and human beings than was ordinarily thought possible" (Cunningham, 181–82). As preachers, we model the intimacy of that relationship of the Trinitarian persons among themselves and with us. Pastors genuinely participate in the lives of those around them, and their preaching is part of that participation.

And so we lift our voices to praise the God who has created us, redeems us, and sustains us. We declare that God is three persons in one nature, in one joyous, divine dance, and that we have not only been created in the image of this dancing, loving God, but been invited to participate in this life of radical, mutually indwelling equality. The doctrine of the Trinity grounds everything we are, everything we do, and everything we say. It, therefore, is the grounding for our theology of preaching.

GIVING SPEECH TO MORTALS: A TRINITARIAN THEOLOGY OF PREACHING

If we have been created in the image of the God who is three persons in one nature, if we have been created in the image of the God who took on flesh and entered into a relationship, communicating with the human beings that God had created, what does this mean for our preaching? It means that we are incarnate, human preachers, who preach the graced word of God by the grace of God within a community of love and radical equality. But more concretely, what does a Trinitarian theology of preaching look like?

We Are Essential

Moses offered numerous objections when God called him to speak, not the least of which was his inability to speak. "O my LORD, I have never been eloquent, neither in the past nor even now that you have spoken to your servant; but I am slow of speech and slow of tongue" (Exod. 4:10). Moses thought that it was all up to him. He forgot the source and grounding for his message: "Who gives speech to mortals? . . . Is it not I, the LORD?" (Exod. 4:11). It is God who has given speech to mortals. It is God who will "be with [our] mouth, and teach [us] what [we] are to speak" (Exod. 4:12). We speak because we have been created in the image of a communicating God.

The temptation, however, is to think that we do not have to do anything, that God's Spirit will do all of the work. That is not true. You are an essential part of the divine dance that is preaching. God has called you to bring your thoughts, your questions, your experiences to the preaching task and preaching moment. Each of us has an important, essential role to play.

Each of the three persons of the Trinity is associated with a particular activity. For example, God the Father is the creator. This is known as the doctrine of *appropriations*. "We 'appropriate' a particular activity to one of the Three, in order that we might better understand its role in the overall divine plan" (Cunningham, 117). Likewise, we have been called, by God, into particular activities. There are times when we are to be the speaker and other times when we are to be the listener. Each is an essential, particular role in graceful communications.

The Preaching Round Table

If we go back to the image of the round table that is the Trinity, we are called to affirm that each member of the Trinity—Father, Son and Spirit—is essential. Who are the "persons" who gather around the preaching table?

God is seated at the table, the God who has called us to speak and who fills us with grace. There is the preacher, who prepares and delivers the sermon. And there is the listener, who receives the preached word of God. Each is an active, essential member at the table. We have been called by the triune God to gather at the table in a relationship of radical equality, echoing the relationship of the three in one. The preacher is essential, but not superior to the listener. Likewise, if you remove the listener, there is no preaching.

We are called to be in relationship with God and gathered around the table set by the God who created us. We are to view the preaching moment, not as the enlightened and learned informing the ignorant, not as the superior educating the inferior, but as all the people of God gathering to praise the God who gives them life and to declare God's saving acts in and among them.

Naming Grace

Earlier I wrote of Mary Catherine Hilkert's description of preaching. Preachers, she observed, are engaged in the important task of identifying and declaring God's saving acts. Preaching is "naming grace":

> Because human beings are essentially embodied and social, however, grace as the spiritual mystery at the heart of reality has to be manifested in concrete, historical, visible ways. God's presence is mediated in and through creation and human history, but that mystery remains hidden and untapped unless it is brought to word. (Hilkert, 47)

The Word became flesh and dwelt among us. We came to know God as one who walked in the world, who ate with us, who spoke to us words of justice and empowerment. We know that God loves us even more than life itself. God suffered and died as one of us and assured us that God would be with us "to the end of the age." Therefore, Hilkert observes, "preachers listen with attentiveness to human experience because they are convinced that revelation is located in human history, in the depths of human experience" (Hilkert, 49). As preachers we proclaim that "the creative Spirit of God who was active in the history of Israel, in the life, ministry, death, and resurrection of Jesus, in the church of the past, in the lives of the saints, is still active today" (Hilkert, 48–49). God is active and participating in every point of our preaching. God is with us as we begin to prepare our sermon, in our study of the Scriptures, in the crafting of the sermon throughout the week.

A CHALLENGE TO GET STARTED

God has created us to be loving, communicating people. This book focuses on one dimension of our communication: preaching. Throughout this book we will explore many of the variables in the moment, the event, the relationship that is preaching; and they are numerous. Whether you are reading this book on your own or as a part of a preaching course, I challenge you to reflect on a series of questions that are crucial to your preaching.

At first it seems rather easy to answer the crucial questions: What is a sermon? and Who is a preacher? A sermon, approximately ten minutes long, discusses the lessons appointed by the lectionary for the day, applies those lessons to the lives of the congregation, and prepares them to receive the Eucharist. The sermon is delivered by an ordained person appointed by the church. Yes, for some. For others, a sermon is fifty minutes long with a text that has been given to the preacher by the Holy Spirit, and it will end in an altar call. The preacher is the one anointed by the Holy Spirit. Yes, that is true for others. And for others the sermon is delivered by the teaching elder, will last approximately twenty minutes, and will explore the meaning of a particular biblical text, doctrinal issue, or pertinent topic. Which is correct? One of the goals of this book will invite you to understand how complex the answers to these questions are and to explore answers to these and many other questions.

You bring to these questions your experiences. You will explore them with your local congregations, and denominational leadership; you will explore them within your denominational tradition. Some of you are involved with congregations that have rejected the past ways that the church has answered these questions and believe that you are starting afresh to address these topics.

A major goal of this book, therefore, in addition to offering you advice and suggestions on how to write a sermon, is to invite you into, and give you resources for, answering these central questions. It is all too easy to learn the nuts and bolts, the "how-tos" of preaching without being challenged to develop a theology of preaching. Consider yourself so challenged.

Let's begin.

QUESTIONS

1. What is a sermon?
2. How is God involved in what is said?
3. What or who is a preacher? Who am I when I step into the pulpit?
4. What does it mean for me to preach?
5. What does the congregation think that I am doing when I preach? Who do they think that I am?

READ MORE ABOUT IT

Buber, Martin. *I and Thou*. New York: Charles Scribner's Sons, 1958.
Cunningham, David S. *These Three Are One: The Practice of Trinitarian Theology*. Malden, MA: Blackwell, 1999.

Hilkert, Mary Catherine. *Naming Grace: Preaching and the Sacramental Imagination*. New York: Continuum, 1997.

Johnson, Elizabeth. *She Who Is: The Mystery of God in Feminist Theological Discourse*. New York: Crossroad, 1996.

LaCugna, Catherine Mowry. *God for Us: The Trinity and Christian Life*. San Francisco: Harper San Francisco, 1991.

———, "God in Communion with Us." In *Freeing Theology: The Essentials of Theology in Feminist Perspective*, ed. Catherine Mowry LaCugna. San Francisco: HarperCollins, 1993.

———, "The Trinitarian Mystery of God." In *Systematic Theology: Roman Catholic Perspectives, Vol. I*, ed. Francis Schüssler Fiorenza and John P. Galvin, 152–92. Minneapolis: Fortress Press, 1991.

McClure, John S. *The Round-table Pulpit: Where Leadership and Preaching Meet*. Nashville: Abingdon, 1995.

Moltmann, Jürgen. *The Trinity and the Kingdom: The Doctrine of God*. Minneapolis: Fortress Press, 1993.

Peters, Ted. *God as Trinity: Relationality and Temporality in Divine Life*. Louisville, KY: Westminster/John Knox Press, 1993.

Rose, Lucy. *Sharing the Word: Preaching in the Roundtable Church*. Louisville, KY: Westminster John Knox Press. 1997.

2

A Great Cloud of Witnesses

Therefore, since we are surrounded by so great a cloud of
    witnesses,
let us also lay aside every weight and the sin that clings so closely,
and let us run with perseverance the race that is set before us.
Hebrews 12:1

Who or what is a preacher? What is a sermon? Who should be allowed to
preach? How is God a part of preaching? Is the listener a passive or an active
participant? You have been invited to join a conversation seeking to explore
the answers to these questions—a conversation, often quite lively, that has
been going on since the first preachers were called. This conversation, while
often contentious and frequently marked by wildly different answers to these
most important questions, has been, and continues to be a lively and heartfelt
examination of most crucial questions.

As preachers in the twenty-first century we join a great company of preachers who have gone before us from Mary, Peter, Paul, (no, not the singers), and
all the rest of that first generation of apostles, through Augustine and the
golden-mouthed Chrysostom, Francis, Dominic, Martin Luther and John
Calvin, Jonathan Edwards and John Wesley, Billy Sunday, Billy Graham, and
Martin Luther King Jr. Our family history is filled with great, and not so great,
preachers whose words joined with the word of God to move, challenge, and
shape not only the body of Christ but the world beyond the church walls. But,
while history students in secular high schools and universities today may read
"Sinners in the Hands of an Angry God," by Jonathan Edwards, not as many
preachers are familiar with their family history. As one of my colleagues in

church history was fond of observing, many preachers think that it begins with Jesus and that there is a direct tube to them, with no stops in between.

The reality, however, is that there were many stops in between, and the twists and turns of that history continue to affect and influence us. Consequently, it is helpful for preachers to become familiar with our colorful family tree—the mothers and fathers we can be proud of, the uncles and aunts we would like to forget—and to discover the ways that our brothers and sisters in Christ shaped their words for their people and their times.

The writer of the letter to the Hebrews used a powerful athletic analogy for the Christian life. As one makes one's way on the journey from Christ to Christ, he wrote, one might think of that journey as a race. The race can be challenging and at times difficult, but, as the writer observes, we are never alone. At every point, whether we are at the starting line or nearing the end of the race, we are surrounded by a great cloud of witnesses. Some of those witnesses are living: our brothers and sisters in the church, other preachers who support us in our task. But that cloud is also made up of the women and men who went before us. Their witness is very much a part of who we are, and it is important for preachers to listen to that witness. They will support, challenge, and enlighten your preaching.

How does one listen to that witness? A real challenge for most preachers is being able to hear the preaching of others. Fortunately, technology is making it easier for preachers, if not to hear preaching within the context of worship, at least to hear other preachers on tapes and discs. One of the ways to become a good preacher is by listening to good preachers. While there are many theories one can study in the classroom, it is always important to combine classroom work and the preaching literature with exposure to outstanding preaching. Listen to a wide variety of preachers: those from your own denomination, famous preachers, and those from different denominations and different cultures.

Don't limit yourself to current preachers. Go back and read the sermons that are available from our two-thousand-year history. My students are amazed to discover how fresh some of the messages are—sermons that, although they are fifteen hundred years old, could be preached today. They are also stunned to read the sermons of "great" preachers only to be left wondering, "Why was that preacher considered to be so 'great'?" The excellent histories of preaching listed at the end of this chapter will introduce you to our colorful past.

Time does not permit me in this chapter to give you a thumbnail sketch of our preaching history. Rather, I would like to introduce you to several key questions or tensions that are woven throughout that history, tensions and questions that continue to affect the preaching of today. Preachers of great faith have "chosen sides" and lived out their answers in very different ways. You are being invited to do the same. We will look at three issues: Are preachers inspired or trained? What are preachers' sources of authority? What is the relationship between preaching and the sacraments, particularly the Eucharist or Lord's Supper?

JERUSALEM AND ATHENS

Where does preaching begin? What are the roots of Christian preaching? We are correct to look toward the preaching of Jesus and then, following the resurrection, of Mary Magdalene, Peter, and Paul. But it is clear that the roots go much deeper. Which root should we choose?

During a debate in the early church, one of the church fathers, Tertullian, posed an important question: "What does Jerusalem have to do with Athens?" The growing church was being shaped and influenced by two very different worlds: "Jerusalem," the church's Jewish heritage, and "Athens," the classical world and its attendant philosophical approaches. John's Gospel sounds very different from Mark's because the authors lived in very different cultural worlds. Once the church moved beyond the confines of the temple and the synagogue, it was subject to new questions and new answers.

When Tertullian posed his rhetorical question, he did so with the implied response of "nothing." Tertullian did not want the church to have anything to do with the classical world. But if we look at the roots of preaching today, we will see that our preaching has been influenced by both of these worlds, Athens and Jerusalem. They set up a tension that remains today.

What do I mean? First, we will go back and see how these two worlds defined preaching, and then we will look at the tension that remains. We will begin by looking at preaching, or rather, human public speaking as it is developed in the Hebrew Scriptures.

Jerusalem

At the beginning of his Gospel, Luke tells us that Jesus began his ministry, not with a startling miracle—water into wine—but by doing the ordinary and expected, giving the message at his home synagogue. After his baptism by John and a time of testing his call in the wilderness, Jesus returned home and did what he always did, go to services. At that service he was invited to both read and expound upon the Scriptures. While it was what he said, not how he said it, that got Jesus into trouble that morning, Luke reminds the new church that the preaching that they were hearing at their worship services was grounded both in the preaching of Jesus and, by extension, in the preaching of their Jewish heritage.

The Old Testament roots of Christian preaching are rich. We are able to identify a number of different types of public speaking. Beginning with the call of Moses in Exodus, we are able to discern an important dimension that is a hallmark of speaking in the Hebrew Scriptures. The speaker has not only been called and appointed by God to speak, but God gives the speaker the message that is to be proclaimed:

> Then the LORD said to him, "Who gives speech to mortals? Who makes them mute or deaf, seeing or blind? Is it not I, the LORD? Now go, and I will be with your mouth and teach you what you are to speak." (Exod. 4:11–12)

Old Testament proclamations take many forms. They may be challenges to the oppressors: "Let my people go" (Exod. 5:1). They may be instructions to the tribes of Israel: "Now therefore revere the LORD, and serve him in sincerity and in faithfulness; put away the gods that your ancestors served beyond the River and in Egypt, and serve the LORD" (Josh. 24:14). Or they may be prophesies to turn the people of God back on the right path: "A lion has gone up from its thicket, a destroyer of nations has set out; he has gone out from his place to make your land a waste; your cities will be ruins without inhabitant" (Jer. 4:7). But whatever the form, they are all prefaced with the same introduction: "Thus says the LORD."

Thus says the Lord. It is God's message that is being announced or proclaimed. It is God who has decided what the people should or should not do. It is God who will give the words to the speaker who functions as God's mouthpiece.

Moses pleaded with God to release him from this calling. The only concession made by God was to bring in Moses' brother, Aaron, as the person who would speak. But notice, they do not receive any training or practice before they are sent into the court of Pharaoh. It is not the eloquence of Moses or Aaron that will move the heart and mind of Pharaoh. They do not make logical arguments. How is Pharaoh to know that they have been sent by God? How will Pharaoh know that the message he is hearing is God's message? It is confirmed by signs and wonders: sticks that turn into serpents, bloody rivers, plagues of frogs, gnats, and flies.

In his review of Judeo-Christian rhetoric, George Kennedy observes that the basic modes of proof in Old Testament speeches are grace, authority, and logos (Kennedy, 123). It is God's grace that will move the hearts and minds of the listeners. No matter what Moses and Aaron say, Pharaoh will not release the people of Israel until the God-appointed time. The authority of the speaker rests in God. God has called the prophet or teacher. God has appointed that person, directing him or her to a particular people in a particular place. God called Jonah and sent him to prophesy to the people of Nineveh. They are delivering God's logos, God's word, not their own. They are proclaiming to the people, not trying to persuade them.

Athens

When Peter returned from the home of the Roman centurion Cornelius, the Jewish Christians in Jerusalem were not happy. They recalled the words of Jesus who told them, "I was sent only to the lost sheep of the house of Israel" (Matt. 15:24). They were Jews who followed the Jewish laws and prayed the Jewish prayers. The stories they told were the Jewish stories. Theirs was the God of the exodus and the exile, not the gods of Olympus. "Why did you go to uncircumcised men and eat with them?" (Acts 11:3) Peter, and then Paul, were given visions of what was possible. God's Spirit was sent to Jews and Gentiles alike, and they were to welcome the Gentile Greeks to their table. In doing so, they tapped into another major root, that of classical oratory.

Rhetoric is a much misunderstood specialty. You won't need to watch the evening news for too long before you will hear one politician accuse another of mouthing "empty rhetoric" or claim that something is "just rhetoric." Well, in one sense, they are correct; it is all rhetoric. Rhetoric is the discipline that teaches speakers and writers how to construct a text and argument that will inform and persuade an audience, whether of one or a thousand. We all employ rhetoric every day each time we think about what we need to say and how we need to say it to achieve the end we desire; it is not "empty" at all.

In 467 BC Syracuse, the Athenian court system was suddenly introduced. In the court structure individuals were responsible for pleading their own cases. There were no lawyers who knew the law and could therefore construct the best case. Needless to say, some people were more successful than others. People needed help in learning how to craft their speeches and turned to two teachers, Corax and Tisias. These two discerning gentlemen sat in the courtroom day after day keeping track of the speeches of those who successfully persuaded the judges. They also noted what was done, or not done, by those who lost their cases. Corax and Tisias then taught people the tricks and patterns of those who had won their cases and how to avoid the mistakes made by those who had lost.

From these informal beginnings developed the classical schools of rhetoric, those of Plato, Aristotle, and Cicero. And their contributions continue to shape the culture of public speaking today. Their theories help us to understand how one persuades and the process one must undertake to prepare a speech, which, in turn, have helped to train speakers for over two thousand years. It is helpful for us to highlight the key contributions of two significant works in the classical literature, Aristotle's *Rhetoric* and Cicero's *De inventione*.

The Greek philosopher Aristotle summarized his teaching notes in 341 BC when he was Alexander the Great's tutor (Kennedy, 61). Rhetoric, Aristotle wrote, is "an ability, in each [particular] case, to see the available means of persuasion" (Kennedy, 36). Aristotle goes on to show his readers that, in order to persuade, a speaker must employ various proofs. Some he identified as "inartistic." Those are things that one might employ to prove one's point, but they are proofs over which one had no control, that is, examples, contracts, or the evidence of witnesses. What one is able to control are the "artistic" proofs.

While you may not be familiar with Artistotle's work, you probably hear of these artistic proofs all of the time. When seeking to persuade, Aristotle wrote, speakers employ three proofs, *ethos*, *pathos*, and *logos*. We persuade in part by who we are, our *ethos*. Do we appear to be someone our listeners can trust? Do we seem to know what we are talking about? Do we have our listeners' best interests at heart? If we don't, Aristotle taught, people are less likely to be won over by our arguments.

But it is not just all about the speaker. We must also be attentive to who the listeners are—using what they find convincing and putting them in the proper frame of mind. That proof is identifed as *pathos*. While we frequently cast that in the negative, saying that something is pathetic, this proof is actually essential to public speaking. Do we want to move a group of people to action? We won't have much luck if our speech leaves them lukewarm or bored. Likewise, if we don't frame our arguments using ideas, concepts, and issues that are of value to the people to whom we are speaking, it will be difficult to engage them.

Finally, Aristotle wrote, the speaker must employ *logos*, or the actual words and arguments constructed for the speech. Do we create arguments that make sense? Is our speech clear and easy to follow? Are our illustrations fitting and enlightening?

When all three—*ethos*, *pathos*, and *logos*, who we are, what we say, and how we say it—are in balance, the speaker has a much better chance of convincing his or her listeners. With this understanding, Aristotle's *Rhetoric* sought to train speakers. This helped second-century-BC Athenian speakers, and as you will see in this book, I think it continues to help preachers today.

By now you should be getting a sense of the profound difference between these two streams that sought to influence the development of Christian preaching. One, the Judeo-Christian stream, stressed the authority of God and the centrality of inspiration. The classical stream, on the other hand, saw preaching as an art that could be taught, with the speaker in control of what was to be said. But, before moving on, it is helpful to look briefly at the contribution of one other classical theorist, the Roman orator Cicero (106–43 BC). Like Aristotle's proofs, Cicero's "Canon of Rhetoric" continues to prove helpful to twenty-first-century preachers.

Significant changes had taken place in rhetoric's move from democratic Athens to imperial Rome, and little of Aristotle's subtlety remained (Kennedy, 92). Rhetoric was now viewed as primarily a tool of the political realm. Cicero discussed the parts of rhetoric, or what a speaker must do. Often referred to as the Canon of Rhetoric they are invention, arrangement, style, memory, and delivery. By invention, Cicero does not mean invention the way we currently use it, that is, Thomas Edison invented the light bulb. Rather, he means that when you are preparing a speech (or sermon), you gather all of the information, stories, facts, and figures that you will need to convince your listeners. That, he notes, is only the beginning. The speaker must then arrange all of these materials in the most beneficial and persuasive order; make stylistic decisions about the tone of language, the metaphors, and figures of speech to employ; memorize the speech; and finally deliver that speech. When we begin to explore the process of preparing and delivering a sermon, see if you don't think that Cicero's contribution continues to help you to understand the process and organize what you do.

There was a significant tension in the early church between the Jewish understanding of inspiration and the classical approach to rhetoric, or the training of speakers. Is the preacher one who can be taught and trained? Is the preacher the mouthpiece of God who is entirely dependent upon inspiration? If we look at the life of Augustine, we see both this tension and the compromise that has lasted over fifteen hundred years.

Like many of the other church fathers, Augustine was a teacher of rhetoric before he, much to his mother Monica's delight, became a Christian. But also like many of the other church fathers, after his conversion and baptism he rejected his former profession. No longer would he teach people to become speakers. Preachers were those who were to rely solely on the inspiration and direction of the Holy Spirit.

Do you know how to swim or ride a bicycle? If you said that you would never ride a bike or swim again, do you think that you could really forget how to do either? Of course not. And likewise, neither could Augustine, Ambrose, or any of the other church fathers who had been rhetoricians forget how to be skillful, persuasive writers and speakers. There is a reason that we still read their works: because they had been trained to be clear, engaging writers.

Although he was no longer a teacher of rhetoric, Augustine continued to be a teacher. When he became the bishop of Hippo, Augustine began to write his influential work *De doctrina christiana* [On Christian Doctrine]. Books I, II, and part of III were written about 396. In those books he develops his method of interpreting Scripture.

One of Augustine's duties as bishop was to visit the congregations under his care. In doing so, he had the opportunity to hear the preaching of his priests. If we turn to book IV, we discover why Augustine returned to write an addendum to his book in 427.

During his travels Augustine had discovered that the preachers he heard were, "sluggish, cold, and somnolent" (Augustine, 118). In other words, they were boring and confusing, and they put people to sleep. (Fortunately, you probably *never* have heard a preacher who suffered from this.) The teacher of rhetoric stirred within him, and Augustine found that he could no longer ignore what he knew would help his preachers. Why, he asked, should rhetorically trained speakers, who are "urging the minds of their listeners into falsehood . . . know how to make their listeners benevolent, or attentive, or docile in their presentation," while preachers who are declaring the truth of God, but who have not been trained, "speak so that they tire their listeners, make themselves difficult to understand and what they have to say dubious?" (Augustine, 118). Clearly it was necessary for preachers to combine the truth of God with the rules and lessons of rhetoric. While he claims that book IV is not a rhetoric of preaching, book IV is, in fact, the first rhetoric of preaching.

In book IV Augustine negotiates a compromise between inspiration and education, suggesting a middle ground in which the preacher, while called and inspired by God, is able to learn and improve his or her preaching skills through education, training, and practice. Although Augustine argues that there is a middle way, this has continued to be a crucial question and tension throughout the history of the church. Augustine did not consider his work to be a "rhetoric" of preaching, that is, a text book, but throughout the centuries since Augustine there have been countless textbooks designed to teach preachers how to preach, often presenting quite complicated formulas. But we also continue to find the rejection of classical rhetoric in preachers from Martin Luther to Karl Barth.

PETER AND PAUL

Another tension in preaching revolves around the issue of the authority of the preacher. If you are reading this book, you may be enrolled in a preaching course. Some of you may already be preaching; others will need to fulfill certain requirements before you are able to preach. In your church who is allowed to preach? Are there restrictions? Does one need to go to seminary, or be ordained, or can anyone preach? The apostles Peter and Paul represent two approaches to conferring preaching authority.

In his foundational work *The Theory of Social and Economic Organization*, sociologist Max Weber described what he identified as the three types of "legitimate authority": legal, traditional, and charismatic. According to Weber's description, *legal* authority is based on rational grounds or the belief in particular rules that grant to a particular person or persons the right to govern or lead. In the United States the president governs by legal authority. Americans accept the rules that describe who may be president, how one becomes president, and what the president may or may not do. For example, if a person was born in France, that person, even if she had become an American citizen and was wildly popular with the American people, could never be elected president. The president must be at least thirty-five years old and must have been born an American. Those are the rules and Americans follow those rules.

Traditional authority rests on immemorial traditions—in other words, we have always done it this way. It rests on the belief that the leader is entitled to lead because of these traditions or precedents. Queen Elizabeth is queen of the United Kingdom because her father was king, her grandfather was king, and her great-grandmother was queen. The "way that we have always done it," is that the eldest child of the reigning monarch becomes king or queen on the death of the king or queen. When Queen Elizabeth dies, her son, Charles, will become king. At that point he will assume control over the people of the United Kingdom to a certain degree, and his power will be based, not on a legal set of rules or regulations, but on traditional authority.

Some exercise authority because of certain traditions, and some assume authority because of a legal system. But if one is able to exercise authority over people by sheer force of character or exceptional powers or qualities or heroic actions, that person is said to exercise *charismatic* authority. This authority rests on the individual because of who he or she is. Unfortunately, it is all too easy to point to people who used their charismatic powers in destructive ways. Charles Manson and Jim Jones were terribly charismatic persons who gathered about themselves people who were willing to kill others or themselves at the order of their leader. But we might also point to Mother Teresa, who, even though, as the founder of a religious order, she exercised both legal and traditional authority within the church, nevertheless gathered about her a large and devoted following that extended far beyond the members of her order.

Weber observed that both legal and traditional types of authority were "forms of everyday routine control of action" (Weber, 361). They are, he wrote, rational, rule-governed behavior. Charismatic authority, however, according to Weber's observation is "irrational." He does not mean to imply that the charismatic person is irrational. Rather, he means that those who claim charismatic authority do so in a way that is "foreign to all rules" (Weber, 361). In Peter and Paul we see very different sources of authority.

Simon Peter

Peter was a family man and fisherman when he met the wandering teacher. Mark tells us that, as Jesus was walking by the Sea of Galilee, "he saw Simon and his brother Andrew casting a net into the sea" (Mark 1:16). Then, without any apparent conversation, Jesus demanded, "Follow me and I will make you fish for people" (Mark 1:17). What is even more amazing is that, according to Mark, Simon and Andrew did just that. They dropped what they were doing to follow Jesus.

Luke offers us a more complicated story. His account seems to suggest that perhaps Jesus and Simon Peter were already friends or acquaintances. After returning from his time of testing in the wilderness following his baptism by his cousin John, Jesus preached his first sermon in his hometown. (Let's just hope that your first "hometown" sermon goes more smoothly!) Jesus escaped the crowd in Nazareth and traveled to Capernaum, where he began his ministry of teaching and healing, much to the astonishment of the people in the synagogue there. Leaving the synagogue, Luke tells us, Jesus went to the home of Simon, where he performed his second healing, curing Simon's mother-in-law.

A large crowd gathered once again, although this time they were much friendlier and were hoping that Jesus would heal them as well. He slipped away and eventually found his way to the Sea of Galilee, but the crowds had followed him. Luke tells us that Jesus got into Simon's boat and began to teach the crowd. By the time Simon received his first command from Jesus, he had seen him heal at least one person, his mother-in-law, perhaps a second person, a man with an unclean spirit, and heard him teach. Nevertheless, Simon is still skeptical when Jesus commands him to "Put out into the deep water and let down your nets for a catch" (Luke 5:4). Simon explains that he has been fishing all night, catching nothing, and the best time for fishing has now passed. "Yet if you say so, I will let down the nets" (Luke 5:5b). Now Simon is visited with a miracle of his own: his nets are filled with fish. Finally convinced that Jesus is, indeed, a holy man, a horrified Simon confesses his sinfulness and begs Jesus to leave. Simon realizes that he is not worthy to be in the presence of this great teacher, but then Jesus invites Simon to follow him.

Throughout the Gospels Peter's story unfolds. It is a story of faith and foolishness. Peter is the one who understands at one moment and is clueless the next. It is a story of devotion and desertion. And, in the end, Peter truly is the rock upon whom the church will be built. He is the first voice to be heard following the flames of Pentecost, the nascent church's spokesperson: "Peter, standing with the eleven, raised his voice and addressed them, 'Men of Judea and all who live in Jerusalem, Let this be known to you, and listen to what I say'" (Acts 2:14).

It was Peter who was the first worker of miracles and, while not the first martyr, was the first to be arrested. But Peter claimed his authority, not only because he was touched by the Spirit's flames, but because he was the first to be called by Jesus and followed Jesus throughout his ministry. He claimed to be the rock because Jesus "appointed" him as that rock and commanded him to "feed" Jesus' sheep and lambs. That was why he was the person who first stood before the people of Jerusalem on the day of Pentecost. It was Peter who was the first spokesperson. It was Peter who declared to the crowd what they must do to be saved, "Repent, and be baptized every one of you in the name of Jesus Christ so that your sins may be forgiven, and you will receive the gift of the Holy Spirit" (Acts 2:38).

Peter was a person for whom rules and tradition were important. While it was Peter who announced that the Spirit fell upon Jews and Gentiles alike, opening wide the church, it was also Peter who determined the qualifications needed to be an apostle. With the death of Judas, their numbers were diminished. In order to restore their number to twelve, Peter declared that they must choose one who "accompanied us during all the time that the Lord Jesus went in and out among us, beginning from the baptism of John until the day when he was taken up from us—one of these must become a witness with us to his resurrection" (Acts 1:21). All could be Christians, but not all could be one of the apostles—a "witness to the resurrection." Qualifications were established, and requirements had to be met. Peter, therefore, would argue that preachers have the authority to preach because they have been appointed and have been approved by the church. To preach, one must have satisfied qualifications and criteria.

While we might argue whether Peter claimed legal or traditional authority, his actions suggest that, according to his conception, ministry is a rational, rule-governed process. One became a witness to the resurrection because one had been a follower of Jesus from the beginning to the end. This is certainly a far cry from the claim of Paul, whose call no one could see or hear but himself.

Paul

In his letters Paul is careful to provide us with his résumé. He wants us to know his *ethos*, his identity and his credentials. He was "advanced in Judaism beyond many among my people of the same age" (Gal. 1:14). Paul was "circumcised on the eighth day, a member of the people of Israel, of the tribe of Benjamin, a Hebrew born of Hebrews; as to the law, a Pharisee" (Phil. 3:5). For a Jew his credentials were impeccable; as an apostle, according to Peter's requirements, deficient. Paul, or Saul, had never even met Jesus. How could he claim to preach? How could he base his authority to preach on his "Jewishness"?

Luke tells us the story of Paul's call. At that point he was Saul, the efficient and well-known persecutor of Christians. It was Saul who directed the stoning of the first martyr, Stephen. It was Saul who was now on his way to search out Christians in the synagogues of Damascus. But along the way he was surrounded by a bright light and, falling from his horse, was addressed by the voice of the Jesus, whose followers he was persecuting. Jesus confronted Saul, excoriated him, and commanded him go into the city where he would be "told what . . . to do" (Acts 9:6).

Paul was a Roman citizen. Paul was a good and faithful Jew. Paul had been knocked off his horse and filled with the Spirit of God, called to become a follower of Jesus, one of those whom he had been persecuting. While he threw himself into his new life and mission with all the zeal he had demonstrated when he was the enemy of the church, what Saul did not have was the proper credentials. He had not been a follower of Jesus from the baptism in the river Jordan through the crucifixion on Golgotha, the resurrection, and finally the ascension. He had not gathered with the other followers of Jesus in the upper room at Pentecost. He had not been touched by the Spirit's flames. How could Saul, now Paul, claim to be a witness to the resurrection? To what authority could he appeal?

Paul appealed to one source alone: Jesus Christ.

> This is the reason that I Paul am a prisoner for Christ Jesus for the sake of you Gentiles—for surely you have already heard of the commission of God's grace that was given me for you, and how the mystery was made known to me by revelation. . . . Of this gospel I have become a servant according to the gift of God's grace that was given me by the working of his power. (Eph. 3:1–2, 7)

Paul believed that his authority to preach was given not by human mandate but by the risen Christ himself.

How does one become a preacher? How is one given the authority to proclaim the word of God? Is it God's call alone? Is it through a process of ecclesiastical validation? Do preachers and the church appeal to legal, traditional, or charismatic authority? The experiences of Peter and Paul, their presence in our history, demonstrate that there is no easy answer to these questions. We do not need to look far to find those who follow in the footsteps of both of our brothers in Christ.

Many of you are currently in the process toward ordination. If it is in the Roman Catholic, United Methodist, Lutheran, or Presbyterian church, you are required to meet certain standards, fulfill certain academic requirements, meet with countless committees and boards, and satisfy church officials that you are a wholesome, worthy individual. Others of you serve in churches in which one need only point to your calling before you are permitted to preach. And others are starting their own churches. Enormous churches are sprouting up everywhere, planted by wildly popular preachers whose only qualifications are that, like Paul, they have been called by God to preach. They have not gone to seminary, they have not met with any boards or councils, they have simply begun to preach the good news of the resurrection.

This tension continues, and you must be aware of how this tension affects you and your preaching. If you are a preacher who claims charismatic authority—that is, God has called you to preach and no human validation is necessary—you must be prepared to answer questions about your authority. Why should people listen to you? How are they to know whether your call is or is not authentic? Likewise, if you are a preacher in a church body that requires the ordained clergy to go through an extensive vetting process, how is God's call recognized or valued? Even though an ordaining board has approved you and an ecclesiastical body or a bishop has ordained you, people will still want to know how God is moving and acting in your life. They will want to get a sense of the Spirit's presence.

We shall return to these important questions in the next chapter.

ALTAR AND PULPIT

A third tension that continues to influence preaching and preachers revolves around the relationship between Word and sacraments. What is the nature of the principal Sunday service at the church you attend or serve? Does it include both a sermon and the celebration of the Eucharist? Or is the preaching of a sermon the norm, while the Lord's Supper occurs only monthly or quarterly? The history of preaching is marked by the tension between these two key elements of Christian worship.

We do not have a clear understanding about the worship of the early church. What we are able to piece together is that the early Christians met in someone's home to share a meal and to share the stories of Jesus. The first preachers were storytellers—often telling the stories of their own experiences following the itinerant rabbi who gave his life for them. When they broke the bread and passed the cup, many of them offered their body and blood in the same way, becoming martyrs, witnesses, through their own deaths.

When, under Constantine, the persecutions ceased and Christianity became the religion of the land, the stories and meals moved from the intimacy of someone's dining room to the grandeur of the basilica, the former Roman courts of law. With that, our worship became more formal; the stories became sermons, and the meal became the Eucharist. Not everyone could preach, and not everyone could consecrate the bread or the wine.

If you have an opportunity to travel to England or France, you will be able to see some of the great cathedrals that dominate the landscape. Sermons in stone, the cathedrals do preach. The windows and stone carvings tell us the stories of the Old and New Testaments. They tell us about Jesus and Mary. They tell us about the saints, the heroes of the church. Those cathedrals also tell us about a theology of worship whose focus was the celebration of the Eucharist. While the pulpits are large and commanding, it was the Eucharist that commanded the attention of all in attendance. Over the centuries, while there were periods when there was increased attention directed toward the sermon—in thirteenth-century Paris or through the preaching of the Franciscan and Dominican friars—the tendency was to focus on the Eucharist to the neglect of the sermon.

During periods of upheaval and reform we have an opportunity to examine what people think is important and what they think has gone wrong. At the beginning of the Reformation, perceived abuses and misinterpretations of worship drove some to advocate for changes in worship life. Luther, for example, believed that people should be attending worship services in which there was equal focus on the Eucharist and the Table, on the one hand, and the Word, Scripture and sermon, on the other. He did not agree with the practice of people attending the Eucharist but not receiving the bread or wine. And he did not agree with conducting a service in which no sermon was preached. It was time, he argued, for the pendulum to swing back to the practices of the early church, where all people gathered around one table to be fed both by the bread and by the word of God.

Soon, in some worshiping communities preachers were preaching sermons weekly. Unfortunately, the weaknesses of many preachers were quickly revealed and an interim measure was suggested. In the Anglican church a weekly sermon was required, but priests were forbidden to preach sermons that they wrote. Instead, they were required to read a sermon from *The Book of Homilies* that had been written by theologians and eminent preachers, principally Thomas Cranmer, the archbishop of Canterbury.

When pendulums swing they often swing too far in the other direction. Consequently, for many, one effect of the Reformation was a return to the focus on Scripture and the preached word, to the neglect of the celebration of the Lord's Supper. The sermon came to be the center of the service. We then entered a period in which some churches featured the Eucharist and, if not ignoring it, did not put too much emphasis on the preaching of the church, while other churches put great emphasis on preaching and rarely participated in the Lord's Supper.

Now many churches are once again seeking equilibrium. Some Protestant churches that have traditionally deemphasized the sacraments are experiencing a renewed interest in more frequent celebration of the Lord's Supper, and the liturgical churches have put renewed emphasis on the preaching of the church.

As we shall see later in the book, preaching does not stand alone. It is always a part of the larger worship service. And whether it is the hymns or the prayers, the sermon or the Eucharist, all preach of the glory of God and the good news of the resurrection.

As you begin your exploration of preaching, both the theology of preaching and the art of crafting the sermon, listen to the great cloud of witnesses that surround you on all sides. Familiarize yourself with how they crafted their messages for their people in their time. Listen to how they interpreted God's word. They have much to teach us.

You will also need to reflect upon the ways that you will negotiate these tensions: the question of inspiration and training, the sources of your authority, and the role of the sermon in the larger worship service. These are important issues with profound ramifications on your preaching. I would, however, encourage you to think more in terms of both/and rather than either/or. We can understand that God inspires our words, while at the same time realizing that we will better serve the people to whom God has sent us to preach if we take the time, not only to learn how to preach, but to continue to work and improve our preaching through continuing education. God calls us to be preachers, but the church, the body of Christ, is also involved in affirming that call, whether it is a church ordination board or a group of people who have gathered for worship. People are always evaluating whether it is God's word or ours. And the sacrament of the Word and the sacrament of the Table have never been, and should never be, a question of either/or.

We have all been invited to join this great cloud of witnesses, cheering on the people of God as they run the race set before them.

> O for a thousand tongues to sing my great Redeemer's praise,
> the glories of my God and King, the triumphs of his grace!
> My gracious Master and my God, assist me to proclaim,
> to spread through all the earth abroad the honors of thy name.
> Charles Wesley

QUESTIONS

1. Augustine offered a way to negotiate the tension between inspiration and training/education. Not all have agreed with his proposal. Where would you place your church? Where would you place yourself?
2. You are preparing to stand before a group of people and preach the word of

God. What has given you the authority to do that? Are you a Peter or a Paul? What can you learn from the other?

3. What is the shape of worship at your principal service? Is there a balance between the service of the Word and the service of the Table? If not, why not? Do you think that there should be?

READ MORE ABOUT IT

Edwards, O. C., Jr. *A History of Preaching*. Nashville: Abingdon, 2004.

Lischer, Richard, ed. *The Company of Preachers: Wisdom on Preaching: Augustine to the Present*. Grand Rapids: Eerdmans, 2002.

Thornton, John F., and Katherine Washburn, eds. *Tongues of Angels, Tongues of Men*. New York: Doubleday, 1999.

Willimon, William H., and Richard Lischer, eds. *Concise Encyclopedia of Preaching*. Louisville, KY: Westminster John Knox Press, 1995.

3

You the Preacher: Growing into the Preaching Life

Out of the mysterious place where words first come to be "made flesh"—that place which is all holiness—I am given the grace to work with words in a spirit of right livelihood that calls me to peace, reflection, and connectedness with communities of readers whom I may never know or see. Writing becomes then a way to embrace the mysterious, to walk with spirits, and an entry into the realm of the sacred.

bell hooks, remembered rapture: the writer at work, 130

GUIDES TO THE HOLY

bell hooks writes that she has been a writer for so long that "I can no longer remember a world without words on the page calling me, calling me to come inside and to find what Rilke names 'the deeps into which your life takes rise'" (hooks, xv). She can see herself sitting at the feet of her grandmother, Miss Zula, reading, reading to Miss Zula because Miss Zula could not read. Her heart aches to remember the embarrassment of her grandmother and all of the other elders because they could not read. But more than their shame she remembers

> their longing—their desire to be led into this world of written words. They never let me forget that they could not enter this world without a guide. And that my ability to guide them was a precious gift. . . . They never let me forget that I was blessed. To them words were sacred. To read and write was to partake of a sacrament as holy as our eating the body and drinking the blood of the divine in communion and remembrance. (hooks, xv)

hooks did not forget. She grew into her call and as she read to Miss Zula, "giving voice to passions she would never know—I knew then I wanted a life in words. I wanted to be a writer. I wanted to be able to enter this sacred realm at will and find there the meaning of grace" (hooks, xv).

For bell hooks, that was her call to be a writer. How have you experienced your sense of call to be a preacher? For some of you, it came as a sudden revelation. For others, it has evolved slowly over time, a gradual process of coming to understand who you are and what God would have you to do. I have known some preachers who described their call in very vivid terms. One woman told me that Jesus sat down next to her and told her what she was to do. For another, the appearance of a white dove on his porch railing confirmed his long-held suspicion that God wanted him to become a pastor, a suspicion he had long held at bay. Often there are others in our life, like Miss Zula, who are instrumental in helping us see what we cannot or will not acknowledge about ourselves.

In the opening chapter we explored the centrality of our relationship with God. It is God who has created us in the image of the one who lives in unity of relationship and who communicates with love. Our relationship with God is, therefore, central to our preaching and proclamation. We speak because we have been spoken to. We are sent out because God first went out into the world. But we must also realize the importance of others in our call.

When I was growing up, it was not possible for women to be ordained in the denomination in which I grew up, the Episcopal Church. Nevertheless, there were times when I was young that, like many of you, I "played" church. Yet, even though I did that, I never really thought of becoming a priest. Consequently, it came as quite a revelation when, as a college student in the late sixties and early seventies, I met young women from different denominations who were planning to go to seminary. But it was not until several women had been irregularly ordained in the Episcopal Church in 1974 that I began to think about ordination as a possibility for me. What I needed, however, was a push, and that push came from my husband, who wanted to know what I was going to do, now that he was finishing medical school. After weeks of asking me, one day, out of frustration, he challenged me, "Don't think, just tell me—what do you want to do?" Suddenly the words came tumbling out of my mouth, "If I would have been a man, I would have been a priest." I think that I was as surprised as he was. I had never actually thought of doing that until that moment. Not very dramatic, was it? No bolt of lightning or descending dove, but it proved to be, in fact, a moment of profound change—my life was never again the same.

Each call is unique, and it is crucial to your life as a preacher that you are *conscious* of your call. In his book *Presence in the Pulpit*, Hans van der Geest explores what he identifies as "aspects" that are crucial to being a faithful and effective preacher (van der Geest, 144–51). First, and perhaps foremost, he argues, preachers must have "*a sense of calling.*" They must have the sense that they have been "personally spoken to and engaged by the gospel and called to proclaim it to others" (Geest, 144). We have all been called to be guides to the holy. How have you experienced that call? When and how did you become aware that you have been engaged by God and by the gospel and that you have been "called to proclaim it to others"?

God has put you in this time and this place. Now what do you do? Therefore, before we explore the important issues involved in the preparation and delivery of sermons, we will first turn to an examination of you, the preacher, because, as Paul so aptly observed,

> But how are they to call on one in whom they have not believed?
> And how are they to believe in one of whom they have never heard?
> And how are they to hear without someone to proclaim him?
> And how are they to proclaim him unless they are sent?
> As it is written,
> "How beautiful are the feet of those who bring good news!"
> Romans 10:14–15

"How are they to hear without someone to proclaim him?" Preachers are an essential part of the preaching equation. Although we might agree with the prophet that "all flesh is grass," that we are weak and sinful creatures, nevertheless God has chosen to send us out into all the world to proclaim this great good news that God loves us and has given us new life.

As you will recall from the previous chapter, an important question throughout the history of the church has been whether preachers should be educated and formed by human teachers or should depend solely upon their call. I think that the answer to this tension lies not in either/or but in both/and. Preachers must be called, but they must also enter into a process of lifelong formation. Therefore, we begin by reflecting upon the task of forming the character of the preacher, and we do that by first turning to a discussion of the preacher's identity. The prophet praises the "feet" of those who went to proclaim this good news. So think of this chapter as a little podiatry work. We are going to be looking at your feet and having a Dr. Scholl's moment.

WHO IS A PREACHER?

Luke's Gospel records a pivotal moment in the life of Jesus. Returning to his home in Nazareth following his baptism, Jesus went into his hometown synagogue—as he had done countless times before. But this morning was different. After being invited to read a passage from the prophet Isaiah, this hometown boy declared to them, "Today this scripture has been fulfilled in your hearing" (Luke 4:21). Today, he was telling them, the man who sat before them spoke not as the little boy whom they had watched grow up, but as one who, filled with the divine spirit, had been sent to declare to them impossible things—that the blind will see and the lame will walk.

Luke tells us that at first they were pleased and astounded. They watched and listened as their friend was transformed before their eyes. But as he spoke with authority and confidence, their astonishment quickly turned to anger. Who does he think he is? Isn't this Joseph's son? How impudent!

If you have not yet had the experience of preaching in your home parish or congregation, you will, no doubt, come to that moment when you stand before a group of people who "knew you when." While we will hope that your experience was not, or will not be, similar to that of Jesus (try to stay away from cliffs), it will be a moment of revelation for both you and your listeners. Who are you? Who do they think you are? Who should you be?

Different denominations, different faith groups, have different conceptions of who the preacher is. In Presbyterian churches, the pastor is the teaching elder. Consequently, teaching features prominently in the sermon, and the preacher will not go wrong if she or he thinks of her or himself as teacher. In many African American churches, the preacher will sound very much like the prophets of old, calling the people of God to accountability and railing against the powers that threaten to overwhelm and crush those in their path. As you begin to think about who you are as a preacher and question who you ought to be, it is important to consider these different aspects of your identity as the preacher: Who are you? Who should you be in the pulpit? Who do your listeners think you are?

Who Am I?

First, of course, is the person you are, with all of your strengths and your weaknesses. You are the sum of your biology, your family and experiences, your education, your failures and your successes. An important part of the formation process, not only for preaching but for all dimensions of the ordained ministry, therefore, is getting to know yourself.

Think, for a moment about all of the different "people" that you are right now. You are a student, perhaps a pastor. You may be married. You may be a parent; you may also be a child. You may be a boss. In each of these different "yous," you speak differently and are spoken to in a different way. For example, I am both a parent and a child. I am very fortunate that my parents are still alive. But when I am with my parents, it doesn't matter that I have been married for thirty-two years, have children who are in their late twenties, have been ordained for twenty-four years, and am a professor; I am still their baby, their firstborn, and they still want to do things for me. (I don't mind, because I know that I do the same thing to my two babies, even though my "babies" are adults.) I am different when I am with my parents and when I am with my own children.

As a preacher you need to get to know and become comfortable with all of these different "yous." Each "you" speaks differently and relates differently to those around you. But getting to know ourselves is one of the most difficult things that we do. What are the gifts that you have been given? What do you do well? What are areas on which you will need to improve? (And you need to be honest with yourself. You hurt not only yourself but all of the congregations to whom you will be preaching if you ignore or dismiss weaknesses.)

You need to be honest about recognizing not only the things that you love to do and the people that you love, but also the things that you hate and the people with whom you are uncomfortable or who make you angry or impatient. What are, as a colleague of mine asks, your preferences and your prejudices, your commitments and your indifferences? Because of our biology and our experiences, we are never able to approach a person or situation neutrally. I certainly don't want to imply that we can never change—isn't that the good news of the gospel? But if we are honest, we must admit that we usually enter into a new relationship or situation with a preliminary impression. Whether we like it or not, we do tend to judge books by their covers. We make assumptions based on our past experiences and relationships. Therefore, who I am is often someone who has already made up her mind, who looks at the world through lenses that I have spent a lifetime developing. And those lenses shape the way I approach the vocation of preaching.

What have been key moments in your life? I do not mean only moments of religious experience, although they are crucial to shaping who you are and what you do. But what are the moments both high and low that you point to as having shaped who you are and how you approach the world? Phoebe Palmer, founder of the Holiness movement, always pointed to the death of her children as catalysts for her ministry. When John Wesley was a small child, a fire engulfed the family home. His mother Susanna saw, in his last minute rescue, a sign that he was destined for great things: "Is not this man a brand plucked from the fire?" (Zech. 3:2) What do these experiences tell you about yourself and what you think is important? How do some of them give you courage and confidence as you enter your preaching ministry, and how do others hobble you and hold you back?

When I sit down to begin preparing a sermon, I always feel the presence of my piano teacher, Mrs. Kneeland. Each Monday my sisters and I would pile into the car and my mother would drive us to Mrs. Kneeland's house. The ride was filled with silent dread. I knew that, despite my parent's pressuring, I had not practiced the scales, the exercises, or my pieces enough. I could play them, but only haltingly, fumbling around, searching for the key on the piano that corresponded with that little black dot on the scale.

As we drove, my sisters and I would play rock-paper-scissors to determine the order in which we would face Mrs. Kneeland. (I was not the only one in the car agonizing over the upcoming lesson.) My mother would drop me off, and with music scores in hand, alone I would walk up the sidewalk and into her house. In her living room she had two pianos. Two. I couldn't imagine. I would sit on the piano bench and she on a chair beside me at my right. We would begin. First the scales. Not bad. Then the chords. Not great. Then I would play the Czerny exercises I had been assigned the week before. Again, not too bad. But finally I would get to my "pieces." I never became a great pianist, but I did love to learn music. I still play for myself, and when I do, I sense Mrs. Kneeland's presence beside me.

While Mrs. Kneeland may have died many years ago, her lessons of hard work, practice, attention to detail, and knowing that everything you do demands your whole being, remain with me. What I learned at the piano bench in that crowded living room with two pianos, shapes who I am as a preacher and every sermon I prepare. I think that she was one of the Miss Zulas in my life.

Who are your Miss Zulas? Who are the people that have shaped you into the person you are today? What are the experiences to which your memory returns over and over because they have formed and molded you?

Who Should I Be?

No matter who you are or think you are, that is not the only "person" who gets up into the pulpit. You also need to think about who you think that a preacher should be. I have already mentioned two possibilities, the preacher as teacher and the preacher as prophet. But there are many other choices that we make.

Paul was born a Jew and was a Roman citizen. He makes sure to tell us those facts because they reveal much about his experiences and his education. (He also tells us that he was a star student, but he does that for a different reason, which we will talk about later.) Saul, a Jew with Roman citizenship—that was who he was. But in his letter to the Christians in Corinth he reveals an important dimension of preaching. "Yes," he says, "I am free and in Christ I have become a new person," but in order to speak to people and offer them Christ, he needed to become a variety of different people, or what he calls being a "slave to all" (1 Cor. 9:19). When he was with Jews, he emphasized his Jewish credentials, or we might say "spoke" as a Jew. When he was with those who followed the law, he spoke as one who followed the law. When he was with those outside of the law, "I became as one outside the law" (1 Cor. 9:21). If he was with the weak, he was weak; and we might assume that when he was with the rich and powerful, he portrayed a powerful Paul.

Who do you think that a preacher is or should be? Are you teaching or proclaiming? Are you announcing the good news or challenging unrepentant sinners? As preachers, in order to speak to different people we, like Paul, become many different people.

Over the years a number of different images and metaphors have been used to describe the preacher. In his *Introduction to the Homily*, Robert Waznak identifies four different images or metaphors for preachers that have been used frequently. As preachers, he argues, we are, at times, *heralds*. He reminds us that the most common word for preaching in the New Testament is *keryssein*, proclaim. "The preacher is like the herald (*keryx*) whose task it is to announce a message from the monarch" (Waznak, 32). The preacher has also been understood to be a *teacher*, the one who instructs both the new Christians and those who seek a deeper understanding of their faith. Under the controlling metaphor of *interpreter*, Waznak draws together a variety of images—pastor, storyteller, prophet—to describe the role of interpreting Scripture and weaving the connections between the text and the life of the listeners. And finally, he argues, we are *witnesses*. The preacher's "experiences, both mighty and mundane, are part of the stuff of life that needs to be interpreted in light of the Scriptures" (Waznak, 62). Take some time and think about the variety of possibilities.

So who do you think God is calling you to be as a preacher? It is important that you don't think of this as a facade or false identity. You are still you. You are still a person of faith who has been called to proclaim the gospel. But there are different ways that you can speak to people, reach out to people, ways that they will be better able to hear.

Are you a herald or a pastor? Are you a storyteller, teacher, or prophet? Many things will help you to answer that question and adopt different "voices" or, as it is described in literary studies, "personas" when you preach. You will need to think about the texts on which you will be preaching, the people to whom you will be preaching, their needs and concerns. You will need to think about the context. Is this a time that calls for the prophet to challenge or the pastor who will comfort? You will also need to think about what is allowed in your denomination or faith group.

Who Do They Think I Am?

That brings us to the final question: who do they think that I am? Your listeners come with their own set of expectations of who you are, who or what a preacher is, and what their relationship is to you as their pastor, their preacher.

If you need to take your car in for servicing, how do you decide who is the best mechanic? You may ask friends. You may check with the Better Business Bureau. You may ask where the mechanic trained. You may also ask the same questions when looking for a new physician. I suspect you may also be attentive to the doctor's "bedside manner." Even a diploma from Harvard or Johns Hopkins can't make up for a physician whose manner is abrupt and dismissive.

I began to get a sense of this when I was fairly new in the ordained ministry. I went to visit Mr. Musgrove. Mr. Musgrove was a spry ninety-five-year-old. I, on the other hand, was only in my mid-thirties. So, when Mr. Musgrove asked me what he should call me, I told him that he could call me Lucy. "No," he said, shaking his head," I don't think that I could do that. I will call you Pastor Lucy."

I had been raised in a time that had come to see a pastor as "one of the gang." I wanted to be his sister in Christ, his equal in the church. That was how I understood my role in the congregation. He, on the other hand, had a very different understanding of the preacher. I was the minister at his church. I could not be his equal. So, in spite of the fact the he was sixty years my senior, he could not bring himself to call me by my first name alone. I came to see that I had to respect his point of view, to be Pastor Lucy.

In the previous chapter I briefly mentioned the Greek philosopher and rhetorician Aristotle and his three proofs in a speech: *ethos* (the character of the preacher), *pathos* (the emotional or psychological state of the listeners), and *logos* (the words or arguments that a speaker makes). Aristotle reminded his listeners that all speakers employ all three proofs, whether they intend to or not. Each is important, and when they are out of balance, that is, if one of the proofs is featured to the diminution of the others, a speech will probably not be as effective at producing the results the speaker hopes for. Which of the three proofs would Aristotle identify as the most important? While we would imagine that he would argue for *logos*, the arguments developed by the speaker, he says that it is *ethos*, the character and believability of the speaker and the trust that the listeners place in the speaker.

Every time a speaker steps before a group of listeners—whether a preacher in the pulpit from which he or she has spoken every Sunday morning for years, an official on the platform at a national political convention, or a teacher standing in front of a preaching class, the people looking at and listening to that speaker are asking themselves a number of questions: Who is this person?

Does this person know what he or she is talking about? What are her or his qualifications for saying what he or she will say? Does this person have our best interest at heart? Is this someone we can trust?

In Greek, the word *ethos* means character. Someone's ethos was his or her character, developed over time. When this concept was imported into the Roman political system, the word *ethos* was translated as *auctoritas*, authority. It was no longer the internal virtue that one developed. It now referred to the permission that one had been granted by an external authority. The diploma from Harvard that hangs on the wall is the authority. The caring, gentle bedside manner is the character. Let's go back and look at Paul one more time to examine how he negotiated the character/authority tension. What did Paul do to establish his *ethos*?

Most of the congregations with whom Paul corresponded were a mixture of Gentiles, who were hearing about Jesus and the God of Abraham, Isaac, and Jacob for the first time, and Jews who had come to understand that this Jesus of Nazareth, who had been executed at Golgotha, was the anointed one of God. Nowhere was tension between these two groups greater than in Galatia. Did Gentile Christians have to practice the Jewish laws in order to be a Christian? Having accepted Jesus Christ as their lord and savior, did Jewish Christians have to continue to observe the dietary restrictions?

Paul opens his scolding letter to the Galatians with a reminder of who sent him to them. It was not a "human commission," nor was it "from human authorities." Those could be ignored or superceded. No, he had been sent by "Jesus Christ and God the Father" (Gal. 1:1). If they were going to be disagreeing with him, they would be disagreeing with the very God whom they claimed to follow.

Paul has established his authority, but that is not enough. He also feels that he needs to establish his character. After all, for many in Galatia, his reputation had preceded him. Like Ananias of Damascus, they were probably leery of Paul, a fact he does not ignore, but places front and center in his autobiography: "You have heard, no doubt, of my earlier life in Judaism" (Gal. 1:13). Paul models an important dimension of Christian anthropology. It doesn't matter who we were; what matters is who we are. Nevertheless, Paul realizes that it mattered what they thought of him.

In order to convince the Jews that one can be a Jewish Christian and not follow the way of the law, he needs to identify with them. He is not an outsider; rather, he is a Jew himself. And here Paul engages in a little self-aggrandizement. While he could just state that he too was a son of Moses, he reminds them that "I advanced in Judaism beyond many among my people of the same age, for I was far more zealous for the traditions of my ancestors" (Gal. 1:14). Why should they listen to him? Not only is he one who has always been a faithful child of God; he has been sent by God, their God, to proclaim the gospel.

Who do they think that you are or should be? There are, as I already noted, denominational differences. The expectations of a Baptist community will be very different from an Episcopal church. There are communal differences. If you are preaching in a small church in a rural community, you might have a different demeanor than you would if you were preaching in a large suburban church. Likewise, the situation might call forth a different person. You will be very different preaching at the church picnic than at a funeral. You need to become aware of the different possibilities and learn how to apply the right person in the situation.

THE DANCE OF *ETHOS*

Who do you think you are? Who do you think you should be? Who do they think that you are? The meeting of these different points of view has a profound impact on preaching, your preaching. A recurring theme in this book is that preaching is like a dance. There are a number of partners in this dance: God, you, your listeners. God calls us as preachers to coordinate that dance, to work together with God and with our listeners. If you are trying to lead without paying attention to what your partners are doing or what your listeners expect you to do, your preaching will look more like a wrestling match than the graceful moves of Fred Astaire and Ginger Rogers. Although we will explore delivery later, I would like to use delivery, particularly where preachers stand, to demonstrate what I mean by this "dance" of preaching.

Many of my students and many preachers I hear want—as I did in my meeting with Mr. Musgrove—to present themselves as the equal of the congregation. They don't want to climb up into a pulpit that towers over the congregation, that seems to elevate them to a higher position of honor. So, rather than preaching from the pulpit, they stand on the chancel steps or walk among the congregation as they speak. Some of my students return to class surprised when they report that their congregations don't like them to "wander" as they preach; they want them to stand in the pulpit. In part, they want them in the pulpit so that they can see them and hear them. But the parishioners also want them in the pulpit because that is where the preacher stands to deliver the Word of God. In this moment the preacher's concept of who a preacher is, the fellow traveler, conflicts with the congregation's conception of a preacher as the leader.

Where you stand, how you stand, your tone of voice, your pitch, your volume, your phrasing, the words you choose, the examples you employ, the look on your face, the clothing you wear, all combine to project an image of the preacher who stands before the congregation. Who you think you are, who you think you should be, who they think you are, all come together, and how you negotiate this will be crucial to your ability to preach to a group of people.

HOMILETICAL HABITS

When I walked up the sidewalk to my piano lesson, I had visions of becoming a concert pianist. While that never came to be, I did learn the lessons of hard work and practice. In order to play those Bach inventions or Chopin preludes, I had to play every day. I had to play my scales over and over again. I had to cultivate the habits of a musician. I had to practice the habits that would help me to become the person I wanted to be. Through scales and exercises I would be able to cultivate a way of being. This is true for musicians. It is true for athletes. It is true for engineers. And it is certainly true for preachers.

William Willimon observes in his book *Calling and Character: Virtues of the Ordained Life* that "Character is essential. We wish it were not so" (Willimon, 38). But, he argues, we need to develop the virtues and habits of the preacher:

> A person who desires to please God in ministry will desire to acquire those skills that make one an effective instrument for God. On the other hand, the skills required of ministry (like biblical interpretation, homiletical ability, pastoral care) reinforce our love of God and form us into more godly people. (Willimon, 41)

What are your habits? From biting our nails to sending thank-you notes, we all have them. The word habit is from the Latin *habere*, to have. In London, people drive on the left side of the road. After numerous accidents, officials realized that the "stop, look, and listen" we all learned as children would not work for tourists raised in cultures that drive on the right. When you come to the curb, before you cross the street what do you do? If you were raised in the United States or Canada, you first look to the left, because that is the direction from which you will first encounter traffic. After years of looking left, then right, you do that without even thinking about it. That is your habit. But in England, if you first look to your left, you may be hit by an oncoming car, because automobiles will be coming, not from your left, but from your right. So, at all of the intersections they have stenciled at your feet, in bold, ten-inch white letters, the reminder "LOOK RIGHT."

Where to look becomes a habit, and habits are difficult to break. A habit is something that you do so often that over time it becomes part of who or what

you are. A habit becomes second nature, so that you do it without even thinking. That is a good thing if it is a good habit, not so good if it is a bad habit.
Bad habits, as we all know, are a very difficult thing to break. Bad habits can
be most detrimental. But good habits can go a long way in helping shape us
into the people we want to be, the people God wants us to be. As you begin
your life as a preacher, this is the time to develop good habits of preaching.

Many things in your life as a preacher will intervene to make sermon preparation difficult: meetings to attend, illness, crises, the death of parishioners.
There will always be something that will keep you from devoting forty hours
a week to your sermon, as did the great preacher Harry Emerson Fosdick.
Now is the time to develop the good habits that will make responsible sermon
preparation part of who you are. This is also the time to cultivate the "habi-
tus," the way of being a faithful, loving preacher.

An important preacher in the early church was named John. Born in Greece
in 347, he eventually became the patriarch of Constantinople. So renowned
was his preaching that he came to be known by his nickname, Chrysostom, the
golden-tongued. Fortunately we still have access to many of his sermons. We
also have his writings on the ordained ministry.

In the *Treatise concerning the Priesthood* Chrysostom alludes to the habits of
preaching. What is important is his assumption about the work that the preacher
will devote to his preaching. In the midst of his discussion about the preacher's
motives, disparaging those preachers who have become preachers in order to
gain worldly fame and human praise, he observes, "For though the preacher
may have great ability (and this one would only find in a few), not even in this
case is he released from perpetual toil. For since preaching does not come by
nature, but by study [you can see on which side of this debate he has come
down], suppose a man reach a high standard of it [preaching], this will then for-
sake him if he does not cultivate his power by constant application and exercise. . . . the man who is powerful in preaching has peculiar need to greater study
than others" (Chrysostom, 71–72). In other words, as one's preaching
improves, and as one becomes a more skillful preacher, one needs more, not
less, study and work.

If you have developed what William Willimon calls "good homiletical
habits," you will be ready, not only to prepare your sermon, but to meet the
needs of those in your care. "Habits" is a shorthand way of speaking about a
way of life, the preacher's life. Too often preacher students are so focused on
learning about the writing of a particular sermon, the prayer, reading, studying, and writing that needs to be done for that particular sermon, we neglect
the development of our character. What are the good habits of a faithful
preacher?

The Habit of Humility

In his helpful and most engaging book *Just Say the Word*, Robert Jacks, with tongue firmly in cheek, reminds those who will be reading Scripture that the purpose of reading Scripture, and we might add of preaching, is to proclaim the Word of God—not to call attention to ourselves. "There's only one God," he observes, "and it's not you." (Jacks, 21). Our preaching is not about ourselves. That is why John Chrysostom was so distressed that congregations were applauding preachers, including himself. When listeners applauded, he believed, the focus was on the oratorical skill of the preacher rather than the good news. In his *Treatise concerning the Priesthood* he demands from priests preaching excellence, excellence that is achieved by long study and hard work, but that same excellent preacher must be "indifferent to praise . . . [if he] is overcome by the thought of applause . . . because in his desire for praise he is careful to speak rather with a view to please than to profit" (71).

You must learn to walk this very fine line by practicing the habit of humility, learning how to be the very best preacher that you can without getting, what we called when I was growing up, "a big head." We will return to this difficulty encountered by many preachers, given the nature of human sin, in the next chapter.

The Habit of Praise

John Chrysostom was worried about worldly praise, but while that praise is not helpful to the preaching enterprise, preachers need to develop the habit of praising God. As important as studying, which we will discuss next, is to the discipline of preaching, all of our efforts, our reading, our exegetical work can prove to be a purely intellectual enterprise if we have failed to ground that work in worship and the spiritual disciplines. As one of my colleagues reminds our students, we must always be attentive to nurturing our preaching spirit before we do anything else.

My predecessor in preaching at Wesley Seminary frequently reminded his students that they were to preach from the overflow of their spirit. How is your spirit filled? How is your soul fed? I always tell my students, when we come to this portion of our discussion, that I am about to give them one of the most difficult assignments of their preaching life. My assignment is that they find some place and some time to attend a worship service *each week*—a service that is not at their home church.

You need to set aside time for God, a time when you are fed by the prayers and preaching of someone else. I would encourage you to worship at a church where you are not serving, because you will find it easier to give yourself over to the worship experience rather than trying to "manage" the moment. Your need for Sabbath worship is no different from the rest of the congregation. The only difference is that your time may be on Wednesday morning. Your preaching will also benefit if you are able to set aside time each day for prayer and the reading of Scripture. How is God going to be able to talk to you if you don't create the opportunity for you to listen?

I might also pass along a suggestion by a friend. Each morning Bill rises very early, when the "busy world is hushed," and devotes that quiet time to prayer. An important part of his prayer discipline is praying for the members of his church family. He does that by working his way through the church directory, praying for the people one page at a time. Along the same vein, I know that some people put the names of different parishioners in front of them as they work on their sermons. It helps them to remember that sermons are written for real people—with joys, sorrows, angers, and hurts, who are struggling to be faithful children of God in a world filled with pain and sin.

The Habit of Time Management

Now if you are like my friend Susan, who is the pastor of an eight-hundred-member parish, you are going to challenge me, "I barely have time to write my weekly sermon. How am I going to find time to pray each day, let alone worship somewhere else?" This is definitely a valid concern, and it can also be asked about the next habit, that of study. That is why, concurrent with developing all of these other habits, preachers need to develop the habit of time management.

All of my former students would be able to tell you that one of the first things that I write on the board, in *very* large letters, the first day we come to discussing the actual writing of the sermon, is TIME. Good preaching, deep preaching, preaching that takes everyone, preacher and listeners alike, to new places, happens when the preacher has devoted time to that sermon—time for prayer, time for study, time for thinking, pondering, reflection, and time for writing and revising.

While sunrises and sunsets are a gift of God, calendars and clocks are tools of human invention. You control them, not the other way around. But how do you control time? How do you find the time to do all of the work that needs to be done? You find that time by making these things a priority and building your schedule around them—in other words, by making appointments with yourself. We always are able to find time for the things that we love doing. You need to develop the habit of "loving" preaching. If you decide that Monday morning, before the church staff meeting, is a productive time to start your sermon, block out that time on your calendar. That way, when someone calls asking to see you early Monday, you can honestly say you already have an appointment. (Remember, you don't have to tell them with whom!)

The Habit of Study

John Chrysostom wrote that excellent preachers need to devote more, not less, time to hard work and study. An important homiletical habit is that of devoted study. It is essential that you read, read, read. You need to continue the studies that you have begun in seminary: biblical studies, theology, pastoral care, church history, homiletics, liturgy. You need to read writers who come from a wide variety of theological and cultural backgrounds, including some very different from your own.

The importance of this was brought home to me recently when I was conducting a workshop on the preacher and the public sphere, at an international homiletic meeting in Singapore. Many of the preaching books in North America that address this subject argue that preachers must address important, controversial issues, must be activists. However, during our workshop I posed the question to the preachers present, "What are you not allowed to preach about from your pulpit." One of the women from Singapore spoke up immediately. "I can't say anything critical of our government. If I did, I would lose my license to speak publically for two years. Two years! Likewise, the preacher from Myanmar (Burma) also said that to criticize the government in a sermon could mean imprisonment. Preaching in those contexts is very different from preaching in Washington, D.C., or in Des Moines, Iowa.

Think of your studies as a conversation with the great cloud of witnesses. You want to include witnesses, living and dead, both from your own culture and from many other cultures.

A good preacher is also one who develops broad reading habits. In addition to the academic reading that you do, you will also want to read fiction, newspapers, magazines. You need to keep your mind active and engaged. I warn my students that I might just drop in on them someday, and when I do, I don't want to find that their libraries stop growing at the date of their graduation.

Preachers need to be aware of cultural and media trends. If everyone is reading *The DaVinci Code*, it is probably a good idea for you to read it. When there was the big furor around the Mel Gibson movie *The Passion of the Christ*, I felt that it was irresponsible when I heard clergy tell me, "I don't think that I will go to see it—it's not my style." They needed to see the movie so that they could answer their congregants' questions thoughtfully and responsibly. It is also important, even if you don't watch them devotedly, for preachers to be familiar with the top television programs. Those programs are shaping the worldview of the people who are listening to your sermons, and you should know what that world looks like.

As important as time is to study and the preaching enterprise, so is space. It is important for you to have a quiet space where you go to pray, read, and prepare your sermon. I have a wonderful book of photographs of writers in their space. Some want that space very sparse and plain; others write in a space that is filled to overflowing with papers, books, pictures, and mementos. One writer says that she always begins a piece seated on the counter in her kitchen with a pad of paper in her lap. (I wouldn't recommend that.) So when, where, with what—what kind of paper or pad, pencils, pens, computer or not—are important rituals to develop, rituals that are important to your life as a preacher.

Finally, recognize that, through your habit of study, you are making the commitment to be a lifelong learner. You are not going to stop learning when you finish seminary. You are going to want to participate in continuing education opportunities within the church and beyond the church.

The Habit of Play

As study is important to preaching, so too is play. We don't usually think of combining study and play, but they are not, in spite of what your parents told you, incompatible.

In the middle of the last century, a Dutch historian, Johan Huizinga, argued that play was as essential to our humanity as work. In his 1938 book *Homo Ludens*, he wrote that machines and robots would soon do most of the work. They would do it better and more efficiently than human beings. All that would be left for human beings to do would be those things that machines are not able to do—activities involving imagination and creativity. You are, he argued, not only a thinking person, you are a playing person as well.

Think of the word *recreation*. It is re-creation. Through play we exercise our body and our mind. We re-create our soul and our spirit. How do you like to play, to relax? What things do you do that give you a new lease on life and a whole new perspective? Perhaps you like to visit art galleries. You may like to go to the movies. Going to a football game or an auto race may be the way you play. My brother-in-law loves to drive his ATV in the Oregon mountains. We need a change of scenery. We need to see things in a new way. Find those ways that you play best. They are not a waste of time. Far from it. They are the way to best spend the gift of time that we have been given.

I would also encourage you to do something physical. You may not have the time or the agility to join a softball or bowling league, but you can certainly find time for what I like to call an "Eden walk." Doctors recommend a half-hour a day, and I think preachers should recommend that—not only for themselves, but for their congregations as well.

The writer of Genesis tells us that God was walking in the garden at the time of the evening breeze. Isn't that a wonderful image? We should all follow God's example and walk in the evening as the day is drawing to a close, or, as the hymn describes, as morning is breaking,

> Morning has broken like the first morning,
> . . . .
> God's re-creation of the new day!
> Eleanor Farjeon (1881–1965)

Find a park with a walking path and walk. Don't talk on your cell phone. Don't listen to your iPod or your MP3 player. Listen for the blackbirds singing, the wind rustling through the trees. Become aware of God's creation around you. Let it re-create you.

Physical exercise is also important for your vocal delivery. Leading worship and preaching a sermon on Sunday morning are very hard work. You will do a better job, and you will not get as tired, if you have prepared your body for what you have to do.

The Habit of Love

Finally, as Paul would remind us, the greatest habit is the habit of love. All too often we have the image of the preacher going into her or his study, shutting the door, and working on the sermon in blessed isolation. While sometimes you need to be working alone, it is important that you realize how important others are to your life as a preacher.

When you are making appointments with yourself for praise and prayer, for study and play, make a commitment to spend time with the people you love and who love you. Your family and your friends are essential to your life as a preacher.

Essential also are the people that you do *not* know. Your preaching will be greatly enriched if you develop the habit of reaching out your hands in love to the least of these. Service to the community is important for all in your church, including you the preacher. In Washington, the St. Ann's Home, a place of refuge for children since 1863, provides a temporary home for over fifty children. I have a colleague who made sure that every week, no matter what else she had to do, no matter what work was waiting to be done, she went to rock the babies. For several hours she would focus her attention on the little ones, the least of them. She said that it kept her focused and connected to God's gracious love.

And finally, as Jesus reminded us, you need to love yourself. You love yourself by taking care of yourself physically and mentally, eating well, and getting enough rest. Remember all of those things that your mother and teachers told you to do? They were right.

On my desk I have a small, smooth stone that nestles comfortably in the palm of my hand. I gathered it up one day when I was walking on the bank of a river, and I keep it in sight as a reminder. Whenever I am feeling as though my feet are not the feet of a preacher, that I cannot do justice to the call that I have been given, that I can't "preach like Peter or pray like Paul," I look at that stone. That stone reminds me of Jesus' encounter with the Pharisees as he entered Jerusalem. When they demanded that Jesus silence his disciples, he reminded them that "if these were silent, the stones would shout out" (Luke 19:40). If the stones can declare God's good news, then I should know that I can.

We need to do our best. We need to nurture our preaching life and work on becoming the very best preachers God would have us become. But in the end, we must rest in the knowledge that the God who calls us is the God who will fill us with grace and add our voices to the chorus of creation.

QUESTIONS

1. Jeremiah, Isaiah, and Paul gave us fascinating descriptions of their call to proclaim God's word. Write your call story as though it was going to be included in a scriptural book. Call forth the poet in you.
2. List three people who have had a profound impact on your life. What did you learn from them? What did they teach you? Where do you see their influence in the things that you do and how you approach life?
3. I explored several preaching habits in this chapter. But surely there are more. What habit or habits would you add to my list? Why?

READ MORE ABOUT IT

Clader, Linda. *Voicing the Vision: Imagination and Prophetic Preaching*. Harrisburg, PA: Morehouse Publishing, 2003.

Palmer, Parker. *A Hidden Wholeness: The Journey toward an Undivided Life*. San Francisco: Jossey-Bass, 2004.

Taylor, Barbara Brown. *The Preaching Life*. Cambridge: Cowley Publications, 1993.
Troeger, Thomas. *The Parable of Ten Preachers*. Nashville: Abingdon, 1992.
Westerhoff, John. *Spiritual Life: The Foundation for Preaching and Teaching*. Louisville, KY: Westminster John Knox Press, 1994.

4

The Virtuous Preacher:
Even in "Terrible, Horrible,
No Good, Very Bad" Weeks

I went to sleep with gum in my mouth and now there's gum in my hair and when I got out of bed this morning I tripped on the skateboard and by mistake I dropped my sweater in the sink while the water was running and I could tell it was going to be a terrible, horrible, no good, very bad day. I think I'll move to Australia.
Judith Viorst, Alexander and the Terrible,
Horrible, No Good, Very Bad Day

You have been worshiping each Wednesday at a nearby church that has an evening service. You have been rising early each morning for fifteen minutes of prayer and reading Scripture. You have just returned from a continuing education seminar on preaching to college students. You meet every other week with an ecumenical group of clergy who serve at churches near yours to study and discuss the lectionary readings for the upcoming weeks. You have even enrolled in a voice class that is going to be offered by the local theater group. You are pleased that you have been doing a number of things to develop the habits of the preacher's life. You can tell that this is helping to deepen, enliven, and enrich your preaching.

Then on Monday morning you arrive in your office early to get a jump start on a busy week's paper work. Seated outside of your office, waiting (oh dear), is the director of music. She follows you into your office and begins her tirade about yesterday morning's service even before you can hang up your coat. And before you have a chance to get a word in edgewise, she demands a raise, "or I'll quit!" She storms out of your office, without your having uttered a syllable. It's not going to be a good day.

51

Monday afternoon, after a succession of angry calls from parishioners, your sixteen-year-old calls to let you know that he's all right. Oh dear, again. He is all right, but the car he rear-ended (because he was paying more attention to the CD changer than the road in front of him) isn't. You then are certain that, to quote Judith Viorst, it is a "terrible, horrible, no good, very bad day."

By Thursday, when things have yet to improve, you know that it is a "terrible, horrible, no good, very bad" week. It has been a week filled with furious and raging parishioners, church meetings that have gone badly, people who shouldn't be ill but are, and you just hope that the wedding scheduled for Saturday evening goes smoothly because the mother of the bride and the bride have been fighting over every detail for two months now.

On Friday, when you were going to write your sermon, the head of one of your major committees and a much beloved "grandfather" in the parish suffers a heart attack while visiting his daughter in a town an hour away. So you spend the day at the hospital with him and his dear wife and daughter. This "terrible, horrible, no good, very bad" week shows no sign of improving, and now you are really worried about the wedding because you catch the weather report that predicts major thunderstorms with possible heavy flooding—on Saturday evening.

But before the storms hit, Saturday morning your precious sixteen-year-old, whom you have threatened to disinherit several times during the week, is playing in a soccer tournament and absolutely, positively has to have you there to cheer him on. You sit there in the stands hoping and praying that you will have two quiet hours in the afternoon to write your sermon at the end of this "terrible, horrible, no good, very bad" week.

When you go into your study, locking the door behind you, turning off the phone and your cell phone, you look at the clock and realize that those two hours have now become *one hour.* You have one hour to write tomorrow morning's sermon. Like Alexander who had that "terrible, horrible, no good, very bad day," you wish that you could move to Australia. But since you can't go surfing on the Great Barrier Reef, you begin surfing the net looking for ideas.

Not only do you find ideas, you find the most wonderful sermon, which says exactly what you would like to say about Sunday morning's readings. The theme fits your congregation, the stories are engaging, and you wonder—you don't have any time, you have just come through the most "terrible, horrible, no good, very bad" week that tested you at every turn, since you are tired, demoralized, and you wonder how much a surfer makes in Australia. As you print out the sermon to read it, you also wonder if it would be all right, just this once, to preach this sermon. No one will be able to tell, and you won't do it again, you promise to yourself. It's just that you have had this "terrible, hor-rible, no good, very bad" week, and if you have to write the sermon yourself, you are going to preach a "terrible, horrible, no good, very bad" sermon. You don't want to do that to your congregation; they deserve better than that. Just this once.

Just this once?

It seems reasonable for preachers to have performance anxiety, to worry about the quality of their words and the success of their sermons. As we sit down to write our sermons, we hear an onerous chorus of voices. We hear in the depth of our heart the warning, "I tell you, on the day of judgment you will have to give an account for every careless word you utter; for by your words you will be justified, and by your words you will be condemned" (Matt. 12:36–37). We are tempted to be conformed to the signs of success in our age—wealth, fame, power—because we compare ourselves to television per-sonalities who daily draw huge audiences with their humor and wit. And we cringe at the possibility of the wagging finger that shouts, "You're fired!" if one isn't creative, unique, cutthroat, obsessed, and single-minded.

The choir of our age sings anthems to individualism, materialism, greed, acclaim, and power. These are the hymns we hum under our breath while we write sermons about the one who came to proclaim that the first shall not be first. And we are apparently not struck by the irony of being consumed with concerns about finding interesting, engaging, stimulating, and successful ways to talk about the one who taught humility, lowliness. We are very full of our-selves while we preach about the one

> who, though he was in the form of God,
>   did not regard equality with God
>   as something to be exploited,
> but emptied himself,
>   taking the form of a slave,
>   being born in human likeness,
> And being born in human form,
>   he humbled himself
>   and became obedient to the point of death—
>   even death on a cross.
>   (Phil. 2:6–8)

How do we both empty ourselves and at the same time write and preach sermons that honor the God who has suffered and died for us? How do we humble ourselves on the one hand and do our very best on the other? How can we be talented, creative, engaging preachers who keep the focus on God and the gospel, rather than on ourselves?

HABITS AND VIRTUES

In the previous chapter we began a reflection on our identity as preachers by exploring our understanding of the character of the preacher as well as the habits that encourage the preaching life. We considered the crucial questions preachers must ask themselves, as well as the questions asked by our listeners: Who am I? Who do I think that I should be? Who do they think that I am?

We turned our attention to the questions that people ask, not only of preachers and public speakers, but many others. Is this someone who knows what he or she is talking about or is going to do? Is this someone who has my best interest at heart? In other words, is this someone who is going to urge me to do the right thing, or take advantage of me? Is this someone who will honor and respect me? And, of preachers, we ask, is this a person of faith? Can I tell whether this is someone who believes in God? Is this someone I can trust?

In his book *Calling and Character: Virtues of the Ordained Life*, William Willimon makes the distinction between clergy ethics and clergy morality. Clergy ethics, according to Willimon, is about "affirmations, beliefs, commitments, and character" (Willimon, 12). Ethics is the way we answer the question, "Who ought clergy be?" (Willimon, 11). Clergy morality is about action and behavior. Morality is about developing virtues. Virtues describe how we might answer the question, "What ought clergy to do?" (Willimon, 11). In the previous chapter we began our reflections upon who we ought to be, the habits of preaching. In this chapter we will reflect on the virtues of preaching, what we ought and ought not to do in our sermons and preaching. Ultimately, however, I would like to echo Willimon's instance that we cannot and must not separate who we are from what we do.

In his book *Preacher and Cross: Person and Message in Theology and Rhetoric*, André Resner explores the conflict between theology and rhetoric around the issue of *ethos*. Because of the antipathy between theology and rhetoric, and Augustine's compromise, *ethos* has been thought of primarily in classical rhetorical terms. He notes, further, that one of the results of homiletical rhetoric's "Barth Attack" was that "*ethos* found itself part of the quarantine" (Resner, 3). As a consequence, "a peculiar state of affairs has existed in homiletics with regard to the person of the preacher. Some, following Barth, have virtually omitted the category [the person of the preacher] from their homiletical schemes because of the donatistic suspicions that attend any *ethos* construct" (Resner, 3). As a result, most recent preaching textbooks devote little or no time to either the spirituality of the preacher or the ethics of preaching.

Clergy ethics, however, has been featured in the news lately. From sexual misconduct to financial misdealing to plagiarizing the sermons of other preachers too many of us have forgotten what we should and should not do.

In response to this situation, the Willimon book is an effort to help clergy examine both the clerical character, who we ought to be, and the virtues of the clergy life, what we ought to do. The Resner book narrows the focus to an examination of homiletical *ethos*—"nature and function of ministerial character for homiletics" (Resner, 3)—one that is "bilingual," both theological and rhetorical.

While this topic deserves an entire book unto itself, in this book we just touch on this important and complex issue of what preachers ought and ought not to do in the pulpit. It is impossible to cover all of the specific instances where preachers may step over the line of appropriate behavior and into irresponsible preaching, but I would like to introduce major virtues, with the hope that they will stimulate conversation and lead you to ask as you write your sermons: "Is this what I ought to be doing?"

In the classical tradition four virtues helped people to become good: prudence or wisdom, temperance, fortitude or courage, and justice. As the church moved into and developed in the classical world, Christians were familiar with the practice of the virtues. But they also knew that without God's help one could not be good. So, to the classical virtues were added the theological virtues taught by Paul in 1 Corinthians. After describing the gifts that were given to various individuals for building up the church—prophecy, teaching, healing, leadership—Paul makes a shocking disclaimer: "Strive for the greater gifts. And I will show you a still more excellent way" (1 Cor. 12:30). Yes, those gifts are important, he writes, but "as for prophecies, they will come to an end; . . . tongues . . . will cease; . . . knowledge . . . will come to an end" (1 Cor. 13:8). Faith, hope, and love are the virtues that will not cease, "and the greatest of these is love" (1 Cor. 13:13). To the classical virtues were added the theological virtues of faith, hope, and charity or love.

In the rest of the book we are going to focus on what you ought to do. In the remainder of this chapter we will look at some of the things that you ought not to do and will develop a list of homiletical virtues. Because, whether we like it or not, we do have to think about the fact that "on the day of judgment you will have to give an account for every careless word you utter; for by your words you will be justified, and by your words you will be condemned" (Matt. 12:36–37). Our words do matter and we must take seriously the charge, "If any of you put a stumbling block before one of these little ones who believe in me, it would be better for you if a great millstone were hung around your neck and you were thrown into the sea" (Mark 9:42). So how can we keep from becoming a stumbling block?

In the opening chapter we explored the Trinity as the grounding for our preaching. We return to the Trinity, to God, as the grounding for the virtues that will help us become the preachers God would have us to be.

THE VIRTUE OF TRUSTWORTHINESS:
WHOSE WORDS?

The easiest place to begin is with the issue of plagiarism. Easy on one level, but not so simple on others. Trustworthiness revolves around the questions of our respect for our listeners and our honesty. Whose words are we preaching? Whose words do our listeners think they are hearing? Our listeners must be able to trust us. As preachers we must be trustworthy because we are created in the image of our God, who is trustworthy.

Even as I wrote this section, the *Washington Post* ran a small news clip with the header, "Pastor Admits Plagiarism" (*Washington Post*, September 11, 2004, B9). It reported that the pastor of a church in North Carolina claimed his battle with depression was the reason that "parts of some sermons were stolen from other preachers." A member of his parish had heard a sermon on the radio that sounded like a sermon he had heard the pastor preach and had investigated the similarity.

There is a long history of reading the sermons of others from the pulpit. In the early days of the Anglican reformation, those in leadership were faced with the same problem encountered by Augustine a thousand years earlier. The preaching of the clergy was not very good, because they were not well educated and lacked homiletical training. While Augustine had encouraged preachers to seek rhetorical training (and read his book), the Anglican response was to prohibit the clergy from preaching altogether. Instead, they required clergy to read sermons from *The Book of Homilies*, a collection of sermons written by theologians and bishops. What is crucial is that those who were listening to those sermons knew that they had *not* been written by the person who was reading them.

The parishioners at a church in Washington recently made the discovery that their pastor, who had been called to that church in part for his great preaching, had in fact been preaching the sermons of another preacher. It was not difficult to prove. He had not only recorded the sermons, which he then sold, he had also sold books that were collections of his sermons. Of course, when "his" sermons were compared with the sermons of that other preacher, sermons that had been available on the Internet long before he preached the sermons, the parishioners discovered the truth of what he had been doing. Their preacher had not written the sermons and, in fact, claimed them as his own without the permission of the preacher who had written them. Unfortunately, it is not illegal to preach another's sermon without attribution—unethical perhaps, but not illegal. What was illegal, however, was the fact that he sold them in tape and book form as his own.

This is the easy case. It is wrong to preach the sermons of others while allowing your listeners to think that they are yours. While preaching textbooks may neglect the issue of the ethics of preaching, public speaking textbooks recognize that this is an important and serious topic that must be dealt with. They devote entire chapters to the issue. In his textbook *The Art of Public Speaking*, Stephen Lucas discusses plagiarism, which, he notes, is from the Latin word for kidnapper (Lucas, 42). In other words, you have kidnaped another's words and claimed them for your own. He encourages his students to learn what plagiarism is, because, "If you are caught plagiarizing . . . you stand to forfeit your good name, to damage your career, or, if you are sued, to lose a large amount of money" (Lucas, 42). Lucas identifies the delivering of another's speech, in its entirety and without attribution, as "global plagiarism."

But, let's move out into murkier waters. If I have written a sermon that you then preach as your own, you have committed global plagiarism. What about the situation presented by preacher and author Rick Warren, who not only gives his permission but encourages others to preach his sermon if they purchase his books or subscribe to his online materials? His preaching, he believes, has been successful in "growing" his church, and he believes that the sermons will help others "grow" theirs. However, even if one has the permission of the author, while preaching the sermon may not be illegal, is it ethical to preach the sermon of another?

Anglicans in sixteenth-century England were right in assuming that the person preaching a sermon was probably not the person who had written the sermon. We too are familiar with "ghostwriters." We are not shocked when we see one of the president's speechwriters interviewed on television. While we may romanticize the image of Abraham Lincoln penning the Gettysburg Address on the back of an envelope while riding on the train (which is probably not true), Ronald Reagan never hid the fact that one of his most famous speeches, delivered following the explosion of the Challenger space shuttle, was written by Peggy Noonan. Nevertheless, most people today make the assumption that the person delivering the sermon is the person who wrote the sermon. If people discover that you are not the author of the sermons you have been preaching, even if you have the author's permission, your listeners will feel as though they have been misled and that you have betrayed their trust. The parishioners of the church in Washington were hurt and confused when they discovered that their pastor had not written the sermons he was delivering. They questioned not only his ability to preach but his whole ministry to them. If they could not trust his preaching, how could they trust him in anything else?

Is it appropriate to preach the sermon of another if you identify its true author? Of course. There will be times when you do have a "terrible, horrible, no good, very bad" week and you aren't able to write a sermon. There will be other times when you do have the time, but you find the sermon that says what you want to say far better than what you could. Or you may be celebrating the feast of one of the great saints of the church; why not let him or her say it in his or her own words? Rather than preaching *about* John Wesley, you might want to read one of Wesley's sermons. As long as your listeners know that you are reading the sermon of another, you are standing on solid ground.

Global plagiarism is only one of the types of plagiarism described by Lucas. If you pick paragraphs or ideas from a number of different sources and weave them together into a sermon, again without attribution, that is "patchwork plagiarism" (Lucas, 43). And if you combine your words with the quotations and paraphrases of others, but do not cite them, you have engaged in what Lucas identifies as "incremental plagiarism" (Lucas, 45).

Unfortunately, the Internet has made these various forms of plagiarism altogether too easy. Preachers are able to surf the net and discover sermons, stories, and quotes that they easily cut and paste seamlessly into their sermon. Soon you forget which were your words and which were the words of another. But beware. While you may forget, others won't.

An administrator at a prominent seminary told me of an embarrassing moment that occurred when they had a guest preacher. During the sermon a number of people in the congregation, both faculty members and students, began to realize that significant portions of the sermon were familiar. They believed that the preacher was using stories and images from the sermons of a prominent preacher, but the preacher never attributed the stories and images to the other preacher. Their suspicions were confirmed when, following the service, they found the passages they thought sounded familiar in the other preacher's books. The preacher indeed was guilty of incremental plagiarism. But what could they do? When one of the hosts mentioned to the guest speaker that the sermon was similar to that of another author, the preacher realized what had happened and apologized for not citing his source.

A good friend of mine always delighted in telling the story of a service he attended. As a preaching professor who frequently wrote lectionary aids, he was used to hearing stories or images that he had suggested being used in other's sermons. He was nonetheless startled as the preacher began the sermon. Finally, as he was leaving the service, he shook the preacher's hand and announced, "That was a fine sermon. I wrote it!"

Preachers are advised to be careful and cautious. You never know who will be sitting in the congregation. And lest we think that this is a recent temptation, John Chrysostom warned his fellow preachers, "For if it has occurred to any preacher to weave into his sermons any part of other men's works, he is exposed to greater disgrace than those who steal money" (Chrysostom, 70).

We must practice the virtue of trustworthiness, being honest with our listeners.

THE VIRTUE OF RESPECT: *A HOMEMADE MEAL*

We are created in the image of the God who loves us and in whom we are able to place our trust. We also are created in the image of a God who respects and honors us. Ours is a God who is faithful and constant, who leads us through the darkest of times and spreads life joyously and abundantly before us. We are invited to follow in God's footsteps by loving and honoring those whom we are called to serve.

My youngest son is still in college, living 500 miles away, which means he does not get a home cooked meal very often. When he does come home, I make sure to ask him what meals he wants me to cook for him while he is here. I always know that sometime during his visit I am going to be making his favorite dishes. There is nothing like a homemade meal.

What, you might ask, does this have to do with preaching? I would argue that many preachers, like those who have gotten into the habit of heating prepared food in the microwave for dinner, have turned to dishing up "canned" stories and serving "store-bought" images in their sermons. We must respect the intelligence, the creativity, and the faithfulness of those to whom we are speaking. We must spread a table of our freshest and our finest before them, just as God has done for us.

Can you tell the difference between a freshly made chicken soup and soup that was poured from a can? Of course. So too can a congregation tell the difference between an example that you saw or experienced and one that was pulled from a resource like *Chicken Soup for the Soul*. While they are often great stories, they have come out of someone else's experience. Our delivery is much different and much more engaging when we have gone through an experience firsthand rather than secondhand. I speak about the assassination of John Kennedy much differently from that of Abraham Lincoln because I lived through the former, not the latter. Likewise, I know from my parents that Pearl Harbor had a profound impact on the American people, but I cannot talk about in the same way that I can about the events and the effects of September 11. I have learned about Pearl Harbor from my parent's stories and from accounts in history books; I lived through September 11 in Washington, D.C.

I don't mean to suggest that we should never talk about historical events or tell stories about others. Our sermons should be a healthy mix of firsthand and secondhand stories. We will return to a fuller discussion of the use of stories, illustrations, and examples later in the book, but at this point I want to focus on the virtue of doing the careful work of "naming grace," looking about your life and the life of the congregation to discern where and how God is acting in your lives—here, now, today.

Like a sweet-smelling bakery, preachers are tantalized by books and Web sites that are filled with stories and illustrations, often already linked to Scripture texts or topics. Are you going to be preaching about Luke 15, the lost son and the all-forgiving father? Enter the Scripture citation, and you will be directed to countless stories about the relationship between parents and children, about people who have forgiven and who have been forgiven. All you have to do is "paste" that into your sermon.

What you discover in these books and on these Web sites may be delightful and engaging stories; however, you are merely reporting the work of someone else. What if you become a grace detective? How different will be the fruits of your investigations! And how much more will you respect and engage those who listen to your sermons! Remember, our message is "Christ is risen. I have seen the Lord," not "Let me tell you about someone who saw the risen Christ."

Mary Catherine Hilkert argues that "God's word of salvation, hope, healing, and liberation is being spoken in new ways today in people's daily lives" (Hilkert, 48). To help people understand God's exuberant, extravagant, all-forgiving love, Jesus told people about a father and his two sons. He told them a story with which many were no doubt familiar. Preachers, Hilkert goes on to say, "listen with attentiveness to human experience because they are convinced that revelation is located in human history, in the depths of human experience—a mystery that should not come as such a surprise to those who profess a belief in the incarnation" (Hilkert, 49). Preaching, therefore, is "naming grace . . . naming the presence of God in human experience" (Hilkert, 49).

If you begin your week by reading Luke 15:11–32, then, whether it is a "terrible, horrible, no good, very bad" week, or a wonderful, joyous, excellent, very good week, you will open the eyes of your mind and your heart to see where God is working in our world. Through your prayers, your reading, the people you meet, the things you see, you will discover God's presence and you will help your listeners learn to discover where God is working in their lives. What is important is that *you* will be doing that work, *you* will be making the discoveries, not reporting on someone else's.

Does this mean that you will be able to talk only about things that you have experienced firsthand? By no means. But we will explore this later in chapter 9. What is important here is that you demonstrate your respect for your listeners by doing the hard work yourself and not depending upon others.

THE VIRTUE OF AWE: *DEEP CALLS TO DEEP*

"My heart stands in awe of your words. I rejoice at your word like one who finds great spoil" (Ps. 119:161b–62). Awe, according to *The New Oxford Amer-*

ican Dictionary, is "the feeling of reverential respect mixed with fear or won-der" (*NOAD*, 112). The great depth and wonder of God's love reach out to us: "Deep calls to deep at the thunder of your cataracts" (Ps. 42:7). Responsible preaching is preaching that approaches its task with reverence and awe, out of the profound depths of our souls and to the depths of the lives of others. Our preaching must reflect our great amazement that our great God has reached out to us, has become one of us, has been willing to both live and die for us, and that in God we have been given the gift of new life. Stepping into a pul-pit or before a congregation to preach calls for a preacher who takes his or her responsibility seriously. It does not mean that one can't laugh in the pulpit, but it does mean that you must always be aware that we are taking about impor-tant, life-and-death subjects.

As I write this book, a small controversy is brewing over two different approaches to the news and current events. On the one hand you have the tra-ditional—or if you will, the serious—news programs of the networks. On the other hand you have programs that, while looking like a traditional news pro-gram with an "anchor" and "reporters," are "reporting" on the events of the day with humor, their tongues firmly in their cheeks. Needless to say, while such programs are very popular, they are not popular with the serious or "real" network news teams. Those who consider themselves serious journalists do not appreciate those who approach serious issues with satire, mocking what they do.

Look around your study. Where is your Bible? Is it under a pile of other books? In Islam, the Qur'an is treated with great respect. It must always be handled carefully and gently, and one must always put it in a place of honor. No other books or papers must ever be put on top of the Qur'an because it represents the word of life. We show a similar attitude when we read Scripture during a worship service. We read carefully, and many of us end our reading by declaring that what has just been read and heard is "the Word of God."

We are called to treat the sermon with the same respect. It is not a time to stand in front of a group of people and talk to them as though we were a standup comedian. It is not a time to don bunny ears to preach a children's ser-mon on Easter morning, as one pastor did. It is not a time to make flip, sar-castic comments about anyone or any group.

But the awe of our sermon does not come from us; it comes from the God who has created and redeemed us. We do not need to manipulate our listen-ers with stories that will make them weep. We only have to tell them the sto-ries of what God has done for us. Theologian and playwright Dorothy L. Sayers, writing in the mid-twentieth century, argued against those who attrib-uted the drama of her religious plays to her skills as a writer. "I protested in vain against this flattering tribute to my power of invention" (Sayers,

"Dogma," 24). Her plays made the gospel come alive, not because she took out the Christian doctrines and dogma, but because "the dogma was the drama" (Sayers, "Dogma," 24). She goes on to remind us,

> Let us, in heaven's name, drag out the divine drama from under the dreadful accumulation of slipshod thinking and trashy sentiment heaped upon it, and set it on an open stage to startle the world. . . . It is the dogma that is the drama—not beautiful phrases, nor comforting sentiments . . . but the terrifying assertion that the same God who made the world, lived in the world and passed through the grave and gate of death. (Sayers, "Dogma," 27–28)

Seeking to make the gospel story come alive for people caught up in the horrors of war, in the early 1940s Dorothy Sayers wrote a cycle of twelve plays surrounding the life of Jesus, *The Man Born to be King*. It was her goal, she wrote of the plays, "not to subordinate the drama to the theology, but to approach the job of truth-telling from his own end, and trust the theology to emerge undistorted from the dramatic presentation of the story" (Sayers, *Man Born*, 4). Sayers sought to take the gospel story beyond, "comfortable persuasion . . . assisted by stately and ancient language . . . and by the general air of stained-glass-window decorum" (Sayers, *Man Born*, 6). She replaced "sacred personages standing about in symbolic attitudes," with people who spoke in modern speech and "determined historical realism." By doing that, she felt, we would be able to see that the gospel story is our story and that we must throw ourselves into that divine drama.

Out of the depths God has come to us, and into the depths of life God sends us.

THE VIRTUE OF COURAGE:
STEPPING OUT WITH BOLDNESS

Dorothy L. Sayers claimed that the classical Christian virtues had been recast into "Respectability; childishness; mental timidity; dullness; sentimentality; censoriousness; and depression of spirits" (Sayers, "Dogma," 26). But we are not created in the image of a respectable, timid God. We are created in the image of a God who is not cowered by the armies of Pharaoh, but turns rivers into dry land, delivers water out of stone, and covers the land with food so that the children of God might be free. We are created in the image of a God who loves us even when we turn away, even when we squander our inheritance. We are created in the image of a God who speaks to the outcast, lifts up the fallen, and mends the broken. We are called to be preachers who develop the virtue of courage, the courage to speak to the powers and principalities of this world, the courage to love the unlovable, to reach out to those whom the world has rejected. We are called to be prophets of the Most High. A prophet is one who names the grace of God active in the world—courageously.

We are to develop the virtue of courage. We must not be timid. We are not to measure our words out with teaspoons. Rather we are boldly to overflow with good news, even when it might cost us our life.

> Give, and it will be given to you.
> A good measure, pressed down, shaken together, running over,
> will be put into your lap;
> for the measure you give will be the measure you get back.
>   (Luke 6:38)

When he became a priest, Oscar Romero measured his words out with a teaspoon. A priest who lived with him when he first came to San Salvador wrote that he did not like Romero. While the eyes of all of the other priests had been open to the injustice and oppression that filled the lives of the women and men in their country, Romero preferred to work in his office. He was uncomfortable with their activism and anger, so he avoided speaking with them. He took his meals long after everyone had left the dining room. But slowly the grace of God began to open Romero's eyes and fill his heart with love for the poor of his country.

When he was appointed the archbishop of the archdiocese of San Salvador in February of 1977, the powers and principalities that ruled his country were not worried. They were not worried about the quiet administrator who never troubled the waters or ruffled any feathers. But shortly after Romero became archbishop, one of his priests was brutally murdered. When it became apparent to all that this murder had been sanctioned and carried out by government officials, Archbishop Romero began to measure his words with bushel baskets —full to overflowing with God's good news of new life and rejection of injustice. He spoke out against the government's injustice in his sermons, in interviews, in his writings, to anyone who listen to him.

Only three years after becoming archbishop he was invited to officiate at the funeral of the mother of a friend of his. At the end of his homily he declared:

> God's reign is already present on our earth in mystery. When the Lord
> comes, it will be brought to perfection. That is the hope that inspires
> Christians. We know that every effort to better society, especially
> when injustice and sin are so ingrained, is an effort that God blesses,
> that God wants, that God demands of us.

On that day, March 24, 1980, as he stood at the altar, Archbishop Romero himself was brutally murdered, because he had grown in the virtue of courage, because he had grown into the image of the God who declares life and declares it abundantly.

PASTORAL WISDOM: *PREVENTING PERCUSSIVE PREACHING*

How are we able to do all of this? How are we able to develop the virtues of trustworthiness, respect, awe, and courage? How are we to avoid being noisy gongs or clanging cymbals who make a great deal of noise but say nothing? How does someone grow into being a virtuous preacher? Is there an overarching virtue that draws together the character of the person, the skills learned, and the will to do the right thing? I would like to suggest that an important, perhaps overarching virtue for preachers is *pastoral wisdom*. I would define pastoral wisdom as the knowledge that all we are and all we do are grounded in the grace and love of God working through us, and the development of practical wisdom. We are to do our best, study, work hard, write careful, engaging, energizing sermons. But those who have developed a sense of pastoral wisdom will always know the source of their accomplishments, the God who called them to preach, to minister, to serve the people of God. It is through grace, love, and practical wisdom that we are able to develop the necessary pastoral wisdom to be faithful preachers.

Paul taught the centrality of grace in all that we do. We are, Paul believed, able to prophesy, teach, heal, and love only because of the grace of God that has filled us and saved us. "I am the least of the apostles, unfit to be called an apostle, because I persecuted the church of God. But by the grace of God I am what I am, and his grace toward me has not been in vain. On the contrary, I worked harder than any of them—though it was not I, but the grace of God that is with me" (1 Cor. 15:9–10). Pastoral wisdom is grounded in the knowledge that all we are and all we do comes in and through the grace of God.

Paul also declared that without love we would not be able to practice any of the other gifts that we had been given. Paul told the new Christians in Corinth that without love their practice of all of the wonderful gifts they had been given by God would be for naught: "If I speak in the tongues of mortals and of angels, but do not have love, I am a noisy gong or a clanging cymbal" (1 Cor. 13:1). Paul understood that even if we are preaching wonderful sermons or caring for the sick, if we do not love the people to whom we are preaching or the ill we are helping, our efforts will fall short. Paul told these new Christians that to keep from becoming gongs and cymbals, they needed to love one another as Christ had loved them—giving all of himself to God and to those whom God had created.

Pastoral wisdom is grounded in love: the love of God, the love of neighbor, and the love of stranger. If we do not love the people to whom we are preaching (and we must not confuse *like* with *love*), our preaching will be, as Paul reminds us, percussive—noisy speech and clanging cymbals. It is difficult, if not impossible, for us to connect with our listeners if we do not love them; that is, care about them, have their best interest at the heart of all that we say, respect them as children of God, and know that ultimately their salvation is in the hands not of the preacher but of God.

Finally, we need to develop the ability to know what to say and when to say it. Aristotle taught that people could learn to be speakers. We become excellent speakers by practicing the art of rhetoric. We learn to discover what we are going to say, analyze our audience, decide on a form and arrangement, and learn the proper techniques of delivery. We learn the art of speaking the way we learn the art of painting or building a brick wall. Each art has a set of skills that we learn. But Aristotle also taught that without *phronesis*, practical wisdom, we would not be able to practice any of the other virtues. *Phronesis* was "street smarts." It was the concrete, down-to-earth, everyday knowledge that "managed" the other virtues. It was knowing what to do and when to do it, matching thoughts and actions to the demands of the situation.

Finally, therefore, pastoral wisdom demands practical wisdom. We must recognize that we are filled with the grace of God. We must love as we have been loved, and we must develop concrete, everyday reasoning. We need the ability to make decisions about what to say and when to say it. Practical wisdom is learning about the people to whom we will be speaking. It is understanding the situation and context. It is the skill to speak *with* people rather than *at* them. It is the art of the careful preparation of clear, engaging sermons.

QUESTIONS

1. The *New York Times* carries a series called "The Ethicist." Under the heading of "Divine Cheat," the writer answered a letter from a woman who described how her church had discovered that their pastor had been preaching sermons written by other preachers. "Is this man to be trusted with a congregation?" wrote the woman. After assuring her that it was "unethical" for the pastor to deliver as his sermon the sermon of another, he then made an interesting proposal. Pastors are not only very busy, he wrote, but many of them may not be particularly good preachers. Perhaps, he suggested, it would be better that some pastors made it clear to their congregations that they *do*

not preach sermons they have written. Rather, his or her job is to search for, discover, and deliver "the profound and stirring words of a more talented author." Do you think that it is appropriate for a preacher to preach the sermons of others? Should a congregation expect their pastors to preach their own sermons, even when it makes so many other demands on them?

2. A preacher was recently sued by the family of a man whose funeral the minister had conducted. During the funeral message the minister had declared that it was well known that the deceased was one of "lukewarm" faith who had been living in sin. He declared that "the Lord vomited" such people out of his mouth and sent them down to hell. What do you think of this approach? Was this preacher correct in preaching this biblical message (Rev. 3:16)?

3. Which homiletical virtue do you think that it will be the most difficult for you to develop? Why? How will you work toward overcoming this weakness?

READ MORE ABOUT IT

Campbell, Charles. *The Word before the Powers: An Ethic of Preaching.* Louisville, KY: Westminster John Knox Press, 2002.

McClure, John. *Other-wise preaching: A Postmodern Ethic for Homiletics.* St. Louis: Chalice Press, 2001.

Resner, André. *Preacher and Cross: Person and Message in Theology and Rhetoric.* Grand Rapids: Eerdmans, 1999.

Willimon, William. *Calling and Character: Virtues of the Ordained Life.* Nashville: Abingdon, 2000.

PART 2

Crafting the Sermon

5

Fish of Every Kind:
Getting to Know Our Listeners

The kingdom of heaven is like a net that was thrown into the sea and caught fish of every kind.

Matthew 13:47

THE OTHER

On that first day of the week, Mary Magdalene rushed back to the disciples with the unbelievable news that, not only had Jesus broken the chains of death, but she had seen him and spoken with him. It was impossible to keep the news to herself. Likewise, fifty days later, touched with the wind and fire of the Spirit, the disciples poured out into the streets of Jerusalem, jubilant, ecstatic, drunk with the Spirit, proclaiming the good news to all who would listen.

These are wonderful stories that challenge us to "go and do likewise." But consider also another person's experience of God's call to preach—Jonah. We know little of the son of Amittai except that he received a call from God. It was a very direct and specific call to go to Nineveh and announce to them God's displeasure. (I think that, while many of us would like to have that direct a call, we would be uncomfortable with those specific instructions.) The story of Jonah is so popular that even people who know nothing of the Bible know the story of Jonah. But, while they love the image of Jonah sitting in the belly of the great fish, most of them do not know why he was there. Jonah was there because he recognized the importance of the audience in the preaching equation.

Preaching is not a solitary activity. An artist, writer, or musician can paint a landscape, write a poem, or play a Bach fugue for no one but himself or herself (although most of them do enjoy a wider audience); preachers cannot. Sermons cannot, and should not, be soliloquies. Sermons are, by their very nature, public. They are prepared to be delivered to a group of people, whether two or three people or a crowd of thousands. Preaching is, as the Greek word *homilia* connotes, a conversation. A conversation requires the other; therefore, the other is essential to the preaching equation.

As he heard that very specific call, Jonah thought about those Ninevite "others." He thought about the reaction he would receive as he walked through the great city of Assyria, the capital, the three-day-journey-sized city. He thought about the response he could anticipate when he announced to those rich, wealthy, and powerful Assyrians that God was displeased with their wickedness. Jonah thought and quickly decided that the wisest response to God's call was to turn and run the other way. That is, of course, how he came to be in the belly of the great fish.

THE DANCE OF PREACHING

Earlier I used the analogy of dancing, specifically Fred Astaire and Ginger Rogers, to picture the preaching relationship. But that analogy is incomplete, as all analogies are. Preaching is more like a square dance, or a reel, or, any other dance can you think of that involves many partners moving in complex movements.

We have been created in the image of a dancing God. In the opening chapter we explored the relationship of the Trinity and *perichoresis*, the great dance. Theologians, we noted, saw the Father and the Son and the Holy Spirit moving in and out of each other and moving in and out of all of creation in a great and loving dance. We have been asked to join hands with God and with one another in the dance of life:

> I am the Lord of the Dance, said He,
> . . . .
> And I'll lead you all in the dance, said He.
> (Sydney Carter, "Lord of the Dance")

Preaching is a dance, therefore, that includes many partners: God, the preacher, the text, the context, and the "others"—those who actually hear the sermon, the wider congregation, and the wider community beyond the doors of the church. And, as David Buttrick reminds us, in our preaching we are "dancing on the edge of mystery" (Buttrick, 189).

In this chapter, as we move from an examination of the theology of preaching and of our identity and role as a preacher into the actual writing of the sermon, a critical move involves a discussion of those to whom we will be preaching. In his book on preaching, Fred Craddock stresses that preachers must recognize there are two important tasks for the preacher: first, deciding what to say, and only then deciding how to say it (Craddock, 85). When one is deciding what to say, he writes, "There are two focuses. . . . One focus is upon the listeners. . . . The other is upon the biblical text" (Craddock, 85). And so we begin. Who are our dancing partners? How do we get to know them? How do we learn to dance together in the divine *perichoresis* to which we have been invited by the Lord of the Dance?

UNIVERSAL OR PARTICULAR?

The scandal of the incarnation was that the universal Word became a particular man, Jesus, and dwelt among us. He lived in a particular time at a particular place and spoke to particular people. He was a man of his time and place. To those who made their lives as fishermen, he spoke about fishing for people. To those who lit their homes with oil lamps, he compared faithful discipleship to bridesmaids who not only kept their wicks trimmed but also made sure that they had sufficient oil to light the way for the bridegroom. To those who tended sheep, he described a loving God who would go to great lengths to search for them even when they, like lost sheep, had wandered away. Fish, lamps, sheep—these were the things of everyday life. But for most of us today, we see sheep only at a county fair, and unless we fish as a hobby, we see fish only after they have been deliciously prepared for our dinner plate. And if we bring out an oil lamp, it means one of three things: we are camping, we are setting the mood for a romantic dinner, or the power has gone out.

How do we prepare sermons about the timeless, universal message of God's good news for fleshly people who live in particular times and particular places? Of course, over the years, some have argued that sermons should preach these timeless, universal truths and therefore should not take into account the particular, historical, geographical, cultural context of the listeners. The word of God, they argue, was meant for all people. Preachers, therefore, should not get bogged down in the particularities of their listeners.

But even from the beginning of the church, of those seeking to proclaim the good news, most have realized that their messages have to be tailored to their listeners. Paul wrote that, when he was speaking to Jews, he spoke differently from when he was speaking to Gentiles. When he was speaking to slaves his messages were different from when he was speaking to free women and men. Compare, for example, the Gospels of Matthew and Luke. Biblical scholars argue that they can tell us much about the communities for whom the authors wrote their texts by what they write and don't write, what they feel they have to explain, and what they assume their listeners will understand. Who the listener is, Matthew and Luke knew, matters. And if we want to reach our listeners we have to pay attention to them.

So, while it is not a new understanding, either biblically or rhetorically, in the last century there was, in homiletical writing, a return to preaching that took the listener into account. Fred Craddock, who was trained as a biblical scholar, found himself in a situation where he was asked to teach preaching. Being not only a "producer" but also "consumer" of preaching—that is, someone who sat in the pew on Sunday morning, like Augustine so many centuries before him—he was concerned that preaching had gotten rather dull and stale. Preachers, he found, spent all of their wonderful, challenging, lively time studying the texts; when they got to sermon time, they merely reported the results of their findings, as if they were presenting a book report to a committee. The preacher had made the fascinating journey to the end point, but left the listeners out of the journey. What preachers had to do, he argued, was make preaching come alive, and they would do that by taking the listeners on the journey itself, not just describing the arrival. At the center of his concern was the listener: "Fundamental to the inductive movement, therefore, are identification with the listener. . . . It cannot be overemphasized that the immediate and concrete experiences of the people are significant ingredients in the formation and movement of the sermon" (Craddock, 59).

CHASTISERS AND ENTERTAINERS

Before we explore how we go about understanding our listeners and discovering their immediate and concrete experiences, a call for balance is in order. We live in an age of consumerism, which teaches us the customer is always right. While this chapter will advocate listening to the listeners, preachers must strive, using the language of the three bears, not to listen to the listeners too much, or not enough, but just right.

In his play *Mass Appeal*, Bill Davis introduces us to two preachers. One is the seasoned, if somewhat cynical, pastor of a large, prosperous Catholic church, Father Farley. His nemesis in the play is an outspoken, idealistic young Deacon Dolson, who is in great danger of not being ordained a priest because of his confrontational approach. One such moment of confrontation occurs when Father Farley helps Deacon Mark Dolson practice his sermon. As the deacon steps into the pulpit, he begins a harangue to the empty pews that sounds much like Jonah's message to the citizens of Nineveh: "God is not impressed with your Gap shirts, your cell phones and your blue hair" (Davis, 18).

Father Farley interrupts Mark to remind him that he should always use the first person plural "we," rather than the accusatory "you." But when Mark begins again with the revised pronouns, he realizes that he can't do it. "I don't wear Gap shirts, why do I have to say 'we'?" (Davis, 19). He understands himself as the Jonah who has been sent to chastise them for their inattentiveness and misplaced priorities. Father Farley, however, does not want his congregation scolded. If you tell them what they don't want to hear, he claims from long years of experience, they will turn on you. Yes, the deacon observes, that is why your sermons are "song and dance" routines.

The playwright has set up these two extremes, the preacher who lets his listeners drive the sermon, and the preacher who sets himself over and against the listeners. While they both have analyzed their listeners, one of them has decided to offer only what people want to hear, and the other views as irrelevant what people want to hear and will tell them what he thinks they need to hear.

In his preaching textbook, Thomas Long offers us several images of the preacher: herald, pastor, storyteller, witness. What images of listeners would we offer? Father Farley would suggest a paying audience ready to be complimented and entertained. Deacon Dolson looks down from the pulpit and sees wayward, selfish sheep. How do we as preachers arrive at an appropriate balance of listening and leading? How do we come to understand and encourage our listeners to be active partners in the preaching venture?

SENDERS AND RECEIVERS

Studies of rhetoric and communication have helped us to understand and appreciate how communication occurs. When we speak with another person, we do not always realize how complex and complicated an activity that is. Communication is far from a simple linear model with a sender, a message, and a receiver.

Communication does begin with the *sender* or speaker. Whether it is as simple as asking someone to meet you for lunch or as complicated as the State of the Union address, the sender must make two decisions: first, what message to send or what to say, and second, how to send that message. In communication models, the first is exactly that, the *message*, but the second is the *channel*.

Whether someone is asking you to lunch or you have joined the rest of the nation that is listening to the presidential address, the *listener* receives the message, but that listener is much more than a passive sponge soaking up the ideas and thoughts of the sender. The first attempts at a communication model described the movement as unidirectional, a message sent from a sender and received by a listener. It quickly became apparent that communication is never unidirectional. Even when only one person is doing the speaking, the listener or listeners are always, through another channel, communicating back to the speaker.

As Deacon Dolson is in the sacristy vesting for his first actual sermon before Father Farley's congregation, Farley gives him last-minute pointers. He should listen for coughs. When it is clear that Dolson doesn't understand, Farley elaborates. Coughing is a sign that they are getting bored and the preacher needs to "pick up the pace."

While we may laugh at that scene in the play or the movie, many preachers will tell you that Father Farley is right. You will know by a congregation's response if they are engaged with what you are saying. It may be very quiet, or there may be lively responses. If you have lost them, you may hear coughs and the rustling of agitated people in their seats.

Through physical and oral channels your listeners are communicating to you that what you are saying is either not clear or is not interesting. Senders, therefore, must also be listeners, receiving and, we hope, adapting and responding to the *feedback* that is being sent by their listeners. We will return to this issue of listening shortly.

To understand the communication event, we must be attentive to much more than simply a person speaking to another person or persons. Think of the different sermons you have delivered or to which you have listened. Some of those sermons were preached in the church, but not all. Some may have been at a park during the service at the church picnic, at a funeral home, at a garden wedding, or at an open-air stadium for a revival. While all still have a sender, message, channel, and listener, each sermon takes place in a very different *communication environment.* Many factors come together to produce that environment. One is the physical space, another the size of the audience. Is this a normal Sunday morning service or Christmas Eve? (Preaching on Christmas Eve is like preaching in a beehive; the church literally buzzes with restless children.) Is this your home church, where you feel comfortable, or are you visiting? Does the church have a public address system, or one that has it failed?

When communication theorists speak of the *communication environment*, they describe it in the terms just mentioned. What happens if we think of God as the environment in which sermons are preached? All that we do and all that we are take place within the environment of God's love and God's call to speak to one another. God calls preachers to preach and the listeners to listen. All of us come to that moment because of the God who has created and redeemed us.

Another important consideration is the *noise* or *interference*. Some of that is actual physical noise. I once preached at a church near the end of the runway for Andrews Air Force Base in the suburbs of Washington. Even on Sunday the congregation was repeatedly bombarded by the roar of military jets. Consequently, periodically I would have to stop and let the jets have their say before continuing with my sermon.

Noise that interferes with the communication process can be much more than screaming jets and crying babies. Those are the *external* noises, easy to identify and deal with. Much more difficult to recognize are the *internal* noises or blocks that come between you and your listeners. Some are individual, that is, specific to one person. Has that person had a bad week at work? Did she have a fight with her husband? Did he hear from the doctor that he has to come in for more tests? Preachers are competing with as many interior conversations as there are people.

CULTURAL NOISE

Another important source of internal interference is the cultures in which we live. When students arrive at Wesley Seminary, one of the first courses that they take requires them to visit a number of different churches. The students must visit churches different from the church they are used to or comfortable attending. If one has grown up in a white Presbyterian church, a black Baptist church will be quite unsettling. If one has attended only the prayer and praise services of a contemporary megachurch, an Orthodox liturgy will seem otherworldly (which is the point).

Our ecclesial culture both shapes our expectations and consequently creates noise when we are not in that culture. Our ethnic culture does the same. We live in a world of tremendous cultural diversity. When I go to my local grocery store, I am often the only person speaking English. I am able to buy foods for people from Mexico, Central and South America, the Middle East, the islands of the Carribean, India, China, Thailand, and Japan. Whether it is chilies or rice noodles, mango chutney or seaweed wrappers, each cuisine smells different and tastes different. While I can't always cook like a native, it is fun to experiment with the different foods. What these foods tell me is that I am living among groups of people who come to a dinner table very different from the Scandinavian Minnesota table at which I dined as I was growing up.

Writing in the middle of the previous century, anthropologist Clifford Geertz, in an article "Religion as a Cultural System," defined culture as "an historically transmitted pattern of meanings embodied in symbols, a system of inherited conceptions expressed in symbolic forms by means of which men communicate, perpetuate, and develop their knowledge about and attitudes toward life" (Geertz, 89). While that may seem a long way from chili peppers and rice noodles, they are outward and visible symbols of cultural patterns.

Over the years anthropologists have built upon and modified Geertz's definition, pushing it beyond his static image. In her book *Theories of Culture*, Kathryn Tanner describes what she would argue are the basic elements of culture. Culture is a "defining mark of human life"; everyone lives within a culture or cultures, however broadly or narrowly defined (Tanner, 25). Culture, she observes, "varies with social group" and is "conceived as their entire way of life" (Tanner, 26–27). Culture describes the way a social group speaks, how it dresses, the music they listen to, the food they eat. There is a Japanese culture, there is a Cuban culture, but there are also a hip-hop culture and a deaf culture.

In her book *Preaching as Local Theology and Folk Art*, Leonora Tubbs Tisdale argues that, more often than not, preaching is cross-cultural communication. She reports the culture shock she experienced when she and her husband spent a yearlong seminary internship as missionaries in Seoul, Korea:

> [T]he language was different; the food was different; the customs were different; the humor was different; the arts were different; and the church—its theology, ethos, and ritual life—was different from that to which we had become accustomed as white North American Protestants. (Tisdale, 1)

Fortunately, she reports, they had been prepared for this before they left. Language classes, books about Korean culture, and conversations with Koreans helped smooth their transition.

What she was not prepared for was the same kind of culture shock following graduation and ordination, when she and her husband went to their first parishes in the United States! Having grown up in large parishes in larger urban areas, Dr. Tisdale did not understand that as she stepped into the pulpit in small, rural churches, she was stepping into a very different culture, as she had in Korea, "For the truth was, we were—pastor and people—from very different worlds" (Tisdale, 3).

More and more preachers are discovering that they must, as authors James Nieman and Thomas Rogers point out, "proclaim the gospel across the boundaries of ethnicity, class, and religious difference" (Nieman and Rogers, 1). These various cultures can produce a great deal of noise in the preaching moment and call for a great deal of sensitivity on the part of the preacher. Later in this chapter we will explore ways preachers might come to appreciate and understand these different cultures.

"LET ANYONE WITH EARS LISTEN"—LISTENING

One of the most important skills of being a preacher, therefore, is listening. In her book *Listening Ministry: Rethinking Pastoral Leadership*, Susan Hedahl asks, "Is it possible that we have overlooked one of the most important areas of pastoral ministry in our training and thinking—listening?" (Hedahl, 7). What's more, she notes that even though we know that listening is "a long-embedded part of almost all spiritual traditions . . . ministry providers and educators have assumed that listening skills just happened" (Hedahl, 7).

Few pastors take a course in seminary on listening, and if they do, it will usually be located within the pastoral care field. Consequently, pastors may not make the essential connection between preaching and listening. Good preachers must be good listeners. So, while we can't devote too much time to this important subject, I would like to highlight several important aspects of listening and encourage you to investigate it further on your own.

We have a joke around my family. If you want to talk to Mother at breakfast, you had better call her name twice. If you put a cup of coffee in one of my hands and a newspaper in the other, I am lost to the world. There is a difference between listening and hearing. If my husband speaks to me, the sound vibrations of his speech are hitting my eardrums, but I am not listening. After thirty years of marriage, my husband has threatened to get a bell that he can ring to signal his intention to speak. Listening and hearing are different. Hearing is physical; listening is a mental or cognitive activity.

Distraction is one source of poor listening. During breakfast I am so involved in the news I am reading that I am not listening. Whether it is the newspaper, television, or the movements and activities of other people, if we are going to listen to someone, we must ignore all of the distractions that assault us.

Another source of poor listening is focus. How often are you hearing someone speak, but really not listening? You are focused, not on the person speaking, but on what you are going to say next. Or you may be focused, not on their words, but on some other aspect of the person who is speaking. Rather than listening, you are looking at the clothes the person is wearing, or you are distracted by some aspect of the delivery—a voice that is too loud or too soft, a physical tick or gesture, or perhaps the fact that the person punctuates his or her speech with the same phrase or conversation marker, "you know" or "like," over and over again. Listening to someone can be hard work.

There are different styles of listening. If we are listening to a friend describe a difficult moment in her life, we don't listen the way we do if we are taking notes at a lecture. A musical concert calls for a different kind of listening than a motion picture or play. There are different listening styles, and we can learn to improve our listening skills.

Listening is not something that just happens naturally. According to Susan Hedahl, "Good pastoral listening is governed by a basic knowledge and command of listening skills and structures. It is a theological activity, emerging from vocational and faith identity, present in all forms of ministry" (Hedahl, 13). A good preacher, therefore, is one who has developed active, appropriate listening skills that enable her or him to get to know the people to whom he or she will be preaching. John McClure and Ronald Allen note that if we are not "listening to the listener," our sermons will not reach hearts and minds. Rather, the congregation will hear but not listen; our words will go in one ear and out the other, without alighting in the middle.

We must listen to the listeners. But before we listen to anyone else, we must listen to God. Too many preachers forget that first and foremost our sermons grow out of and respond to our prayerful and meditative conversations with and listening to God. Dr. Hedahl describes this as "Godward listening" (Hedahl, 44). Without Godward listening underpinning all that we do, "other forms of listening are rendered ineffective or insincere" (Hedahl, 55).

WHO ARE THE LISTENERS?

As I noted in the previous chapter, when Oscar Romero was named archbishop of San Salvador in 1977, the wealthy were pleased with the selection. He had been a quiet, fairly conservative bishop who had not been involved in the political struggles that were rocking the country, and they had no reason to believe that he would change his habits. Unfortunately, shortly after Romero's consecration, a fellow priest who was an outspoken critic of the government was murdered in an attempt to silence this troublemaker. As bishop, Romero presided at the funeral mass. His friends would later say that this event, this painful moment, became a moment of conversion for the now powerful archbishop. He came to understand that he could no longer remain silent about the violence and oppression visited upon the poorest of the poor.

Romero also came to appreciate the various "channels" that were available to him in his position as archbishop. He could preach sermons during the mass, and he could also speak to the people through his weekly radio broadcasts. But who was his audience? Did he speak only to the poor to encourage them, or did he also speak, indirectly, to the wealthy who controlled the vicious government and robbed the poor of what little they had? While Romero would have said that he was preaching to the poor campesinos, his message reverberated through the halls of power.

To whom do we preach? Is it just the people who sit before us on a Sunday morning? Should we speak of them as our *audience*? In *Mass Appeal*, Father Farley thought they were his audience and he was their entertainer. I prefer to speak of them as the *listeners* or the *congregation*. *Audience* has an entertainment connotation, and while I do think that a sermon must to a certain extent be entertaining, we must not equate preaching with entertaining. The word *audience* implies a certain passive quality, and those listening to sermons must be far from passive. But to whom are we preaching? How do we define or characterize our listeners?

It is not enough to say that we are preparing our sermons for those who will be present on Sunday morning. After all, we really don't know who will be present on Sunday morning. Which members of the congregation will be there? Some will, no doubt, be missing. And there may be visitors who have never been in a church before.

Communication theorists identify four different audiences. First, there is the *empirical audience*. Those are the people who actually listen to a sermon or speech. They are the people that are there on Sunday morning, sitting in the pew.

But there is also the *target audience*. That is the group of listeners envisioned by the speaker, the group he or she pictures in her or his mind as the sermon is written. You see the effect of having different audiences in commercials and advertisements. Look at the various commercials produced by McDonalds. Each commercial has a specific target group in mind. Some are produced for young children and focus on the characters and the toys. Other commercials want to encourage families to come in. Some commercials are for African American audiences, other for Hispanic. The target audience determines the people shown eating in the restaurant, as well as the music.

In her textbook *The Rhetorical Act*, Karlyn Kohrs Campbell urges speakers to think beyond the empirical and target audiences. There is also the *created* or *constructed audience* (Campbell, 59–60). In her work with the speeches of women in the nineteenth century, for example, Dr. Campbell has demonstrated that before women could rally women around the issue of suffrage, those women first had to convince the women to whom they spoke that the women could help to effect those changes. The speakers had to construct an audience that "not only had the power to act, it must also believe that it has that power" (Campbell, 60). When Oscar Romero preached to the people of San Salvador, he spoke to all people, rich and poor. He not only wanted to reach those who held the grips of guns, but he also had to construct a group of listeners who would understand that they could take the actions he was recommending; they could put down their guns. As we preach, therefore, we are constructing an audience of people who are being transformed into those who realize that they are able to change and are able to carry out the ministries to which God is calling them.

We might also think about the listeners beyond the church. Preachers have always known that their sermons have an impact on the *broader community*. While this is less true now than it was in the past, as soon as there is a crisis or disaster, preachers are once again reminded how important their sermons are in the community in which they live. One hundred years ago, the Monday morning newspapers would report on the content of the Sunday sermons, but no more. However, on the weekend following the disaster of September 11, the Sunday *New York Times* reported what preachers around the country were planning to say about the tragedy. And on Monday morning they reported about what had been preached from the nation's pulpits. As my friend said, "Tell preachers that people are listening." People are listening, and not just the people in the pews.

Be aware of the various ways that we might envision our listeners as we prepare our sermon. It helps to think about the broader possibilities, but as speakers, we can be sure that we will have a group of living, breathing people in the pews before us. How do we get to know those people?

FISH OF EVERY KIND

In the Gospel of Matthew, Jesus tells us that "the kingdom of heaven is like a net that was thrown into the sea and caught fish of every kind" (Matt. 13:47). What a wonderful image! In that net are flounder and eels, jellyfish and salmon. Central to that image of ministry is that everyone is included—not just one group, one kind of people. It is Asian, black, white, Jewish, Gentile, Roman, Greek, Native American, Brazilian, Nigerian, and Thai. What makes preaching challenging is that different "fish" listen differently. You have been sent to fish for people. How to you get to know those people?

Demographics

The first step in getting to know a congregation is the easiest. Who are they and what do they look like? We might "count" the fish:

- Number in the congregation
- Women / men
- Age groups
- Racial / ethnic groups
- Location: urban / suburban / rural
- Educational levels achieved

- Economic levels
- Occupations

A church can subscribe to services that will give it a very detailed description of the community in which it is located. It will tell you to which magazines your neighbors subscribe, to which radio stations they listen, where they go on vacation, what cars they drive, and to which colleges they send their children.

Through Thick and Thin

The demographic descriptions, while important, go only so far toward helping us to know a group of people. When we speak to another person or group of people, we must speak to them in terms that they will understand. They listen to us through "perceptual screens." Culture is like a pair of glasses through which you see the world, perhaps not even aware that you have them on. Earlier we discussed the noise that will interfere with our communication; preachers must get to know the people to whom they will be speaking in order to minimize that noise. They need to know the attitudes and beliefs of those who will listen to their sermons. What are their likes and dislikes? What do they respond to favorably? What turns them off? What do they value most highly? What are their basic views of life?

Earlier I mentioned Clifford Geertz's definition of culture. Geertz used the work of Gilbert Ryle to describe the ways that one can analyze a culture. We make, he wrote, "thin" and "thick" descriptions (Geertz, 6–9). When doing a thin description one describes a particular action as being cultural, as opposed to behavior. For example, if one was to travel to a certain kind of church in the Appalachians, one might observe that people pick up and hold poisonous snakes. That would be, according to Geertz, "a fleck of culture" as opposed to "a speck of behavior" because most of us do not, I hope, naturally carry around deadly snakes (Geertz, 6). But, if one is going to do a thick description of that behavior—holding snakes during a worship service—one needs to understand that it is symbolic behavior. To make a "thick" description, one not only describes the action, but only also speculates on its meaning and significance in the culture. Holding poisonous snakes might be interpreted as being an outward and visible sign of one's absolute trust in God: "And these signs will accompany those who believe: by using my name they will cast out demons; they will speak in new tongues; they will pick up snakes in their hands, and if they drink any deadly thing, it will not hurt them; and they will lay their hands on the sick, and they will recover" (Mark 16:17–18). By doing both thin and thick descriptions of the communities in which we preach, we are able to identify the rituals and activities that are central to a congregation and, more importantly, the worldviews and values that underlay those actions.

In her book *Preaching as Local Theology and Folk Art*, Leonora Tubbs Tisdale encourages preachers to become amateur ethnographers, which gives them "a new way of seeing and perceiving." By examining the symbols of their congregations they will have "new questions, new perspectives and new tools for interpretation" (Tisdale, 61).

To begin to get to know the culture of a congregation, Tisdale encourages preachers to look at the architecture of the building and the arts that adorn, or don't adorn, the walls of the church. Preachers, she argues, should look, not only at the demographics of the current congregation, but at archival material as well. They need to ask parishioners to tell them stories about important moments in the life of the congregation. It is crucial to know which rituals, events, and activities are central to the community's life together. These provide the pastor with the thin description.

With that portrait in hand, the pastor is ready to begin to develop a thick description of the congregation. By examining those various symbols the preacher is able to begin to understand the congregation's view of God and humanity. How they organize their life together will tell you about their view of time, their ecclesiology, and their understanding of Christian mission. While they may not be able to articulate it coherently, your analysis will help you to understand how they would declare, "This is who we are."

You need to know who they are so that you can shape your message in such a way that they will be able to identify with you and what you are saying. If, for example, your sermon assumes scriptural texts are the work of fallible human authors, but you are preaching to a group of people who believe in the inerrancy of Scripture, there will be a serious disconnect between you and your listeners.

The Tisdale book encourages preachers to get to know the worldview, values, and ethos of their listeners, so that together they move toward the "theological construction for preaching—the engagement of the horizons of the biblical texts and congregation context in a fitting and transformative way"—the preacher will have a better understanding of the people whom he or she has been called to serve (Tisdale, 90). But those are not the only categories by which preachers may get to know their people.

In their work *One Gospel, Many Ears: Preaching for Different Listeners in the Congregation*, Joseph Jeter and Ronald Allen locate the differences in modes of apprehension: "People express themselves and process communications in ways that are influenced by racial experience, gender, personality type, ethnicity, education, and social and economic situation" (Jeter and Allen, 2). Preaching, they argue, "calls for variety that corresponds to the variegation in the listening community" (Jeter and Allen, 6).

Likewise, James Nieman and Thomas Rogers also call preachers to a heightened sensitivity in their book *Preaching to Every Pew: Cross-Cultural Strategies*. As already noted, Nieman and Rogers observe that our changing world, with its fluid immigration patterns, presents a diversity that "reaches even into the soul of worship whenever preachers speak to those whose cultural realities are profoundly different from their own" (Nieman and Rogers, vii). In order to understand the neighbor to whom we are called to speak, preachers need to look at the frames of ethnicity, class, displacement, and beliefs that shape our cross-cultural congregations. "We must learn," they argue, "to speak anew; for how we name a situation [the challenge of diversity] affects how we act toward it . . . we need to choose our words with care" (Nieman and Rogers, 11).

We have been created in the image of a God of many colors, many abilities, many cultures. We are called to listen with care, so that we may carefully choose words that will connect with this variety of listeners that represent our God.

EXEGETING THE MOMENT

Paul Scott Wilson reminds us that preachers must exegete both the scriptural text and the preaching context. We have been speaking about exegeting the congregation—getting to know, in an in-depth way, the people to whom we are preaching—but we must also think about the particular moment in time during which we are preaching. Each preaching occasion is shaped by the many forces surrounding that moment. Like the concentric circles that radiate from a pebble dropped in a pond, our sermons reach out into our congregation, our local community, and our global community. Therefore, as we begin to think about what we are going to say and how we are going to say it, we need to follow those waves.

- What is going on in the life of the congregation? What economic, theological, and interpersonal issues are facing the community? Are members of the community facing difficult times? What is the mission of the congregation? How is it interacting with its neighbors?
- What is happening in the community that lies beyond the church doors? What are the day-to-day issues that confront those who sit in the pews— issues of economic growth or decline, schools, jobs, housing?
- What issues confront the nation in which we live? Is it at war or living in a time of peace? Some argue our world was forever changed after the events of September 11. How do those hours continue to reverberate through the lives of those to whom you preach? What are the political questions that demand to be addressed? What are the questions the people avoid? What divides, what unites? Who has a voice, and who does not?

- What are the issues facing the broader church? Many congregations are connected to denominations that are in serious conflict over issues of sexuality. How does that influence the preaching in the local church? How does your local church relate to the wider mission of the church?
- What are the worldwide issues that demand a hearing? Where are people at war? Where are people suffering from oppression and starvation? Where are we forsaking our call to stewardship of God's resources? Whom is the world ignoring?

It is reported that Karl Barth said preachers must prepare their sermons with the Bible in one hand and the newspaper in the other. Don't step over the Sunday paper on your way to church. Or, listen to the news on the car radio as you drive to your first service. Make sure that you are aware of the events that are confronting those to whom you are preaching. The membrane between the church and the world is, and should always be, permeable.

OUT INTO THE WORLD

Long before the events of the resurrection and Pentecost, the followers of Jesus were sent out into the world. They were to enter towns and villages announcing that the kingdom of God was very near. Jesus instructed them about what they were to take (very little) and how they were to act (as bearers of peace). He warned them that some would listen, some would welcome, some would ignore, and some would reject their message. People are different, and we who have been sent out into the world need to become skilled at learning about and appreciating those differences.

In the next chapter we will begin to examine the preparation of particular sermons, but we undertake that preparation knowing that we are preparing our sermons for particular people in a particular place at a particular time. We are preparing our sermons for the church which is the living, growing, changing body of Christ. Coming to know those whom we have been called to serve will always be, therefore, an ongoing process.

QUESTIONS

1. Father Farley viewed his listeners as an audience ready to be entertained. Deacon Dolson saw sinners in the hand of an angry God, and it was his job to set them straight. What metaphors would you use to describe those who will be listening to your sermons?

2. Do a thin and thick description of the church where you are either attending or serving.

READ MORE ABOUT IT

Allen, Ronald J. *Hearing the Sermon: Relationship, Content, and Feeling*. St. Louis: Chalice Press, 2003.

Jeter, Joseph R., Jr., and Ronald J. Allen. *One Gospel, Many Ears*. St. Louis: Chalice Press, 2002.

McClure, John S., et al. *Listening to Listeners: Homiletical Case Studies*. St. Louis: Chalice Press, 2004.

Mulligan, Mary Alice, et al. *Believing in Preaching: What Listeners Hear in Sermons*. St. Louis: Chalice Press, 2005.

Nieman, James R., and Thomas G. Rogers. *Preaching to Every Pew: Cross-Cultural Strategies*, Minneapolis: Fortress Press, 2001.

Tisdale, Leonora Tubbs. *Preaching as Local Theology and Folk Art*. Minneapolis: Fortress Press, 1997.

6

Where to Begin: Empty Pitchers and Living Water

We come this morning—
   like empty pitchers to a full fountain.
James Weldon Johnson, God's Trombones

Time, Albert Einstein told us, is relative. If you want to understand that, he said, compare a minute spent kissing someone you love to a minute your hand is placed on a hot stove. Preachers also appreciate the relativity of time, because nothing comes as quickly as the next Sunday morning. No sooner has a sermon been preached than it is time to begin preparing the next.

So far we have been developing a theology of preaching, the habits of the preaching life, and exploring ways of getting to know the people to whom we will be delivering our sermons. These help preaching in general, but now it is time to turn our attention to the development and writing of a particular sermon. How do preachers write their sermons? Where do they begin?

As I mentioned in the previous chapter, Fred Craddock stressed that preachers must decide what they are going to say before they decide how to say it. We will get to the latter, how to say it, in chapter 8. In chapters 6 and 7 we will be focusing on the process of deciding what to say. In classical rhetorical studies, that process was called *inventio*, invention, or the discovery of arguments. What point are you, as a preacher, trying to make, and what reasons can be gathered that the listeners will find convincing?

BOWED KNEES AND BENT BODIES

Not only should every sermon should begin with prayer, but, as Paul reminds us, we should pray without ceasing throughout the entire preaching process, from the moment we begin until the last syllable is spoken. Before we read Scripture, before we exegete the text and the context, we should begin by, as James Weldon Johnson reminds us, bringing the empty pitcher of our hearts and minds to the living water of God in prayer. We need to open ourselves to the movement of God in our lives and in the life of our congregation.

All too often our minds are filled to overflowing with all of our duties and responsibilities. Whether you use a Palm Pilot, a Blackberry, or old fashioned paper calendar, it is usually jammed with things to do, meetings to attend, people to see. I know husbands and wives who even have to make appointments to have lunch or dinner in order to find time to talk to each other. Is it any wonder that the living water of God has difficulty pouring into our lives? If we can't find time for our families, how can we find time for God? Our busyness keeps God out.

When we are so hurried, so busy, we find it difficult to listen to the still, small voice of the Spirit that is speaking words of love, encouragement, challenge, and direction. Beginning the preaching process with prayer, therefore, reminds us that we speak only with and through the movement of the Holy Spirit. "Do not worry about how you are to speak or what you are to say; for what you are to say will be given to you at that time; for it is not you who speak, but the Spirit of your Father speaking through you" (Matt. 10:19–20).

TWO STARTING POINTS:
LECTIONARY VS. TOPICAL PREACHING

There are many ways of identifying the type of preaching that occurs. Some say, "I am a biblical preacher." Others might say, "I tend to preach topical sermons." Does that imply that a biblical sermon does not have a topic or that a topical sermon does not use the Bible? Of course not. But it does signal different starting points. To be more specific, rather than talking about biblical preaching, I would like to set up a distinction between *lectionary* preaching and *topical* preaching because they offer us a shorthand way of discussing different approaches to starting the preaching process.

Lectionary-Based Preaching

First, what is lectionary preaching? The majority of Christians around the globe employ some sort of lectionary for their Sunday worship. A lectionary prescribes the Scripture texts that are to be read during the worship service. The lectionaries used by most Western churches rotate on a three-year cycle. Included in the lectionary are an Old Testament reading, a selection from the Psalms, a reading from an epistle, and finally, a passage from one of the Gospels. Each of the three cycles highlight one of the synoptic Gospels while readings from the final Gospel, John, are woven into each year's cycle. The first year features Matthew, the second Mark, and the third Luke. While the readings strive for breadth and comprehensiveness, large portions of Scripture are neglected.

The use of the lectionary affects preaching in a number of ways. First, the weekly texts are already chosen. The preacher does not have to, in addition to deciding what to say and how to say it, also decide from what text or texts he or she will preach. Second, there is a sense of connection to the wider ecumenical church. You and your congregation are reading the same texts that are being read around the world. Third, the succession of readings focus as the morning's worship on the liturgical calendar, the story of salvation. Finally, a large number of liturgical resources tied to the lectionary readings are available to coordinate the worship, music, sermon, and education of the church.

Lectionary preaching is preaching in which the given biblical texts provide the starting point. But preachers do not always have to preach from all of the texts stipulated. An attempt is usually made to align the readings, but the epistle text often stands independently of the Old Testament and Gospel readings and may not coordinate easily. Consequently, an attempt to use all of the texts may end up looking much like the old game of Twister.

The Preaching Plan: Developing Your Own Lectionary

For many, the lectionary is a given. But many other preachers, who do not preach in lectionary-based churches, have found that the development of their own preaching plan, a year's approach to working through various books of Scripture or scriptural themes, helps them to know where they are going throughout the year and prevents them from experiencing "Friday fright."

Preachers need to be open to the movement of the Spirit in their preaching and connected to events and crises that are happening in their community and the world. But at the same time, the pressure of commitments and responsibilities limit preacher's opportunities for reflection and rumination. The development of a preaching plan, that is, your own lectionary, removes one of the tensions experienced by preachers, what shall I preach about this week? It does not mean that one cannot deviate from the given readings if events dictate, but it does relieve one from the burden of picking a text, because this has already been done during a time of quiet reflection devoted to just that purpose.

Developing a preaching plan means that one can think about the events in the church year—Advent, Christmas, Lent, Easter—and plan the readings accordingly. It also means that one is able to review your individual congregation's church calendar and tie the preaching themes to important events in the life of your church—for example, Homecoming Sunday, the start of your education program and commissioning of those who will teach, a fall bazaar, a spring church social. Those are significant occasions that can be made even richer by connecting them through your preaching to the good news of the gospel and our mission as disciples of Christ.

A preaching plan also forces the preacher to move beyond favorite or comfortable texts and themes. On a recent Sunday the lectionary readings included the stern condemnation by Amos, "Alas for those who lie on beds of ivory, and lounge on their couches. . . . They shall now be the first to go into exile" (Amos 6:4a, 7a), and the parable of the dishonest steward, "Make friends for yourselves by means of dishonest wealth so that when it is gone, they may welcome you into the eternal homes" (Luke 16:9). While leafing through Scripture looking for texts, I suspect that many of us would pass those by, and most certainly would not put the two together. A preaching plan encourages you to work through Scripture in a more organized way.

Topical Preaching

For some, therefore, the starting point of a sermon is a Scripture text or texts. They begin by wrestling with a text. What is God trying to say to us through these texts? But another starting point is a topic or theme, an issue, a question, an event. On September 16, 2001, all preachers in the United States were topical preachers. Following the collapse of the Twin Towers, the attack on the Pentagon, and the crash in Pennsylvania, all preachers were like Habakkuk asking, "Why do you make me see wrongdoing and look at trouble? Destruction and violence are before me; strife and contention arise" (Hab. 1:3).

By identifying a sermon as topical, we do not mean to imply that it is not biblical. A good topical sermon will always draw in scriptural texts. The texts, however, are not the starting point. They are chosen to ground the sermon rather than initiate it.

Long-range planning is important for those who consider themselves topical preachers. While they will want to be alert to current events that intercede and take precedence, topical preachers need to map out the flow of their preaching and make decisions about those topics and themes that need to be addressed in a systematic way.

If you are a topical preacher, by what criteria do you make decisions about the topics and themes that will drive your preaching? Preachers need to be careful that their sermons are not limited to a few theological themes and do not avoid issues that will challenge the congregation. Two resources that will help in designing comprehensive preaching plans are *Essentials of Christian Theology*, edited by William Placher, and *Preaching to the Hungers of the Heart* by James Wallace.

In his introduction, Placher questions our resistence to theology. After all, he observes, "all Christians do theology all the time, for *theology* just means thinking about our faith" (Placher, 1). He continues: "The responsibility to think about our faith and how its elements fit together falls particularly on those who preach and teach. The twentieth-century Swiss theologian Karl Barth used to call theology "the conscience of preaching" (Placher, 2).

Placher's book explores the principal questions that inform the conscience of our preaching (Placher, v–vi):

- How do we know what to believe? Revelation and Authority
- What do we mean by God? The Doctrine of God
- Is God in charge? Creation and Providence
- What's wrong with us? Human Nature and Human Sin
- How does Jesus make a difference? The Person and Work of Jesus Christ
- Why bother with church? The Church and Its Worship
- How should we live? The Christian Life
- What about *them*? Christians and Non-Christians
- Where are we going? Eschatology

Placher wants us to see that theology and preaching are ways to help people answer the questions that fill their lives. These might be the questions that will drive your preaching.

James Wallace connects preaching with Jesus' feeding of the multitude: "Jesus moves his listeners beyond physical hunger and calls them to faith, to belief in the one that feeds their deepest hunger" (Wallace, 7). Through our preaching of Jesus, the bread comes down from heaven, we seek to feed the hungers of the heart. According to Wallace, those hungers are:

- The hunger for wholeness
- The hunger for meaning
- The hunger for belonging

Comprehensive preaching, preaching that is carefully planned, will seek to answer these questions and feed these hungers.

THE PLANNING RETREAT

Whether one is a lectionary preacher, is developing one's own lectionary, or is a topical preacher, all preachers benefit from a planning retreat. If possible, devote a week of your summer, away from the responsibilities of work and home. Don't think of it as a vacation or even a spiritual retreat. This will be a working retreat in which you will plan a year's preaching schedule. With your various calendars in hand—the church year, your congregation's calendar, the secular calendar—chart out the texts, themes, and subjects of the year's sermons.

Why do I recommend this, even for those who have a lectionary? Because it is important to sense the ebb and flow of the lessons with which you will be challenged. Quite often lectionary readings will divide a story over several weeks. If you haven't looked ahead, you might find that you have preached on the conclusion to a story one week when it will be read the following week.

With a preaching plan in hand, you can begin to gather stories, examples, experiences, and resources that will be invaluable as you begin to prepare the sermon for a particular week. The plan helps you to coordinate your reading and makes you alert to lectures and continuing education opportunities that will tie into your preaching. A preacher with a plan, whether it is one that you have designed or one that is prescribed by your denomination, is less likely to approach preaching with the sense of being in free fall. The plan or lectionary always provides the parachute or safety net by giving one a starting point. There is nothing as uncomfortable as a totally unlimited universe of possibilities.

MONDAY MORNING

Sunday morning has come and gone. Your sermon has been preached and you have, I hope, had an opportunity to enjoy at least some of the Sabbath rest. Suddenly, however, Monday morning has arrived. Although six entire days lie ahead, you know that all too soon Sunday will be here again, and you will need to have prepared another sermon. So, where to begin? Since most preachers begin by turning to the Scriptures, that is where we will begin. In the next chapter we will discuss the other dimensions of the process of sermon invention. The remainder of this chapter will focus on the preacher's interaction with the Scriptures.

In his book *A Short Introduction to Hermeneutics*, David Jasper observes that we have come to understand that the reading, understanding, and interpretation of texts is very complicated:

> Reading is not just a question of seeking meanings. Texts can affect us in many ways. They can make us angry, or frightened, or they can console us. *Writing*, then, is a kind of action that can work on us in ways

far beyond our mere understanding. . . . Indeed, what we actually
mean by "reading," "text," and even "author," is very complex and
actually not at all self-evident. (Jasper, 8)

This complexity becomes apparent to students when they begin courses in
Scripture. They are confronted by a variety of questions: Who wrote a text?
How were the works of several authors combined into one "book"? How is the
author's intention for one community different when read by another community? Why should the injunctions handed down to people two or three thousand years ago apply to us? How do we know what we must accept and what
is no longer applicable? These questions confront, confound, and disturb students, who may feel a shaking in their foundations.

I would encourage you to begin working on your sermon as early as possible. You will need all the time that you have to read, reflect, and wrestle with
the text and the message. If you begin reading over the text or texts on Monday morning, they will become the lens through which you encounter the
events of the week.

Taking the Bible off your bookshelf on Monday morning to begin your sermon preparation is an enriching and energizing moment. In the previous
chapter we noted that there are different ways of *listening*. There are also different ways of *reading*.

How we read the Scriptures is informed by our understanding of the
authority of the Scriptures and by our hermeneutical approach. I often hear
students declare, as they prepare to read a passage of Scripture, "I don't interpret—I just read and let the Scripture speak for itself." What they don't realize is that the moment we read Scripture, whether silently or aloud, we cannot
but help interpret what we are reading. Preachers do not come to any reading
of a text as blank slates. It is essential, therefore, that preachers address the
questions of authority, hermeneutics, and the development of an exegetical
method.

THE PREACHER AND THE BIBLE:
THE QUESTION OF AUTHORITY

Underlying the preparation of your sermons is your understanding of Scripture and the role that it plays in preaching and in the life of the church. How
would you describe your understanding of the authority of Scripture?

Each day, either as individuals or as the church, we turn to Scripture for
words of comfort and inspiration, correction and direction. These words,
which were first pressed into clay tablets or scratched into the skins of sheep

or goats thousands of years ago, remain alive, powerful, and challenging. Scripture is one of the full fountains from which we are able to fill our empty pitchers. Whether you are a lectionary preacher or a topical preacher, you will use Scripture in some way, and as a preacher, you have decisions to make about how you will approach that Scripture.

During his tour of the United States, an enthusiastic, if somewhat ill-informed, reporter attempted to interview theologian Karl Barth. "Could you," he asked, "sum up your theology in a sentence or two?" A sentence or two? One only needs to look at the bookshelf-length *Church Dogmatics* to realize what a ridiculous question that is. However, Barth did answer the artless reporter's question in one sentence: "Jesus loves me, this I know, for the Bible tells me so."

If you are someone for whom Scripture is authoritative, Barth's answer makes complete sense. The Bible tells the story of God's actions in the creation of the world and the creation of human beings. It tells over and over again the stories of the ways that God rescued God's people from slavery, brought them up from exile, healed them, fed them, and finally came to be one of them. The Bible tells of Jesus' love. It tells us that "he humbled himself and became obedient to the point of death—even death on a cross" (Phil. 2:8). The Bible tells us that death could not hold him and that God raised him on the third day. The Bible tells us that we, who are buried with him in his death, have, through his love, eternal life. "Jesus loves me, this I know, for the Bible tells me so."

But what if you are not sure about the authority of Scripture, or the Bible, while filled with important lessons, is not the supreme authority in your life? For you, Barth's answer leaves many questions. How do I know that Jesus loves me? Why should I listen to what the Bible says? How can I be sure that it is telling the truth? How can I trust a book that was written two thousand years ago? My life isn't anything like the lives of the people who wrote the books or for whom it was written. How can a book that is thousands of years old, about people who lived in the desert and rode donkeys, have anything to say to a person who can fly around the world in a day and has instantaneous contact with anyone, anywhere, anytime through phones and computers?

We preach in a world where authority is problematic. Whether we know anything about deconstructionism, postmodernity, or any of the other numerous philosophical schools that describe the culture in which we teach, learn, and think, we know that it is difficult to make authoritative claims. As the popular bumper sticker commands, "Question Authority." Ron Allen observes, "In a postmodern setting, the preacher cannot simply invoke an external source (tradition, empirical observation, or logical deduction) as sufficient basis for the congregation's assent. The questions of the deconstructionists haunt the sermon" (Allen, Blaisdell, and Johnston, 37).

In this postmodern climate in which we preach, how do we make a decision about whether to trust someone's claim? One way is through commonly held standards known as warrants. Let's return to Karl Barth. His claim was "Jesus loves me." Obviously if one was not being cute or clever, one would need to expand upon "Jesus" and "love." Who was/is Jesus? What does one mean by love? That may have been Barth's claim, but how did Barth get from the Bible to the declaration that Jesus loves him?

Data, Warrants, and Claims

In the mid-1950s, philosopher Stephen Toulmin sought to explore how we "assess the soundness, strength and conclusiveness of arguments" (Toulmin, 1). There is a difference, he observed, between formal logic, the argumentation of philosophers and mathematicians, and practical logic, the arguments of scientists, politicians, and theologians. We use practical, not formal, logic, in the arguments that we all make everyday. He sought to understand the process of practical logic. How are we able to state a claim that is then accepted by others, even if it is not a claim that can be subjected to the certainty of formal logic?

Central to Toulmin's book, *The Uses of Argument*, was his layout of arguments. A *claim*, he wrote, is the conclusion that we are trying to show. For Barth, that claim was "Jesus loves me." (Notice that Barth's claim is personal; he is not saying anything about Jesus' love for anyone else.) To establish our claim, we put forward *data* or *grounds* for making that claim. Barth's data were scriptural: I am able to make the claim that Jesus loves me because it says so in the Bible. Toulmin observed that although claims and the data to back up those claims may be all that we hear or see, there is more to an argument.

Barth's claim of love and data of the Bible depend upon what Toulmin identified as the *warrant*. A warrant, he wrote, is the "practical standard" or "justification" for moving from the data to the claim. Unlike the data and claim, the warrant may be assumed or unstated, as it was in Barth's claim. Nevertheless, Toulmin noted, the warrant is always there; furthermore, it is frequently at the level of the warrants that arguments fail, because the receivers do not subscribe to the same warrants as the person making the argument.

What is Barth's warrant? His claim is that Jesus loves him, and his data are the report of the Bible. The warrant that allows Barth to move from that data to his claim, although unspoken, would seem to be "the Bible is an authoritative book, one that is trustworthy and tells the truth about essential things. I trust what it says."

For Barth, then, the Bible was supremely authoritative. How did he know anything about God? He knew it because of the Bible, *sola scriptura*. As you approach your use of Scripture, you have decisions to make about your understanding of the authority of Scripture. You probably have already done that to a certain extent, but you may not have done it critically or systematically.

What does your community, your denomination, think about the authority of Scripture? What place does Scripture have in the worship of your community? Do people think that it is important to include the Bible in your sermon? Must the sermon have a scriptural text? Or is it permissible to use another book, poem, or movie as the main "text" of your sermon? If we, as a church, declare that Scripture is authoritative, why do we make that claim? There is a continuum of possible answers to that question.

At one pole, Scripture is authoritative because it is the very word of God. It does not need to be affirmed by any outside authorities, nor does it need any outside interpreters. Through the Bible God is speaking directly to us. For people who ascribe to this understanding of authority, the direct, divine inspiration—and for some, even the inerrancy—of Scripture is self-evident.

At the other pole are persons for whom the Bible has no more authority than any other book. They read it as a work of literature for its fascinating stories, the beauty of its poetry, or the glimpses it provides into ancient cultures. This is not to say that they cannot be moved by the calls to justice and fairness contained within its words, but the Bible moves them as any classic work of literature has the power to move and transform.

In the great middle of this continuum is a wide variety of persons and positions who accept the Bible as the authoritative book of the church but to a greater or lesser degree also understand it as the work of human authors who wrote within and out of their limited cultural context. Consequently, just as the Bible can be translated into other languages to make it understandable to people who do not read Hebrew or Greek, it also may be translated from one culture or worldview into another and requires interpretation in order to be understood by contemporary readers.

Preachers must be aware of their own beliefs on the authority of the biblical texts and also of those beliefs in the communities in which they are preaching. It is one of the fundamental factors that will inform how preachers interact with the Scriptures.

THE PREACHER AS INTERPRETER: THE QUESTION OF HERMENEUTICS

Some preachers claim that Scripture is self-interpreting. But must of us are aware that we are called to examine and interpret Scripture. Interpretation involves another dance, a dance involving the text, the author or authors of the text, and the reader or readers of the text. Hermeneutics challenges us to think about what it means to be an interpreter of a text.

In classical mythology, Hermes was a demigod who got the job as the messenger between the gods and people because he was able to interpret the divine will. Because of his ability at translating the divine messages, Hermes lent his name to the discipline of translation and interpretation, *hermeneutics*. While the root of the discipline of hermeneutics was in the study of Scripture, whether we know it or not, we now use hermeneutics in any number of areas of our lives, from poetry to films to the law. When the justices of the Supreme Court seek to render a judgment about a particular case, they interpret the case in the light of the Constitution. Does the judgment that was rendered by another judge and jury conform to the text of the Constitution, to the intention of those who wrote the Constitution? In asking questions like these, the justices are hermeneuts. Likewise, when you being to study and interpret a particular biblical text, you are a hermeneut. Hermeneutics, then, is the study of the theories underpinning that task.

Like the authority of Scripture, hermeneutics is a topic that deserves a course entirely unto itself. Although we can't go into this important subject in great detail, we can introduce preachers to some of the important hermeneutical questions to which they must pay attention.

Contemporary biblical scholarship presents the preacher with a variety of hermeneutical options. The challenge lies in navigating among them. If, for example, we take an objective, scientific approach to scriptural analysis, such as that advocated by the historical-critical method, the emphasis tends to be on the text as an historical document. Some scholars argue that the intention of the author or the character of the community for whom the text was written takes precedence.

Biblical scholars have also helped us to appreciate the text itself and how texts accomplish what they set out to do. Literary and rhetorical analysis of the text helps us to appreciate the strategies, the plots, the figures of speech, and the world constructed by the text itself.

All these hermeneutical approaches (and more) contribute to our reading and interpretation of the text. But the preacher cannot stop there, because for the preacher the text is also a living word that calls for a response by the contemporary reader. Homiletical hermeneutics is permeated by application for the contemporary readers/listeners. It is not enough just to talk about the "what God did back then" of a text, but must point to "what God is doing now" in and through the same text.

As we noted in the last chapter, each of us is the member of several communities. We read Scripture out of our church family. But we also read Scripture out of our secular, cultural, racial, and ethnic families as well. We read

Scripture informed by the great cloud of witnesses who have read before us, and we read Scripture with the inspiration and encouragement of the Holy Spirit. Consequently, we come to every reading with our particular point of view, biases, and suspicions. Postmodern writers have helped us to appreciate that there is no such thing as a neutral stance.

Each of the communities in which we reside provides us with points of view, rules, guidelines, and standards for reading and interpretation. If we as preachers must negotiate the tension between reading Scripture as a historical document and a living word, we also must negotiate the tension between relying only on the insights and knowledge of others, and rejecting them. Hermeneutics, therefore, helps us to understand and develop the process of disciplined study and interpretation that will open up text. Practically speaking, how does one go about developing an understanding of the interaction between the interpreter(s) and the text?

As one begins the process of interpretation, we must, as Frederick Tiffany and Sharon Ringe describe it their work *Biblical Interpretation: A Roadmap*, "begin at home" (Tiffany and Ringe, 25). We must understand ourselves and our context. Philosopher Hans-Georg Gadamer argues that readers should not try to "clear their minds" or adopt an objective, unbiased stance as they come to a text. That, he would say, is impossible, for we always come to a text with prejudices. "To interpret means precisely to bring one's own preconceptions into play so that the text's meaning can really be made to speak for us" (Gadamer, 397).

By virtue of our social location, we all have a vantage point from which we view life and its experiences. A vantage point implies a horizon that determines how far and how much we are able to see. The goal is not to step out of that vantage point, but to recognize where we are and what our limitations are. That perspective, according to Gadamer, does not hinder our ability to interpret; rather, it makes interpretation possible. It does demand that we are open to being changed, open to extending our horizon, open, if you would, to moving up the mountain and getting a "better view."

We come with a view of ourselves and our situation and a desire to get a better view. But we must start somewhere. Paul Ricoeur, in his description of the hermeneutical arc, says we start with a guess, with a first sense of what the Scripture means. But we do not stop at that first, often naive, guess.

Rather, we turn to those many methodological approaches in the process of explanation. We have mentioned the historical-critical, literary, and rhetorical methods, but they are only a few among many. We are today either blessed or challenged by the opportunity to hear from many vantage points, not just the vantage point of North American/European male academics. While they still have much to say to us, we also need to include the insights of feminist, liberation, and postcolonial scholars. Schleiermacher described the hermeneutical circle as the process of moving from the whole to the analysis of its parts, and then back to the whole. We might also think of a hermeneutical circle as one that includes these various voices. One might enter at any point—feminist, rhetorical, liberationist—but it is important to move around the circle and listen to all voices.

Understanding our hermeneutical approach prepares us for the discipline of exegesis. What do we do when we take the Bible off the shelf and begin our sermon preparation? How do we develop a method that enables us to plumb the depths of the text? How are we able to open ourselves to God's message, for ourselves and for our listeners?

READING THE TEXT: THE QUESTION OF EXEGESIS

James Weldon Johnson reminds us that we, preachers and congregants alike, are like empty pitchers seeking to be filled by the living water of God's good news. But another poet compared reading Scripture to trying to take a sip of water from a fire hose. That living water is often not a gentle stream but a cascading waterfall. Open any page of the Scriptures, and countless ideas and images, colorful characters, and life-changing challenges flood over you. How are we to take that sip? How can we possibly absorb all that we need to in order to do justice to God's word? An essential part of any preacher's preaching routine, therefore, must be an attentive reading and analysis of the text or texts that will be preached.

Listening to the Text

Nothing is as damaging to the preaching process as turning to the text assigned for a Sunday and immediately closing up your Bible with the observation, "Oh, it's the parable of the prodigal son; I know that!" Yes, in one sense you do know that. You have heard it many times, you could retell the story, but the you who is coming to the text is not the same person who read it, or heard it, or preached from it the last time you read, heard, or preached the text. As Tiffany and Ringe observe in urging preachers to begin at home:

> One reason for the decision to begin at home is that every journey into and with the biblical text will be new, principally because each community of interpreters at every moment of its life is unique. . . . Each person will have changed, the composition of the group may have varied, and the wider historical and social context will be different. (Tiffany and Ringe, 25)

You are different, your community is different, our world is different; so it is important to be open to the text and take time to dwell in and with the text. I would encourage you to do that three different ways.

Begin by reading the text out loud. Did you know that we use different parts of our brain when we read aloud than we do when we read silently? So read the text out loud, perhaps several times. This will force you to concentrate and avoid the temptation to skim over the text. Note the sound and shape of the words. What do you highlight as you read? What is stressed, what is not? As you read, do you hear patterns emerging? Write your observations down.

Two colleagues introduced me to a wonderful exercise for reading Scripture that forces you to focus on the text to the exclusion of all else. Seated, place the text in front of you. Now, put your fingers in your ears. (That is why you should do this exercise in the privacy of your own study!) With your fingers in your ears, begin reading the text aloud. What images come alive? What words attract your attention? Again, with your fingers in your ears, read the text aloud once more. Do different words pop out the second time? Again, write your observations down.

In this first fresh encounter with the text, pay attention to "speed bumps" (Tiffany and Ringe, 56–57), the details in your reading that catch your attention, make you think, perhaps warm your heart and comfort you, or make you angry or uncomfortable. What are the ideas, people, images that seem out of place? What are the moments that cause you to hit your forehead with the exclamation, "Oh no, do I have to preach about this?"

Why do I keep telling you to write down your observations? Remember, we are trying to drink from a fire hose or pounding waterfall. As you read and study the Scriptures, you are going to discover many ideas and images. If you don't write them down, one idea will quickly replace another, and the first will be lost or forgotten.

Another colleague has introduced me to another way of reading Scripture. While the last exercise provided a way of blocking out all interference, this exercise does just the opposite. It challenges you to read the text in the midst of life's interference. Take your text into a variety of places, and read it in the midst of the life swirling around you. What is it like to read the story of the prodigal son as you sit at a bench in a shopping mall? What happens when you read the story of the raising of Lazarus in the waiting room of a hospital? What about reading the story of Moses and the burning bush on a subway platform or at a bus station? How does your physical location change how you hear God's words? What happens when you put God's holy word together with God's creation? Do you hear things differently? Do you make different connections?

Attentive reading is the beginning, but it is not the end, of a preacher's engagement with the scriptural text. Now you must turn to the development of an exegetical method.

DEVELOPING AN EXEGETICAL DISCIPLINE

My father was a pilot during World War II. That experience taught him the importance of a checklist. Before he could take off, my father had to get out a big book and run down a checklist that insured he inspected everything in the plane, both inside and out. He would flip all of the levers, push all of the buttons, and check the radio. Then he would walk around the whole plane, checking the flaps and the tire pressure, making sure that everything was intact and ready to fly. He was the pilot, and it was essential that he completed that task. He could not leave it to anyone else.

The next time you are waiting for a flight, watch the plane on which you are going to be flying, and you may have a chance to see the pilot of your B-747 or DC-10 doing the same thing. They go over the same checklist, and the pilot herself walks around the outside of the plane visually checking every detail. They don't want to miss a thing—and aren't we glad for that!

Preachers need to develop a similar checklist for analyzing Scripture in preparation for preaching. We need to make sure that we cover many things in a regular, rather than hit-and-miss, fashion. In the rest of this chapter I will suggest many different dimensions of an exegetical discipline, but I encourage you, with the help of many wonderful resources available to preachers, to develop your own exegetical method. In going through their checklists, pilots increase the chances of discovering any potential problems. Likewise, by working through the many different approaches to the reading of the Scriptures, the preacher increases his or her chances of discovering wonderful ways of encountering new insights and revelations in God's living word for us.

Preachers today are fortunate in that they have access to so many different ways of approaching a text. As we saw in the previous section, the hermeneutical circle invites us to view a text from many points of view. However, when the many possible ways of examining a text intersect the time constraints experienced by most preachers, there is the potential for paralysis. Have no fear. If you develop your checklist, this will prove to be a wonderful way for you to turn a text over and over, upside down, and inside out.

What is important to remember, as you go through the text in an ordered way, is that you are only gathering potential information, not making final decisions about what will appear in the sermon. Too often preachers uncover so much interesting, fascinating material that they are tempted to include all of it in their sermon. The goal of homiletical exegesis is to hear what the text is saying to you and your community at this time, not to immerse the congregation in minutiae that may be more overwhelming than inspiring. What are some strategies for this? Let's look at three worlds: the literary, the social, and the theological.

Words, Words, Words: The Literary World

- *Translate.* Many of you are fortunate enough to have become comfortable negotiating your way through the Hebrew or Greek texts. If so, the first thing that you might do is develop your own translation of the text. If you are not that fortunate, try reading the text in a number of different translations. This will give you a feel for the various ways that the text has been imported into various languages.
- *Key words.* Identify key words, for example, the words you are tempted to highlight, and identify unfamiliar words. What is the original Hebrew or Greek word? What does it mean? Here, a Hebrew, Greek, or biblical dictionary such as *Vine's Complete Expository Dictionary* will be helpful. In her work *Amazing Grace*, Kathleen Norris argues that most of us do not understand the vocabulary of our faith. Words such as *grace*, *salvation*, and *repentance* are abstract and somewhat threatening. But if we go back to their origins, why the authors chose the words they did to tell our story and give shape to our faith, they become real and alive.
- *Part of a whole.* What is the location of the text? Rarely in a worship service do we read a book of the Bible in its entirety. Consequently we get an incomplete picture every time we pull out a portion of the text to read and study. First, then, put the part back in the whole. What precedes the portion you are reading? What follows? Often your text is the answer to an earlier question. You should be aware of that. Likewise, a question may be asked in your text that is not answered until later, outside of your reading.
- *One author or many?* Many texts are like a quilt, constructed of the works of a number of authors. How is the text put together? Does it contain the threads of a number of works? On whose work has another author drawn? When the author quotes another text, have there been changes to the text?
- *Related texts.* Often a story or refrain appears in a number of different texts. How does your text differ from those other appearances? What has changed? What remains the same?
- *Genre.* What literary genre is the author using? Is the text a narrative, a letter, a poem?
- *Structure.* What is the shape of the text? How is the text put together? What introduces the portion of the text? If it is a story, how does it proceed? Is there a point of conflict in the text? If so, is there a resolution to that conflict? Paul Scott Wilson is always urging preachers to "make the movie." If you were the director who turned this text into a play or movie, how would you block it out? What would be the camera angles? How many scenes are there, and how would you change scenes?

- *Tone.* What tone is the author seeking to convey? Is it comforting or challenging? Does the voice of the author seem joyful or angry?

People and Power: The Social World

In the first round of analysis, the literary reading of the text, most of your analysis was done inside the text, with the help of a few resources. As you move into an analysis of the social and political context of the reading, however, commentaries will be helpful.

- *Author.* What can you tell about the author? Why is the author writing this text?
- *Audience.* What can you tell about the audience that this author envisioned?
- *Social context.* In the previous chapter we examined the various ways that we might talk about an audience: the audience that actually listens to or reads a text, the audience the author envisions or hopes to create, and the wider audience or the culture in which a text is created. What do we know about the culture that existed when the text was written? What was their daily life like? How did people live, marry, raise and educate their children? How did people make a living? How was the culture governed?
- *Power and powerless.* An important element in understanding any culture is a knowledge of who is powerful and who is not. How, in that culture did one achieve a status of power? In the text, who are the powerful individuals? Who are the powerless?

God Talk: The Theological World

- *God's actions.* Where is God in this text? Is God acting or does God seem absent?
- *Author's theological agenda.* What do you think this author wants you to know or understand about God and a particular theological question? What is the author's concern or confession?
- *Cloud of witnesses.* You and your community are approaching God's word from your particular social location. You are calling out to God from your world. How have others in different locations read and interpreted this text and God's call to them? Read commentaries both across time and across cultural or geographical location in order to listen to the interpretations of your brothers and sisters in the faith.
- *Theological questions.* Earlier in this chapter we reviewed the questions that William Placher argued we should always be asking. Review your text in the light of those questions. Does, for example, your text help us to know who God or Christ is? Is that the concern of the text? Or does this text challenge us to think about how we are to live our lives as followers of Christ, or where we are going, the end of our life?

Back Home: Our World

Finally, before you leave the analysis of the text you need to come back to your starting place, you and your community. You need to finish Paul Ricoeur's hermeneutical arc, identifying the connections between the biblical context and your context, noting that we have come out at a different place. Each time you come to a text, you are a different person who has undergone different experiences; therefore, you must always be open to a fresh reading. The same is true at the end of your reading and analysis. After your initial guess and after your study, you have met the Word and the God who speaks it. You have been changed and transformed by it. How has your understanding of the text changed since you first read it aloud? What have you learned? How do you see your world, your life, your community, your brothers and sisters in Christ differently? How do you connect the questions and challenges of the author with the questions and challenges faced by you and your community?

THIS IS ONLY THE BEGINNING!

You have been reading and studying your texts. You have been praying and thinking. You may have pages and pages of notes. But this is only the beginning. You aren't ready to write your sermon.

The challenge at this point it to begin to formulate a theme, topic, or direction for your sermon, but remain open to other possibilities. There is still more detective work to do, and you do not want to close down the process too soon. The next chapter will do two things: first, give you more resources for the invention phase of sermon preparation, and second, discuss that difficult step of identifying the goal of the sermon.

QUESTIONS

1. We began a discussion of the authority of Scripture. Is it the inerrant, divinely inspired Word of God? Is it a great book of literature? You need to answer the important questions raised by this issue. In conversation with your denomination, your tradition, you need to decide where you stand on the authority of Scripture. You also need to realize that, whether or not they have done so consciously, your listeners also come to worship and to your sermon having considered this question. What is your understanding of the authority of Scripture?

2. If you adopt an historical-critical hermeneutical approach to the interpre-

tation of the Scriptures, you are likely to be more interested in what life was like "back then." What was life like, what did they eat, what did they wear? But this is only one of the many hermeneutical approaches that have been developed. After a review of the many options, select two or three of the interpretive screens that you feel best resonate with your understanding. What are they? Why did you choose them?

3. I have offered you the beginning of an exegetical checklist. Develop your own checklist, one that takes into consideration the hermeneutical approaches you chose.

READ MORE ABOUT IT

Allen, Ronald, Barbara Shires Blaisdell, and Scott Black Johnston. *Theology for Preaching: Authority, Truth and Knowledge of God in a Postmodern Ethos.* Nashville: Abingdon, 1997.

Dulles, Avery. *Models of Revelation.* Maryknoll, NY: Orbis Press, 1996.

Gadamer, Hans-Georg. *Truth and Method.* Trans. Joel Weinsheimer and Donald G. Marshall. New York: Continuum, 1994.

Jasper, David. *A Short Introduction to Hermeneutics.* Louisville, KY: Westeminster John Knox Press, 2004.

Norris, Kathleen. *Amazing Grace: A Vocabulary of Faith.* New York: Riverhead Books, 1998.

Placher, William, ed. *Essentials of Christian Theology.* Louisville, KY: Westminster John Knox Press, 2003.

Toulmin, Stephen. *The Uses of Argument.* Cambridge: Cambridge University Press, 1986.

Wallace, James. *Preaching to the Hungers of the Heart.* Collegeville, MN: Liturgical Press, 2002.

Wiles, M. F. "Origen as Biblical Scholar." In *The Cambridge History of the Bible: From the Beginnings to Jerome*, ed. P. R. Ackroyd and C. F. Evans. Cambridge: Cambridge University Press, 1978.

7

Detectives of the Divine

One Sunday [the pastor] asked me to sit up close to the pulpit. He wanted me to hear his sermon, he said, and as I listened to him talk about the beauty of God's creation and our duty to be awed by it . . .it was as if someone had turned on all the lights. . . . I became a detective of divinity, collecting evidence of God's genius and admiring the tracks left for me to follow.

Barbara Brown Taylor, The Preaching Life, 14–15

TIME, TIME, TIME

We have been given the assurance by the one who has sent us that the Spirit of God will always be speaking through us: "what you are to say will be given to you at that time" (Matt. 10:19), but that does not mean that we do not need to do our part. A student once told me a joke that unfortunately hits close to home. A pastor mounted the pulpit and began his sermon by announcing to the congregation that he was going to try something new that morning: "I have written the first half of the sermon, and I am going to allow the Spirit to deliver the second half." He then proceeded to deliver the "hybrid" sermon. At the end of the service, amidst the shaking of hands and the words "good sermon, pastor," a parishioner took the pastor by the hand and leaned into him. "I want to tell you something pastor. *You* are a much better preacher than the Spirit!"

Of course we are not better preachers than the Holy Spirit; in fact, we cannot be preachers without the Spirit, but we can be poor preachers if we do not put our time and effort into our preaching. As I mentioned earlier and will now remind you again, good preaching needs *time, time, time*. You need time for prayer, for reading and meditating upon the Scriptures, and for study. Good preaching needs time for reflection; for turning ideas, thoughts, themes, directions over in your mind; for testing those ideas with others. It takes time to let those ideas percolate through your life, through the news you hear, the people to whom you speak, through the meetings you attend, the errands you run, the e-mails you write.

Aristotle wrote that rhetoric was the process of reviewing "all the available means of persuasion." A good speaker, he argued, was one who began by thinking, reading, exploring, and examining all of the ideas, stories, issues that might potentially move the people to whom he or she would be speaking. But please note—and we will return to this over and over again—he does not write that all of this will end up in the speech! The point Aristotle is trying to make is that there are numerous resources available to the speaker and the speaker should attempt to uncover as many of them as possible before deciding the focus and goal of the speech and before moving on to the arrangement of the speech.

In the previous chapter we began our examination of the process of invention—how preachers read, study, research the Scriptures that will challenge and inform their sermon. The Scriptures are certainly an important part of the preacher's process of invention, but they should not be the only place where we encounter what Barbara Brown Taylor reminds us are the tracks of God's genius. In this chapter we will discuss three other important dimensions of invention: the creative process, theological reflection for preaching, and finally, how one goes about deciding the theme, purpose, and goal of a sermon.

Again I remind you, good preaching takes *time*. If you do not devote time to your sermon, its preparation will be rushed and unfocused. It will have neither the depth nor the richness of a sermon that you have turned over and over and over in your mind. You will not give the Spirit time to work on you.

THE CREATIVE PROCESS: HOLY SPIRIT TERRITORY

For most people in seminary, the majority of the writing that they have done during their educational career has been research oriented. They have focused on only one-third of Augustine's triad. They have learned to "teach." While study and research are certainly an important part of sermon preparation, sermons are much more than reporting on the ideas of others. Preaching needs also to "delight" and "move." It is a creative activity that demands imagination, inventiveness, and integration. As Jana Childers observes, we need to follow the creative process and "conceive, nourish, and give birth to a sermon" (Childers, *Birthing*, ix).

In a study some years ago researchers set out to discover the difference between those who called themselves creative and those who did not. Did the creative have a particular quality, an innate or special ability, that others did not have? In the end, the study was forced to conclude that the only difference between creative people and noncreative people was that the creative people thought of themselves as creative people.

We have no choice but to consider ourselves creative people, because we have been created in the image of a creating God and filled with the Spirit that "blows where it chooses, and you hear the sound of it, but you do not know where it comes from or where it goes" (John 3:8). We are called upon to enter into the creative process. Linda Clader reminds us that preaching is "Holy Spirit territory. The dynamic space where faith can grow, where a creative impulse can engender trust and incite action, where a bolt of electricity can move the unmovable" (Clader, 3). But without trying to control the Spirit, is it possible to learn more about the creative process that will help us move into and be a little more comfortable in that scary, dynamic space?

A great deal of work has actually been done on analyzing the creative process. Whether one is getting ready to paint a picture, plan a building, organize a new business, or design a computer game, one goes through a rather predictable series of steps. Knowing what those steps are helps as one begins a new project, because one is able to work with, rather than against, that creative flow.

The creative process begins with a period of *preparation*. During this time we engage the project or problem on which we are working. We attempt to gather the information we will need to successfully complete our task. This is a period of conscious thought. We are thinking, reading, searching for resources, often in the most unlikely places. At the outset, writers read the works of other writers, preachers listen to the sermons of others, painters may wander the halls of a museum searching for inspiration and direction in the paths that other painters have taken.

You are probably familiar with the notion of *brainstorming*. When a group is trying to solve a problem, members propose any number of solutions. One of the rules of the process is that as each solution is suggested, no solution can be ruled out for any reason. No matter how impractical or impossible the suggestion may appear, all can be brought to the table. The same should be with the preaching process. All ideas should be allowed to float into the picture—perhaps jotted down on paper. We don't want to rule out any direction. So we engage in the process of collecting materials that will stimulate our thinking and provide us with the resources that will eventually provide the examples and illustration for our sermon.

At the outset the creative process demands openness and a sense of play. Many of us are tempted to inhibit or block this play of ideas. We want to be sensible and practical. We want to find immediate resolution. We are uncomfortable with this dynamic flow. But that is where we need to be at this point. The reminder that the Spirit blows where it will came in the middle of Jesus' nocturnal conversation with Nicodemus. When Jesus told him that he must be born again, he refused to follow the Spirit into that wonderful image of new birth and freedom. "How can anyone be born after having grown old? Can one enter a second time into the mother's womb and be born?" (John 3:4).

Unfortunately, like Nicodemus we eventually find this part of the process very frustrating. People studying the creative process found that the period of preparation eventually reached a *plateau*, a period when the artist or engineer, faced with so many possibilities, so many solutions, became discouraged. What direction should he take, what topic should she chose? The reality is that there are many good choices, but we are uncertain which is the best one to make.

If one is not aware that this is a predictable part of the process, one will become discouraged and possibly quit. Runners often talk of the "wall" that they must work through. But too many runners reach that point and quit. At this point some preachers are tempted to think that they will never find a good sermon and turn to the sermons of others. This is why allowing enough time for the process is so important. While consciously the preacher may feel frustrated, unconsciously the mind is in fact wrestling with the options.

While traditionally this period is identified as the period of *incubation*, a colleague of mine compares this to making coffee. We need all of the grounds— that is, all of the information we find during our research—but to make coffee we have to let the grounds percolate. The grounds and the water have to mix together. Again, you see how important time is. If the water and the grounds aren't given enough time, one ends up with weak coffee—brown water. Likewise, not enough incubation or percolation leaves one with a weak sermon.

An interesting thing about the creative process and the brain is that even when we don't realize we are working on our sermon, we are. If you begin a sermon on Monday, you may have a day or two when you do not put pen to paper (or fingers to keyboard), but you can still be writing the sermon. Ideas, images, solutions, and answers are swirling about. Then, often suddenly, we finally arrive at the moment of *illumination*, the "Aha!" moment when we see what we need to do, where we need to go. It is the moment when things fall into place.

The creative process does not end in "Aha!" The moment of illumination is in many ways the beginning, not the end, of the process. Now one must begin the process of *elaboration* and *articulation*. This is the time of testing and judgment. Is this, in fact, a good idea? Is this building "build-able"? Will the bridge support the weight of the cars? Will the sculpture stand? Is this an appropriate message for the people to whom one will be preaching? Is the sermon faithful to God, to the text? One also must decide how this idea will be *communicated*. One has found what to say. Now one must decide how to say it. Deciding what one is going to say is only the beginning. One must then begin the process of selection: What will be included in the sermon? What will not? In what form and what order will the materials appear? That we discuss in upcoming chapters.

THEOLOGICAL MINDFULNESS

Thomas Troeger compares imagination to sailing a boat, "We cannot make the wind blow, but we can trim the sails and tend the helm" (Troeger, 14). We can't, he observes, control the Spirit, but we can open ourselves to God's presence:

> "What, then, are the principles for using our imaginations so that we can receive the *ruach*, the Spirit of the living God to whom our preaching is witness? The primary principle from which all the others are derived is that we are attentive to what is" (Troeger, 15).

Attentive to what is, we need to develop the practice of theological mindfulness

In the epigraph at the opening of this chapter, Barbara Brown Taylor recalls an experience that she had as a young girl. She had said or done something that had intrigued her pastor, who then decided to use it in his sermon. He wanted to make sure that she was near him when he preached so she could hear her contribution. She recalls the thrill of excitement when she realized that she was part of the sermon. But even more important than hearing her story in the sermon was the recognition that God was involved in her life. It was then, she writes, "I became a detective of divinity, collecting evidence of God's genius and admiring the tracks left for me to follow" (Taylor, 14–15).

As preachers we are all called to be detectives of the divine, or as Mary Catherine Hilkert describes it, we are to be about "naming grace." Gerard Manley Hopkins wrote, the "world is charged with the grandeur of God." God's footprints are everywhere. So theological mindfulness is as important a dimension of the preaching process as scriptural exegesis. How do we go about naming grace? Where are we to look for God's footprints? Let's look at the experience of Moses. His is an excellent model of divine detection, theological mindfulness.

In the middle of his working day tending his flock, Moses noticed a bush that was burning. Now I must confess that I don't know how possible that was. Was this something that would normally happen, or was the burning itself unusual? What was unusual, what caught his attention, was that although the bush burned, it was not "consumed." It kept burning and burning, and still the bush remained. What was important for Moses, and what must be for us, was that Moses said, "I must turn aside and look at this great sight, and see why the bush is not burned up" (Exod. 3:3). Theological mindfulness is about three things: looking or noticing, turning aside or stopping what we are doing to reflect upon this great thing, and thinking or wondering. It is about asking questions: How is God involved in this? What is God trying to say to me, to us, in this moment?

LOOKING FOR GOD'S FOOTPRINT

"How beautiful upon the mountains are the feet of the messenger." As we approach the concept of becoming "mindful" preachers, let us return to the image of the preacher's feet. Too many of us live in cultures where we rarely use our feet. If we want to go somewhere, we jump in the car. Think about the difference between flying down the highway at fifty or sixty miles per hour and walking. What do you see when you are driving fifty miles per hour? You see road signs, stop signals, huge billboards, but the trees and grasses that line the side of the road become a blur. There is no way that you would be able to track any footprints at that speed.

As a preacher, you have been given beautiful feet. Use them. Slow down. Don't race through life; walk. When we are walking, we are able to stop and notice a lovely flower that is blooming beside us. We are able to appreciate the people around us. We have more of a chance of seeing God's footprints that surround us. The Scriptures will always be our most important resource. But where else might we look for God's holy marks, God's footprints?

- *Books.* Novels, short stories, plays and poetry can be a wonderful resource for the preacher. The more widely you read, the more you will be able to draw others into the conversation. The temptation is to go "quote mining." *Google* can be very helpful for finding quotes to include in your sermon, but it will never replace the experience of reading the entire work. When we separate a sentence or phrase from its place in the larger whole, we do violence to that text. As preachers we need to have a sense of the flow of the entire work and why a sentence or paragraph is so meaningful. It is also important for preachers to be aware of what books have captured the corporate attention. If everyone in your congregation is reading *The DaVinci Code*, you had better read it yourself and be prepared to answer the questions presented by such a book.

- *Movies*. Preachers cannot overestimate the importance of motion pictures for today's listener. In fact—and we will return to this later—many preachers are now making film clips a part of their sermon. Some movies are explicitly religious and are based on the Scriptures—as *The Ten Commandments* and *The Passion of the Christ*. Others, while not based on Scripture, have religious themes—*Dogma*, *The Mission*, and *Jesus of Montreal*. Finally, some movies that capture the attention of the moviegoing audience, while not explicitly religious, enable the view to reflect on theological issues. It is essential for preachers to be attentive to the movies people are watching. When a motion picture such as Mel Gibson's *The Passion of the Christ* captures so much attention, the preacher is presented with what educators like to call "a teaching moment."
- *Television programs*. Much of our common life today revolves around what people watch on television. Television programs, both positively and negatively, present preachers with teaching moments. Their themes and images provide the preacher with the cultural vocabulary. While we might not like to think that God could be speaking to us through popular television programs, our earlier brothers and sisters in the faith were not too thrilled to think that God could use Cyrus to rescue God's people (Isa. 45:1–7).
- *Life*. It seems rather silly to have to tell preachers to look at the lives they are living, but unfortunately preachers have neglected the habit of looking for burning bushes. What burning bushes are being put in *your* path? We have discussed the burning bush of Scripture and how we are to turn aside and look at that, but what of the other bushes that God places in our paths? As children of God, we are called upon to turn aside and investigate what captures our attention. What intrigues you? What makes you angry? What horrifies you? What makes your heart sing? What brings you great joy? What makes you cry? Jesus declared to the woman at the well that he would give her living water. Our tears are living water, a sign that God is touching our hearts and minds. We must then attend, question, and ponder.

TURNING ASIDE: THE PREACHER'S SKETCHBOOK

Before I attended seminary I was an art teacher. An important tool for every artist, and therefore a critical part of every art class, is a sketchbook. It has been one thing that I have carried over into many of my preaching classes. Why keep a sketchbook?

Art teachers quickly realize that they must teach their students to look. Our discussion about the difference between hearing and listening applies also to seeing and looking. If you ask six- or seven-year-olds to draw a tree, they will happily draw a tree. However, even if they are sitting in front of a beautiful spreading maple tree, they will draw a tree that looks a lot like a lollipop—a straight, squat brown trunk with a round green top.

As you begin to teach people to draw the tree that is actually in front of them, you must train them to really look at the tree. People's temptation is to see the tree, that is, to let the light waves bounce off the tree, hit their optic nerve, and register in the form that they have come to identify as a tree (and if one is even more sophisticated, to know that it is a maple, or oak, or magnolia). But when they put pencil to paper, they will draw not what is in front of them, but their idea of a tree. The goal of the artist's sketchbook is to force students or artists to both see and look and then to draw what is really before them. The goal of the preacher's sketchbook is the same, to teach preachers to both see and look at the world around them, at the burning bushes and the divine tracks.

Moses was probably getting bored watching sheep and goats nibbling on grasses and scrubby bushes and wandering away from the rest of the flock. Nevertheless, he came alive when he saw a strangely burning bush. He came alive and both saw and looked at that bush. In my class I make the assignment that the students need to record an entry every day. Like Moses, they may be bored or perhaps preoccupied with the duties of life, but they must train themselves to be attentive to the life around them. In their sketchbook they are to record those moments or incidents that capture their attention—a beautiful tree aflame with its autumn colors, a bird pecking at the remains of a cookie dropped by a child, two people engaged in a heated discussion (read argument), someone in a coffee shop who is clearly distressed about something.

These moments that fill our lives all too quickly pass us by and are then lost, if we do not turn aside, attend, and mark their significance. The sketchbook gives one an excellent place to record the moment. Some students draw the moment, while others sketch with words. They are to record what unfolded in front of them. Details are important. Remember that you are training yourself to really look, not just see—the same way you need to train yourself to attend to what is in a scriptural text, and not just notice that it is the parable of the wayward son. Think of those incidents that grabbed your attention: Are the leaves still on the tree, or have many of them fallen already? Are the leaves still under the tree, or has some efficient person already raked them up? What is the person in the coffee shop wearing? Is the person reading, talking on the phone, or just staring into space? Can you tell the relationship between the people who are arguing? Do you think that they are strangers, or do they seem to be related—husband and wife, mother and son? The more details you notice and record, the more attentive you will be, and the more details you will be able to report if you use this moment in a sermon. It is the detail that makes a moment come alive and be believable.

THE NEXT STEP: WONDERING

It is not just enough to stop and look. Why did this moment or scene capture your attention? Why were you intrigued, how did you feel? While watching the forlorn person in the coffee shop, did you want to go over and comfort the person and make sure the person was all right? While looking up at the bright red and orange tree, did you remember the joy of childhood when you would roll in the fallen leaves? Moses was confused. How could a bush burn and not crumble into a heap of ashes? Through that bush, God was trying to get Moses' attention. How many bushes did Moses miss? Through the bushes around us, God is trying to get our attention. How many bushes do we miss?

The final step is to connect this moment with our preaching responsibility, with the questions of the faith, with the stories and parables of Scripture. As my students are fond of saying of a moment or story, "That'll preach." But why will it preach? How is this moment a parable of the kingdom? Jesus attended as a poor old woman put her humble contribution in the temple treasury. He questioned the moment. He was both thrilled to see her commitment to God and angry at the arrogance of the wealthy officials who ignored this lowly woman. He thought about how this moment told him about her overwhelming faith in God, who is our ultimate protection. Does the autumn tree send you to the Psalter, "The earth is the LORD's and all that is in it, the world, and those who live in it" (Ps. 24:1)? Are the people arguing an image of the anger in our world and a sign of how difficult it is for us to live into Jesus' command "Love one another"?

BECOMING SHERLOCK HOLMES

In the art class, the goal of the sketchbook is twofold: one, to teach students to look, to attend to what is really in front of them; two, to develop the connection between eye and hand, to teach one's hand to draw what one sees. The preacher's sketchbook does the same. It will develop your ability to report what you are seeing in words that are engaging and alive. The wonderful thing about a sketchbook is that the more you do, the more competent you become. You will see the details of life that you would have easily missed. You will begin to notice the grace all around you and it will be firsthand, not secondhand reporting. You will become the Sherlock Holmes of preaching.

Finally, the sketchbook is an excellent way to keep you from forgetting and to help you file your observations. You will need to think about a way of keeping track of the materials you gather. Some preachers use actual files to clip newspaper articles or sketchbook entries. You may develop files for individual scriptural texts, theological questions, and doctrines, or you may have files that follow the lectionary cycle. But rather than have paper files, you might do this in the computer. If you come across a moment or story, it is better to file it so that you can use it when it really fits the scriptural text or theme, rather than using it that very week, even if it doesn't fit, leaving your listeners wondering, "This is a great story, but what does it have to do with this text?"

A HIGH-TECH SUGGESTION

In addition to carrying an artist's sketchbook and writer's journal, I would suggest one more item to take along wherever you go. Why not take a digital camera with you? If you see an interesting sign, building, or moment, you are able to capture it and might be able to project it for your congregation. In a later chapter we will discuss the use of images in preaching.

Professional photographers are never without a camera. They know that they must always be ready for what life has to offer. We might take a lesson from them. And digital cameras make it so easy to capture the image.

SO WHAT?

One of my favorite cartoons shows two scientists standing before a blackboard. The left half of the board is filled with a jumble of equations; so too is the right side. But in the middle, where the two sets of equations should meet, there is a large empty space with the notation "This is where the mystery happens." "I think you have to say more than this," one scientist is telling the other.

While it often feels like a mystery, there comes the moment in every sermon preparation when you have to decide what the sermon will be about and what the goal and purpose of that sermon are—the "so what" of the sermon or the "why will people care" of the sermon. This moment of illumination comes with time and hard work. It comes because we have been listening to God, to the text, to our listeners, and to the context in which we will be preaching.

There will be a few sermons that seem to come as a bolt out of the blue—sermons where you suddenly have that "Aha!" moment and you know with confidence what the sermon should be about, sermons where you truly feel that God has given you the word to preach. But those are the exceptions that

prove the rule. The message and purpose of most sermons come about usually by your hard decision-making work.

When you become an adept spiritual sleuth, when you hone your ability to
recognize that we live and move and have our being in a world permeated by
grace, you will also develop your skills at perceiving the countless sermons that
surround us. In every Scripture text there are numerous sermons, and each
week there are so many issues, questions, burning bushes about which we could
preach, but your listeners will thank you if you don't try to preach them all. We,
therefore, must not underestimate that crucial moment when we move from
the left side of the equation—the reading, thinking, questioning, pondering,
gathering of materials, and brainstorming—to the right side of the equation:
how the sermon will be constructed and preached. This is the moment of decision and choice, when we put aside all of the other possible sermons that could
be preached that week and settle on the one we will preach. But do we have to
wait for the "mystery" to occur? I don't think so. This is an active moment of
engagement with God and with all that you have learned so far.

In this moment I would encourage you to sit down and begin a process of
lively engagement that will end in the making of your choice.

- Begin with silence and prayer. This is a process that needs to begin with
  listening and being open to what God is saying to you and your community in this moment. Let this attitude of prayer and reception permeate
  your reflections. It is what one of my colleagues calls "brooding over the
  sermon."
- Review all of the information and reflections gathered from your exegesis of the texts.
- Review all the burning bushes you have encountered in the books you
  have been reading, the movies and television programs you have been
  watching, the experiences that have filled your week.
- Think about the people to whom you will be preaching. What are they
  like? Draw on the congregational analysis that you have done. Will
  you be speaking primarily to adults? If not, don't forget the children to
  whom you will be preaching. They, too, are filled with questions and
  wrestling with the way to be faithful followers. Think about providing
  both meat for those farther in their journey and milk for those who are
  new to the faith.
- Think about what has been happening in your congregation, your community, the nation, the world. What good things have been happening?
  What crises are on the hearts and minds of the people who will be walking through the door of your church that week? What needs to be
  acknowledged in the sermon?
- What is happening liturgically? Where are you in the church year? Is this
  a particular holiday or holy day? Is something special happening in your
  congregation—a baptism, the commissioning of teachers, the sending
  forth of a mission team?

- What is the intersection between the gospel and the life of God's people? What is God saying to us here and now? How does this relate to the life of discipleship that people are trying to live?

First, with all of that information before you, you decide what the message is. Can you describe in a very brief sentence what the sermon will be about? Be clear and concise from the outset. If you are not, your sermon will have a tendency, like the children of Israel in the desert, to ramble around searching for that clarity. And believe me, you will lose many of your listeners along the way. Will this be a sermon about God's love or God's forgiveness? Is this a sermon about discipleship or stewardship?

The more we narrow the subject of our sermon, the easier it will be for people to follow what we are saying. Following a spoken text is much more difficult than following a written text. A book can handle a more complicated, complex message. If you encounter something unclear in your reading you can go back and read it over and over again; your listeners can't do that. The physical layout of the book also helps your comprehension. Headings and subheadings give you a clue about where you are in the argument and text. They let you know when you are moving on to a new subject. They also signal when you have come to the end of one chapter and are moving on to a new one. You also have punctuation to let you know what is a question and what is a quotation, bold or italic type to show emphasis. You have none of those when you are speaking. Everything must be done with your tone of voice, your inflection, and your gestures. The clearer you are about your subject, the clearer it will be for your listeners.

Second, you identify the purpose or goal of the sermon. What do you want this sermon to do? Too many preachers stop once they have decided what the sermon will be about, and forget the "so what?" Why will this sermon speak to the people listening to it? What do you want people to take away from your sermon? What is the aim of your sermon?

- Do you want to inspire them and strengthen their faith?
- Do you want to persuade them to set off in a new direction?
- Do you want to challenge them?
- Do you want to affirm something that they are already doing?

RED FLAGS

As you think about the message and goal of your sermon, stop for a moment and discuss what I have come to call "red flag" sermons or "red flags" in sermons.

Think about the issues or topics which, if raised in your congregation, could generate a lot of controversy and anger. What if your sermon were about war, abortion, homosexuality? If you happened to mention a political issue or candidate in passing, how would your listeners react? Would they be upset or energized? You need to identify the red flags for your listeners. There will be different red flags in every congregation. You should not put yourself in the position of being surprised by a reaction.

If you are going to raise a red flag in a sermon, you must be prepared to discuss the issue. Nothing can derail a sermon more than raising a controversial issue in passing and then moving on without addressing that issue. That is why I call it a red flag. It is as though you have raised and waved a big red flag. You have gotten people's attention, and you then race away from the flag without acknowledging its presence.

Not mentioning an issue can also be a problem. If a big red flag is being raised in the lives of those to whom you are preaching—an upcoming election, a raging war, a major issue confronting the congregation—and you don't mention it, there will be a great disconnect between what is happening in your sermon and what is happening in the lives of your listeners. It does not necessarily mean that your entire sermon must be about that issue, but you must find some way to acknowledge its presence and the questions it raises in the lives of your people.

I recently listened to a sermon about discipleship. It was a good sermon and dealt well with the Gospel text. But as the sermon went on, I grew increasingly uncomfortable—not because of what the preacher was saying but, rather, what he was not saying. In two days the people in the congregation were going to be voting in a very heated election, and the preacher seemed to be totally ignoring that reality. When he finally did bring that into the sermon—by observing that one of the ways we lived out our discipleship was by making difficult political decisions—I was able to relax. The election was not the focus of his sermon, but he did make the connection between what was happening within and without the walls of the church.

THE FLEXIBLE FOCUS

As you prepare to decide what the sermon will look like, it is important to have a flexible focus. The meaning and purpose may be, in fact, will probably be, revised or refined as you move forward. God has not stopped speaking to you. New issues and new crises may arise—even on Sunday morning! The process of putting your sermon together may even help you clarify your message, but you cannot move forward without a concise working message. If you do not know where you are going, how will you know when you have arrived?

So, now you have a direction, and you have already begun to assemble materials that will provide you with the content of your sermon. The next step is to decide the order or form of your sermon. In the next chapter we turn to the question of sermon structure, form, and arrangement. How are you going to put together a sermon that will accomplish the goal and purpose you have identified?

QUESTIONS

1. You may remember the old children's brainteaser of pictures hidden within another picture. You might be given a drawing of a woodland scene, but hidden in the drawing—in the trunks of the trees, in the clouds, in the brook—would be pictures of boats, birds, fruit. You had to hunt for all of the hidden pictures. A crucial dimension of brainstorming is the recognition that there is more than one right answer. Choose a Bible story. Read it over. Now begin to think of all of the possible directions, all of the possible sermons that you might preach from that one story.
2. Prepare an entry for a preacher's sketchbook.
3. What are the most popular movies playing in the theaters? If you have seen one of the movies, what scriptural passages might you connect it to? What theological doctrines or concepts appear in the movie? How might you develop a sermon around this popular movie?

READ MORE ABOUT IT

Childers, Jana, ed. *Birthing the Sermon: Women Preachers on the Creative Process.* St. Louis: Chalice Press, 2001.
Meglin, Nick. *Drawing from Within: Unleashing Your Creative Potential.* New York: Warner Books, 1999.
Schlafer, David J. *Playing with Fire: Preaching Work as Kindling Art.* Cambridge: Cowley Publications, 2004.
Troeger, Thomas. *Imagining a Sermon.* Nashville: Abingdon, 1990.
Wilson, Paul Scott. *Imagination of the Heart: New Understandings in Preaching.* Nashville: Abingdon, 1988.

8

The Sermon Journey

But all things should be done decently and in order.
                    1 Corinthians 14:40

For there is a music wherever there is a harmony, order or propor-
    tion;
and thus far we may maintain the music of the spheres;
for those well ordered motions, and regular paces,
though they give no sound unto the ear,
yet to the understanding they strike a note most full of harmony.
        Sir Thomas Browne (1605–1682), Religio Medici *(1643)*

Form . . . is the turning of content into a material entity,
rendering the content accessible to others, giving it permanence.
                    Ben Shahn (1898–1969)

In Paris are two buildings that, in addition to being centuries apart, are archi-
tecturally polar opposites. The Cathedral of Notre Dame sits on Île de la Cité.
Begun in 1163, the magnificent Gothic structure houses the worship of the
community and tells the biblical story through jewel-like stained-glass and
stone carvings that cover the walls, inside and out. Taking almost two hundred
years to complete, the transcendental interior is made possible by the architectural genius of the flying buttresses that support the structure. You could
not have the vast open interior without the buttresses. They transfer the enormous weight of the stone and forces it away from the interior. Their own
beauty hides their purpose, and they become an integral part of the design
while their architectural function is forgotten. Theirs is a form that, as Ben

Shahn observes, makes the content permanent, but the form of the buttresses is concealed. Consequently, the church seems to rise from the island, pulled heavenward by celestial forces.

Leaving the cathedral, if you walk off the island on Pont d'Arcole, make your way past the Hôtel de Ville, and up Rue du Renard to the old market section of Paris, you will come to the Centre Georges Pompidou. When the building was completed in the 1970s, Parisians were horrified. The architect had decided not to conceal or mask either the skeletal structure or the mechanical necessities of the building. The architect wanted people to see the workings or the form of the building. Instead of the "innards" being hidden under a "skin" of stone, wood, or steel, as happens in most buildings, the steel framework, heating ducts, water pipes, and wire conduits are all clearly visible, prompting many at the time to think that the builders had forgotten to remove the scaffolding when the building was completed.

All sermons have inner workings that provide what David Buttrick calls the framework and structure. As in a building, that framework and structure keep the sermon up and moving. Clearly the architects of Notre Dame Cathedral and the Pompidou Center had very different goals and very different ideas of how to reach those goals. In this chapter we will explore the form and arrangement of sermons.

Deciding the form and arrangement of a sermon is as crucial a part of preaching as deciding the content of the sermon. Unfortunately, many preachers, and most listeners, are unaware of the presence or the importance of form and arrangement. They tend to think of form as neutral, an empty vessel into which one "pours" the content. Consequently, many preachers rely on a "default" preaching form: what they have "always heard." Therefore, an essential dimension of preaching is not only becoming familiar with the concepts of form and arrangement, but also developing a sense of the variety of options available to today's preacher. As we see in Notre Dame Cathedral and the Pompidou Center, form matters.

We have come a long way from "three points and a poem." Given the multiplicity of service types and the diversity of our listeners, both the ability to utilize a variety of sermon patterns and the knowledge of the aptness or appropriateness of various forms, will be crucial to the practice of preaching in the future.

THE ROAD TRIP

Before deciding on the form and the arrangement of your sermon, you will have decided what you are going to say and why you are going to say it. You then must think about how you are going to say it. What will the sermon journey be like?

Have you ever tried to lead someone on a car trip in which you know where you are going, but the driver following you has no idea? In many ways, preaching a sermon is like being the lead car. You know where you are going, but your listeners do not. Therefore, you must be very careful about giving timely signs and signals. What must you do when someone is following you?

- *Preview.* Although you can't always give complete directions—that is, after all, why you are leading; you can give people a general sense of what is going to be happening, the general direction you will be going, and some sense of the final destination. (There may be some sermon forms in which you don't want to reveal the conclusion until the end of the sermon, but we will return to that later. However, if your listeners do not have any idea where they are going, you need to be even more careful to make sure that they are with you every step of the way.)
- *Check the rearview mirror.* As you set off on your sermon, you need to keep checking your rearview mirror to make sure that those who are following are still with you. Don't stay locked in your manuscript. Look into the eyes of your listeners. Are they engaged, or do they have the look of someone who has no idea where you are and about what you are talking?
- *Don't get too far ahead.* When you are leading and another car is following, you can't let the interval between the cars get too large. If you get too far ahead, other cars may get in the way, and you may make it through a yellow light while the other car is stuck when the light turns red. You need to build in points at which people can catch up with you. You also need to have points at which you review where you have been. Remember, listening to an oral presentation is very different from reading something. When you are reading and get confused, you can go back over what you have read and find where you went off course. An oral presenter has to perform that function for the listeners.
- *Timely signals.* When you are going to make a turn, you need both to make sure that you are in the correct lane and that you signal far in advance. Transitions are a crucial part of the sermon. They give your listener a heads-up that a change is going to be taking place, that you are starting into a new idea or what David Buttrick identifies as "moves."

UNDERSTANDING FORM AND ARRANGEMENT

All sermons have a form, whether it is a very simple "beginning, middle, and end" or a more complex narrative. Even if a preacher doesn't consciously choose a particular form, there needs to be some way, some order in which you present the material and ideas you want your listeners to hear. Recognize that different forms do different things. The form of a church is different from a house; a crime drama is different from a comedy program or reality show. Whether it is a church or house, drama or comedy, each is doing something different and has a different goal. While form and arrangement are always necessary, over the centuries there has been disagreement over the role of form and arrangement in preaching.

Classical Roots

In the classical canon of rhetoric, once one had decided what one was going to say (*inventio*), one needed to decide how one would set forth those ideas (*dispositio* or the orderly arrangement of what had been found). The Greek word for arrangement, *taxis*, usually appeared in works on military strategy to describe the arrangement of one's troops for battle. In other words, after marshaling one's troops, or arguments, one had to decide what would be the most appropriate order in which to "march" them out.

For some speakers there was the understanding that, if you dealt with your subject, the words would fall into place. The subject would dictate the order; the speaker only had to follow that natural order. Plato, for example, identified the parts of a speech as the definition, collection, and division; but preferred a more biological description, the head, the body, and the legs of a speech. Aristotle essentially agreed with this "natural" approach and devoted very little time to *taxis*. In chapter 13 of book 3 of *Rhetoric*, he states quite simply, "There are two parts to a speech; for it is necessary to state the subject [*prothesis*] and to demonstrate it [*pistis*]" (Aristotle, 258). But for others, the parts of a speech were complex and carefully prescribed. According to Cicero, in *De inventione*, there are six parts of a speech that must be "arranged in proper order": exordium, narrative, partition, confirmation, refutation, peroration (Cicero, 41).

We have been discussing arrangement, the sequence in which items appear in a speech. But we might also discuss form. Different kinds of occasions call for different kinds of speeches. Traditionally, rhetorical scholars identified three types of speeches: judicial or forensic, the speeches of the courtroom; deliberative, political speeches; and finally, *epideictic* or ceremonial speeches. Since each type of speech was directed to a different audience and had different ends, each needed its own forms.

We are not preaching to ourselves. We are preaching to others and need to make our sermons clear, understandable, and engaging. How we arrange our sermon makes a difference in how it is received and how successful we will be in achieving our goal. Classical rhetorical theorists helped us to understand that form and arrangement matter.

Satisfying an Appetite

Different forms demand different things from the listener and produce different results. Think about milk and eggs. Combine them in different proportions with different ingredients and in different orders, and one is able to make cakes, cookies, pancakes, or even a soufflé. Crucial to understanding and employing form is developing the awareness that, first, form is not a neutral player in the preaching enterprise and, second, one cannot separate content from form.

Rhetorician and literary critic Kenneth Burke claimed that form is neither a skeleton nor a container designed merely to hold the content. Form, he argued, is linked to the psychology (*pathos*) of the listener; it is "the creation of an appetite in the mind of the auditor, and the adequate satisfying of that appetite" (Burke, 31). If you have been prepared by the cook to expect a huge four-layer cake with plenty of frosting, you will be disappointed if you discover you are going to get a plain square of cake with only a little frosting. Similarly, if a preacher whets the congregation's appetite for narrative—that is, a story sermon—they will be disappointed if the sermon that follows is a recitation of "three points and a poem."

Burke argued that the scientific age has driven everyone—not only scientists, but poets, playwrights, and perhaps preachers as well—away from the joy of form and arrangement to an "emphasis on the giving of information" (32). We are so focused on transmitting information and explaining Gospel texts or church doctrines that form, or how we convey the content, becomes secondary, "a luxury, or, as some feel, a downright affectation" (Burke, 33). Consequently as Burke observes, form "remains . . . sluggish . . . its true vigor is gone, since it is no longer organically required" (Burke, 33).

Milk or Solids

People come to the preaching table with different appetites and different needs. As Paul observed about his preaching to the Christians in Corinth, "I fed you with milk, not solid food, for you were not ready for solid food. Even now you are still not ready, for you are still of the flesh" (1 Cor. 3:2). On some Sundays the preacher will need to carefully nurture those who, because of illness and tragedy, need soft food. There will be others in the congregation each week who need the "milk" of the gospel, things laid out clearly and simply, while others will need the solid food of a more complicated, complex sermon. This reality makes preaching a challenge, and it is important for the new preacher to be aware of the arrangement options available. As Edward Corbett observes in *Classical Rhetoric for the Modern Student*: "Disposition [arrangement] then becomes something more than the conventional system for organizing a discourse, something more than just a system of outlining the composition; it becomes a discipline that trains writers in the judicious selection and use of available means to the desired end" (Corbett, 317).

Thinking about form and arrangement demands that the preacher thinks about who are the listeners, what is the context in which they and the preacher find themselves, how is God acting in this moment, and what should be the "desired end."

Preaching's Debate

But, as we noted in chapter 2, a tension has marked the relationship between rhetoric and homiletics. Not all preachers and teachers of preaching believed preaching to be a rhetorical art. Consequently, questions of form and arrangement were not only ignored but discouraged.

Many of the early church fathers, who had been teachers of rhetoric before their conversions, rejected rhetoric and the rhetorical forms. They equated rhetoric with human philosophy and human wisdom and understood that the words spoken by the preacher were to be supplied by God, not human knowledge. It was the Holy Spirit who persuaded, not the preacher. Therefore, one should not be concerned about crafting an introduction or conclusion, because in doing so one replaced the appropriate theological orientation with a rhetorical one.

While many were persuaded by Augustine's armistice, some continued, not only to question, but to totally reject any appeal to rhetoric and its precepts. We do not have to go very far back in our history to find one who "gladly drove a stake into the heart of rhetoric and called upon the newly widowed homiletics not to mourn but to dance on the grave" (Long, 177). Karl Barth rejected rhetoric because it replaced God's Word with human word. He argued, for example, that a sermon must not have an introduction. Not only does an introduction, according to Barth, suggest that a "point of contact" between humans and God is possible, but introductions are also a "waste of time" that distract the listeners.

However, whether he would admit it or not, Barth was making rhetorical judgments. When one decides what will be included in a sermon and what will not, what will have priority and what will be rejected, one is making decisions about form or arrangement. Nevertheless, Barth's position challenges us to think about who or what drives our decisions about sermon content and form.

Therefore, before one moves into a discussion of sermon forms and their use, the first question to be addressed by a preacher is whether or not he or she believes, for theological reasons, that sermons should have a specific form or arrangement at all. I would argue that all sermons employ a form and an arrangement, whether one intentionally applies one or not. Therefore, it is to the preacher's and listener's advantage that the preacher apply that form thoughtfully and carefully, lest the form work against, rather than for, the purpose of the preacher and the sermon. Sermons take listeners on a journey, and the preacher is responsible for moving people through that journey.

RETURN TO FORM AND ARRANGEMENT

Recent homiletical shifts that have placed a greater emphasis on the listener have brought with them shifts in the construction of sermons, from the logical and propositional to the dynamic and narrative. Recent preaching, therefore, has called for a move from the deductive to the inductive, and that move has returned arrangement and form to the forefront. Since we are faced with the need to decide on a form and arrangement, it is important to understand the different sermon forms available and why one might choose one particular form over another.

There is no magic form that will make every sermon a success. Form and arrangement are very important, but they are not the end all and be all of preaching. Many preachers do not set out to use a particular form. They take more of an Aristotelian approach, getting people into their sermon with some sort of introduction or statement—and off they go.

"How One Preaches": A Look at One Solution

Centuries ago, Augustine, upon completion of his episcopal visitations, was prompted to add one final chapter to his *On Christian Doctrine*. Listening to countless boring, dull, and confusing sermons convinced him that he needed to return to his former occupation and instruct preachers how to write sermons. Similarly, when in the mid-1960s Fred Craddock joined the faculty of the Graduate School of Phillips University as professor of New Testament and preaching, he began to realize that preaching was "an anachronism." Craddock observed, in *As One without Authority*, that "on an average corner on an average Sunday, preaching has been tolerated and the ministers have given sermons that were tolerable. Where the expectation is low, the fulfillment is usually lower" (Craddock, 5). Craddock believed that preachers and the church had lost respect for words. But they could not fix this "simply by turning up the volume." In the contemporary cultural context, a world of flexibility and change, in which the relationship between preacher and listener had also changed, old forms would no longer work.

When Augustine recognized that preaching was in trouble, he turned to style. A significant portion of book 4 of *De doctrina christiana* examines the description and directions for use, of the grand, subdued, moderate, and plain styles. Craddock, on the other hand, saw preaching's rescue in arrangement. While he first qualified his proposal, "forms of preaching should be as varied as the forms of rhetoric in the New Testament, or as the purposes of preaching or as the situation of those who listen" (Craddock, 53), Craddock advocated that what is needed is the inductive form of preaching. "Perhaps the alternative sought is induction. In an inductive form, thought moves from the particulars of experience that have a familiar ring in the listener's ear to a general truth or conclusion" (Craddock, 57). Craddock believed that traditional forms of preaching had ignored at best, or dominated at worst, the listeners and that the time has come to "invite the hearer to participate in the sermon" (Craddock, 55).

What Craddock appreciated, and hoped to communicate to preachers, was not only that form mattered, but that arrangement is crucial to the listener's involvement. If one preached what he identified as the "deductive" form, "There is no democracy . . . no dialogue, no listening by the speaker, no contributing by the hearer" (Craddock, 55). The "general truth" or "conclusion" is presented at the outset, and the remainder of the sermon consists of demonstrating or reproducing how the preacher arrived at that conclusion. If one employs this form, according to Craddock, the expectation is that all responsibility for the sermon lies with the preacher, who is the knowledgeable expert. The congregation is expected to be the ignorant, passive recipient of the preacher's superior knowledge. To revive preaching, Craddock argued, one needed to change the form of the sermon and choose the inductive form, because that involves our listeners. It is the way they think, it captures their imaginations, and it connects with their concrete experiences. It is better to invite the listeners into a story about a man who welcomed home his wayward son than simply to tell them that, "God loves us."

PREACHING RECIPES

As the stone masons were beginning the construction of Notre Dame cathedral, scholars, teachers, and students were flocking to Paris, which had become a center of learning. In the first thousand years of the Christian church's preaching, most sermons had been relatively simple exposition or explication of a text with an application to the life of the people. But the rise of learning brought with it a sophistication and interest in both the content and the form of preaching.

In the early part of the twelfth century there was a new "recipe" for preaching. The thematic form of the Paris sermon took preaching to new heights of complexity. The goal of the preacher was to examine logically and systematically a particular theme or question. Therefore, after introducing the chosen theme, the preacher began to divide, subdivide, and subdivide again the theme and questions in such a complicated manner that the outline for the sermon would look like the flow chart for a software program.

While I don't think that it would be helpful for you to attempt the thematic Paris sermon, it is important for you to become familiar with the various preaching forms that are available. Preachers today have many options for framework and structure, but deciding what option to use requires a number of decisions.

Currently there are two excellent resources available for introducing the preacher to that range of options, *Patterns of Preaching: A Sermon Sampler*, edited by Ronald J. Allen, and *Creative Styles of Preaching* by Mark Barger Elliott. Each book not only describes the different patterns but also offers sample sermons. However, as Eugene Lowry notes in the opening of his book, "Reading a textbook on how to prepare sermons often is like looking up a word in a dictionary in order to find out how to spell it—you have to have the answer before you can probe the question!" (Lowry, 8). Nevertheless, I would argue that the beginning preacher, like the beginning cook, benefits from having a recipe for preparing sermons.

When I first began to cook I was very frustrated. I had grown up in the house of a very good cook, but my mother never seemed to use a cookbook. She took a little of that, a pinch of that, and made my favorite dishes: meatloaf, tuna casserole, and vegetable soup. When I tried to cook those dishes, however, I discovered that I needed to open the pages of the cookbook to discover the ingredients. What went into each of those dishes, how much, and in what order? Thirty-two years later, I am like my mother. For most dishes I don't need the cookbook, but that is because after all these years I have learned how to cook.

The same is true of learning how to put together a sermon. At first, you will need a recipe to tell you what needs to go into the sermon, how much, and in what order. I would encourage you to try out a number of different "dishes." See what works for you. And soon you won't need the cookbook. You will feel adventurous and creative, experimenting with various options. But for now, I would recommend learning a few basic recipes. There are many sermon forms, but here are three recipes that will give you a place to start.

Traditional Style

Perhaps the oldest form, this sermon is also known as the "plain style." It is a simple and direct way to deal with either a scriptural text or texts or theological doctrine.

- *Beginning.* The sermon opens with an introduction that focuses the topic and gives the listeners an idea of the direction and/or claims of the sermon.
- *Exposition of text or doctrine.* If working with a text or texts of the Scripture, the preacher provides the listeners with a brief exegesis of the text. If working with a doctrine, he or she explores and explains the doctrine. This is the teaching portion of the sermon.
- *Application.* The preacher then moves to apply the biblical and theological insights of the text and its claims to the life of the congregation. What is God challenging us to do? This is the "so what" of the sermon.
- *Ending.* The preacher ties up the sermon, reviewing what has been explored and examined in the sermon and rounding out the message.

Narrative Style—The Lowry Loop

Whereas the previous recipe is rather simple and straightforward, Eugene Lowry observed that the stories we tell are not. In the early 1980s, Lowry urged preachers to be attentive to the need to design sermons that employ an arrangement attentive to time, the same way that a novel or play is. He regarded the sermon as "a narrative art form, a sacred story" (Lowry, 6). In *The Homiletical Plot*, Lowry introduced the form that lovingly came to be known as "the Lowry loop." The "loop" is a sequence, not a structure, in which the preacher engages the listeners by first "upsetting the equilibrium, [and] analyzing the discrepancy" (Lowry, 25). Drawing on Scripture, the preacher then discloses "the clue to the resolution, [leads them to] experience the gospel, [and] anticipate the consequences" (Lowry, 25). Fortunately, Lowry's students provided him with a shorthand definition: oops—ugh—aha—whee—yeah!

- *Oops.* A good story begins with a conflict in which one is thrown off balance. In the opening of a narrative sermon, the preacher names the conflict or problem. What is the question that is bothering people?
- *Ugh.* The preacher analyses the discrepancy that drives the sermon. In this section, which, according to Lowry is the most important and will demand the most time in the sermon, the preacher diagnoses the problem—the *why* of the sermon.
- *Aha.* The preacher begins to give the listeners a glimpse of the way out of the problem. The gospel provides an experience of the clue to the resolution. We experience those "aha!" moments when solutions begin to fall into place.
- *Whee!* It is time for the congregation to begin to experience the gospel. The preacher cannot go directly from the problem to the application. That, according to Lowry is the *"homiletical short circuit."* You wouldn't like a mystery story that began with the murder and went directly to the revelation of the murderer—how boring! You need to work through the process with the detectives. So too does the preacher need to pull the con-

gregation into "the intersection of gospel and human predicament" (Lowry, 66), where they will experience the good news. This section is the climax or high point of the sermon.

- *Yeah!* Now, according to Lowry, the listeners will be able to anticipate the consequences. The preacher is able to show what "can be expected, should be done, or is now possible" (Lowry, 67). In the final section, the preacher gives closure and direction to help people answer the important question, "What am I going to do with this?" In a story, this is the time when we see what happens as a consequence of the "big news."

The Four Pages

Finally, I suggest that you become familiar with a format provided by Paul Scott Wilson, "The Four Pages of the Preacher." By four pages he does not mean to suggest that a sermon should be only four pages long. What he suggests is that each page is roughly a quarter of the sermon. According to Wilson, this is a way of preaching on a biblical text.

- *Page one.* Page one names the theological problem of the chosen text. What is wrong? What was the trouble faced by our biblical sisters and brothers? Where was the conflict? On this page the preacher will need to do some teaching, discussing some of the information gained by his or her exegesis.
- *Page two.* The preacher now names the problem or conflict in our world, conflicts that are analogous to those experienced in the biblical world.
- *Page three.* The preacher begins to explore the good news and God's redeeming grace. First, the preacher examines the good news seen in the text. How does God's action in the text bring healing and wholeness to the people of God?
- *Page four.* The last "page" of the sermon is devoted to exploring the ways that God's grace is present and active in our lives today. How is God responding to the trouble and conflict in our world the way God responded in the biblical world?

Over the years my students have found these three recipes to be good starting points for their preaching careers. They give them a range of options.

REACHING TODAY'S LISTENERS

My preaching classes are far from homogeneous. Looking out over my classroom, I see students from a variety of denominations that represent a broad spectrum of theological and liturgical perspectives. But the diversity does not end there. I have women and men, different races and cultural backgrounds,

urban students from inner-city Washington and students serving small congregations on the rural eastern shore of Maryland. I have students from Korea,
Japan, and a number of African countries. The class may include students from
countries in the former Soviet bloc, students who grew up in an atheistic country, as well as students who, although they grew up in the United States, also
experienced an atheistic upbringing, not attending church until they were
adults. I have students who have just finished college sitting next to students
in their fifties and sixties who have retired from a wide variety of positions in
the government. There may be students who already hold a number of
advanced degrees and students who only after raising a family returned to finish college so that they could attend seminary. In the second chapter of Acts
we are told that there were dwelling in Jerusalem "devout men from every
nation under heaven." While I may not have any Parthians or Medes in my
classroom, they are speaking, metaphorically, a multitude of languages. How
do we speak to each in her or his language?

The final question, therefore, concerning arrangement and form is, how
does one take into account the effects of diversity? The same diversity that I
encounter in my preaching class is quite possibly the same variety that today's
preachers will encounter on a Sunday morning.

Telling in Their Own Tongues

In his preaching opus *Homiletic: Moves and Structures*, David Buttrick set out
to examine the "moves," the components of a sermon, and the "structures," its
form and arrangement. He did so from a phenomenological point of view, that
is, by being attentive to *"how sermons happen in consciousness"* (Buttrick, xii). It
is, he argued, important to link our sermons to the way people think, learn,
and create the world that they know.

This presents us with a question: do we all think, learn, create the same
way? Are we, as the children of God, made or "hardwired" the same way?
Some suggest, for example, that women and men may not "think" the same
way. Recent works have sought to examine those differences, works such as
Women's Ways of Knowing: The Development of Self, Voice, and Mind by Belenky,
Clinchy, Goldberger, and Tarule, and Carol Gilligan's *In a Different Voice: Psychological Theory and Women's Development.*

Joseph Jeter and Ronald Allen explore the challenges faced by today's
preachers in their book *One Gospel, Many Ears: Preaching for Different Listeners
in the Congregation.* Although we preach one God, one gospel, "a given congregation has many different listeners who process the sermon with their own
particular sets of receptors," and the preacher "has her or his tendencies of

speaking and listening, cultural proclivities, and modes of apprehending the world" (Jeter and Allen, 9). In the book they explore differences in generations, learning styles, gender, culture, class, and political differences. Their work will be helpful as a new preacher seeks to examine ways to "build" sermons that take these many "different ears" into account.

The Wired World

Another significant challenge to today's perception of form and arrangement comes from the wired world in which we live. When Aristotle and Cicero were describing the fitting structure for a particular context, they described a linear layout, because that was the world they inhabited. But that does not describe the world in which we or our listeners live. What are you doing as you read this book? Is there a television, radio, or iPod playing? You may even be reading this on a computer screen rather than the printed page. In that case, you may also be instant messaging in the midst of your reading or switching over to the Internet to order some of the books that are recommended. Today we rarely do one thing or hear one thing at a time.

We now experience numerous messages all at once or as what Marshall McLuhan called a "mosaic" of messages. According to Jeanne Fahnestock, we "form opinions from a chaos of fragmented impressions and bits of information" (Fahnestock, 47). Many of the sermons that will be prepared in the future will not be made up just of the spoken word. That spoken word will be accompanied by visual images of other words, pictures, and film clips.

FORM—MORE NOT LESS IMPORTANT

The electronic capabilities now available to preachers—computers, Power-Point, sound and film clips—have great potential for radically altering the sermon event. Listeners will expect more than the simple spoken word, a format that has changed little since the earliest centuries of the church's history. It is imperative that preachers become familiar and comfortable with these new possibilities.

As we look at the future of preaching and the increasing use of audiovisual components in the preaching event, in order for congregations to experience a challenging and coherent message instead of "a chaos of fragmented impressions and bits of information," arrangement and form will have to take an even more prominent role in the preparation of sermons. Preachers will not be able to focus on content and let form "take care of itself."

QUESTIONS

1. Pick one of your sermons for analysis. If you have not written a sermon, find the text of a sermon written by another person. Analyze the sermon. Pick it apart. Identify the various parts of the sermon. Is there an introduction? Where does it end? Work your way through the sermon. Then, using a book of sermon forms, see if you are able to identify what sermon form you or the other preacher employed.

2. Again, using a book of sermon forms, experiment with writing sermons using different forms.

READ MORE ABOUT IT

Allen, Ronald J., ed. *Patterns of Preaching: A Sermon Sampler*. St. Louis: Chalice Press, 1998.

Elliot, Mark Barger. *Creative Styles of Preaching*. Louisville, KY: Westminster John Knox Press, 2000.

Jeter, Joseph R., Jr., and Ronald Allen. *One Gospel, Many Ears: Preaching for Different Listeners in the Congregation*. St. Louis: Chalice Press, 2002.

Lowry, Eugene. *The Homiletical Plot*. Atlanta: John Knox Press, 1980.

Sample, Tex. *The Spectacle of Worship in a Wired World*. Nashville: Abingdon, 1998.

Schultze, Quentin J. *High-Tech Worship? Using Presentational Technologies Wisely*. Grand Rapids: Baker Books, 2004.

Wilson, Paul Scott. *The Four Pages of the Preacher*. Nashville: Abingdon, 1994.

PART 3

Communicating the Gospel

9

Putting It Together

Putting it together
Piece by piece
                      Stephen Sondheim, Sunday in the Park with George

Wait! You're not done. You have done so much hard work on your sermon. You have prayed and prayed. You have decided about the content of your sermon—what you are going to say. You have thought about the form your sermon will take and its arrangement—how you are going to say it. But you have several considerations left. As Stephen Sondheim reminds us, in a sermon, as in a work of art, "having just the vision's no solution." It all comes together only when we think of every detail, every part, every piece and take care in putting together all those bits.

This chapter will discuss a number of the important "details" that put together your "vision." Continuing with the cooking metaphor, we will be examining a number of the essential ingredients in a sermon.

INTRODUCTIONS

Many preachers who use minimal notes for the body of their sermon report that there are often two parts of their sermons that they do write out carefully and completely—the beginning and the end, the introduction and the conclusion. They know that how you begin is crucial to leading everyone into what you are going to say and how you end cements your words in the hearts and minds of your listeners. Rather than rambling and fumbling about, they want to make sure that they are clear about where they are going and where they have been.

Introduction is from the Latin meaning "to lead to the inside." Introductions lead us into the sermon. When the congregation is seated and ready for you to begin, there are a million different directions that you could go. There are as many sermons anticipated as there are listeners seated in the church. Right away you need to begin to narrow the field and give them an idea of the direction of the sermon. You also need to give your listeners the sense that this is something that will be of interest to them, that it is important for them to listen.

The introduction is also the way you introduce yourself to your listeners. That sounds strange if you are preaching in the same church week after week, but each time you meet, you are different, your listeners are different, and you have a different combination of people. You need to give your listeners a moment to settle into your speech patterns. You need to give them time to focus their attention away from the "noise," the many things, both external and internal that distract them, and turn their attention toward you. Those distractions will return even as you speak, but at least at the beginning you want to work at drawing them all together. Too many preachers make the mistake of declaring crucial or essential information in the first few sentences of their sermons; consequently, those important pieces of information are lost because people are not yet ready to take that in. They are still busy getting settled in their seats, quieting children, putting down hymnals or service leaflets. They may be hearing, but they are not yet listening.

When I describe an introduction, I do not have one form in mind. An introduction does not necessarily state specifically, "In this sermon I am going to be speaking about . . ." or "The point that I would like to make this morning is . . ." There are numerous ways that we can lead our listeners into our sermon. We may briefly retell the Bible story that is at the center of our sermon. We may ask a question. We may tell a story that raises certain issues or concerns. We may show a clip from a movie or television program. Whatever you do, it is essential that the introduction introduces the entire sermon; if it just functions as the first section of the sermon, that will only confuse your listeners.

Most listeners have been trained to expect some sort of introduction, something that draws them in. While it will also lead you into that first section, most importantly, the introduction leads the listeners into the sermon as a whole. Therefore, the first ten or twenty percent of your sermon is the time that you narrow the focus and give people a sense of what you will be talking about, where they will be going.

While introductions can be quite varied, there are several things that you should not do in your introduction. Don't begin by telling us all of the sermons that you could have preached. You run the risk of derailing the message you are giving by having people in the congregation fix their attention on one of the "also rans" with the thought "that sounds interesting, I wish she would have preached that."

Don't tell a funny story or joke that has nothing to do with your message just to "warm up the congregation." This is a sermon, not an after-dinner speech. Don't open with anything that isn't crucial to your sermon. Too often preachers find a great story with which they want to open, even though it doesn't quite fit with where they are going in the rest of the sermon. Consequently they leave their listeners scratching their heads, trying to put together things that don't actually go together. In many ways a sermon is like a short story. Short-story writers will tell you that, unlike a longer novel, which can contain many subplots, a short story must be tight and cannot include anything that is not integral to the plot.

Think back to the image of driving that was discussed in the previous chapter. Even if we don't know the exact route, introductions make your listeners more comfortable because they give them some idea of where they are going. Like a common movie technique, the zoom, an introduction functions like a camera that begins with a view of the broad landscape and narrows, narrows, narrows its field of vision until it finally focuses on one person or one house. This, the director is telling, is to be the center of attention. When we have some idea of where we are going, we are much more likely to relax and let you take us there. If we have no idea where we are going, we are more likely to be distracted while we keep asking ourselves, "Is this what the sermon is about?" We need to know how to listen, and you are the one who gives us the clues.

CONCLUSIONS

How you end your sermon is just as important as how you began. While the conclusion of your sermon will probably not be as long, only five or ten percent of the total sermon, it is your opportunity to bring everything to a close and let people come to a gentle landing. Nothing is as jarring as listening to a preacher say, "Amen," when one least expects it. "Is she done? I didn't think she was finished!" As one writer has observed, there is a great deal of difference between merely stopping and coming to an end.

There is an old joke about how to put together a speech, "tell 'em what your going to tell 'em, tell 'em, and tell 'em what you told 'em." While this is rather simplistic, there is great wisdom in these directions. We do appreciate it when a preacher summarizes what we have heard, and the conclusion is a time to do that. The conclusion rounds out your sermon and reinforces what you have been saying. It is not the time to introduce new material. If you are writing your concluding section and find that you are discussing something that had not already been covered, back up and place that in the body of the sermon.

Beware of false endings. Nothing is as frustrating to a listener as having a preacher give the sense that he or she is finishing up the sermon, only to go on and on and on. If you listen to the final movement of Beethoven's Fifth Symphony, you will hear what this feels like. Over and over it sounds has though the symphony is finally finished, only to have Beethoven begin a new section. We are ready for him to end, but he doesn't. When you say "Finally" or "In conclusion," you should mean it.

The conclusion is a time for you to inspire your listeners and rouse them to action. You want to leave them with the desire to get up out of their seats and join the great cloud of witnesses who are declaring to a heartsick world the good news. While we don't know all of the answers, our preaching is grounded in the certainty that we can "do all things through him who strengthens [us]" (Phil. 4:13). Above all things, your sermon is declaring this central message, and it should shine through at the end of every sermon. Don't leave them depressed or confused. We are preaching good news!

TRANSITIONS

Have you ever driven by a building site only to see several separate small brick walls? They aren't parts of the wall that the builders forgot to connect. Rather, they are the mason's "auditions." The bricklayers are asked to build a section of wall so that the contractor can examine their skill with the mortar. Do they use too much or too little? Are they sloppy? Is their wall clean and sturdy? The contractor knows that not only does the quality of the brick matter, but so too does the quality and application of the mortar that binds them together.

Transitions are a crucial part of your sermon. How you move us from one section to another is like the turn signals when you are driving. They let us know that you have finished one idea and are moving on to another.

A word about numeration. Sometimes in a sermon we wish to make several distinct points. Speakers will frequently introduce each point with its number, "first, . . . second, . . . etc." If you have occasion to do that, remember to do several things. If you have more than two points, give us a preview of the various points. Without the preview we are often scrambling to try to figure out the various points. Label each point with its number. Speakers have a tendency to introduce the first point, but then forget to identify the second. When they then return with "my third point," everyone is left wondering, what was number two? And if you say that you are going to make three points, make three points. Too often people say that, but then make only two—very frustrating.

SUPPORTING MATERIAL

As the early church struggled with ways to tell the story of Jesus, his life and ministry, his death on the cross, and his resurrection three days later, they frequently employed metaphorical images. Jesus is our shepherd, they declared, leading us through the valley of death to our new life in him. Did they mean to tell us that Jesus had actually been a shepherd? Not that we know. It was more likely he was a carpenter like Joseph. Since the Scriptures had been filled with images of the heavenly shepherd: "He will feed his flock like a shepherd; he will gather the lambs in his arms, and carry them in his bosom" (Isa. 40:11), the early church adopted that image in speaking of Christ. Likewise, Paul and the Johannine community wrote of Jesus as the lamb of God, not to suggest that Jesus was a member of the sheep family, but to connect the passion and death of Jesus with the sacrifice of the Passover lamb, when God rescued the people of Israel from slavery and bondage and delivered them into a new life of freedom. "They are to take a lamb for each family. . . . This day shall be a day of remembrance for you. You shall celebrate it as a festival to the LORD; . . . for on this very day I brought your companies out of the land of Egypt" (Exod. 12:3,14,17).

As preachers we make use of abstract ideas. We speak of people, places, events that are not actually present. We speak of what God has done in the past and what God has planned for our future. We must, therefore, use words to make the abstract concrete, and bring the absent, the past and the future, into what philosopher Chaim Perelman identifies as our *presence*: "One of the preoccupations of a speaker is to make present, by verbal magic alone, what is actually absent but what he considers important to his argument or, by making them more present, to enhance the value of some of the elements of which one has actually been made conscious" (Perelman, 117). Likewise, Aristotle said that a speaker must do two things in a speech, state the subject and then demonstrate it. Unlike Perelman, we no longer must rely on verbal magic alone. We have the ability to project images and run film clips. We will discuss this in chapter 12. For now, we will discuss the "verbal magic."

Through the use of examples, illustrations, metaphors, and narratives we make sermons come alive and "demonstrate" our subject. They help us to show people what an idea "looks like" and are an indispensable part of a sermon. They help us to clarify what we are trying to say, and they involve both cognitive and affective reasoning. They aid our listeners by helping them, not only to envision what we are saying, but to become part of the sermon. Illustrations and examples help people participate or put themself in the picture.

Illustrations, examples, metaphors, and analogies, while indispensable, can also derail a sermon. They must be used carefully and judiciously. Let's take a moment to explore the what, when, and how of these important building blocks.

What?

While we explored the issue of illustrations earlier in the book, it is important to return to this question. What can we use to give presence to our sermons?

We tend to use the words *illustration* and *example* interchangeably. However, technically there is a difference between the two. We use an example when an issue is under dispute or when there is disagreement. An example demonstrates that something has occured before. We use an illustration, on the other hand, when we agree about an issue but want to strengthen and clarify. We may also use similarities, resemblances between different things, for comparison in order to understand. The two most commonly used are metaphor and analogy. The metaphorical figure of speech brings together two similar terms to create a new meaning or understanding. Jesus is word, bread of life, the true vine; the Scriptures make extensive use of metaphor. An analogy compares one relationship to another. When Paul wants to describe the relationships between members within the church, he uses the analogy of the body—that we are eyes, hands, and feet.

Through the use of illustrations, examples, images, metaphors, analogies, we hope to make our ideas come to life. We must make sure that the stories and images we use meet certain criteria.

- *Plausible.* Whether we are using an example or illustration that is real or one that is fictional, it must seem likely. Is it something with which people can identify? This doesn't mean that you cannot use rural images for urban dwellers or that you can never talk about snow to people who live in warm climates. But it does mean that the examples and images you use must relate to people's experiences. This brings up the question of the truth of a story. Preachers now have access to countless stories on the internet. Should you tell a story as though it really happened to you, even though it didn't? I would recommend against it. People will be suspicious if they are led to think that you have reported on something that happened to you—only to find out that it didn't. They will then wonder what other "stories" you have been telling them.
- *Timely.* You are surrounded by illustrations. Use them. Using events that are current in the lives of your listeners helps to strengthen the ties between God's word, your message, worship, and the daily lives people are leading. If you don't connect your sermon with what is going on in the world beyond the church, you create a sense of detachment. Let me give you an example. I was listening to a sermon about Christian contentment—learning how to trust God and know that we can be utterly and totally dependent on God. As Christians we can be ready to lose everything because our lives are in the hands of God. The preacher used as his example some friends of his who had a particularly difficult life. That would have been a perfectly adequate illustration any other time. However, the people in the pews were day after day witnessing images of the

destruction of the enormous tsunami that had ravaged Asia only three weeks before. We were watching and contributing money to people who had lost everything—family, friends, villages, homes, livelihood. When the preacher did not turn our attention to those images, but spoke only of two individuals, he totally disconnected his sermon from the life we were experiencing and the questions that we were asking—How could this happen? How could God allow this? How would we live after experiencing that?

- *Detailed.* We become involved in a story or image when there is a lot of detail. The more detail you include, the more it comes alive, the more we are able to picture it in our minds.
- *Authentic.* Countless books and Internet services provide preachers with sermon illustrations. While those stories may be interesting and may fit with a particular Scripture passage or theme, preachers should be careful when they make use of those stories, because they do not come across as authentically as an anecdote or image that you have developed yourself. If you are going to use a story you have discovered in a book or the Internet, make sure that you put it into your own words. Otherwise it will sound "canned."
- *Varied.* Jesus spoke about farmers and fishermen because that is what he knew and those were the people around him. Our lives are much more complex, and we have the ability to know many more things. The examples and illustrations that we use should draw on a number of sources. You may, like me, love to cook, but if you draw images and illustrations only from cooking, they will after a while lose their appeal and not resonate with all people in the congregation. If we draw illustrations from a variety of sources, we have a much better chance of finding images that will connect with more people in the congregation.
- *Hospitable.* Make sure that the images and stories you use are kind and welcoming of all people. Do not use some group of people as an object of scorn or ridicule. Some preachers do that to create unity and identification with their listeners: "we aren't like that group!" Unfortunately, you may end up alienating someone in the congregation who identifies with that group.
- *Weighty.* We are preaching the gospel of our Lord Jesus Christ. We are talking about things that are of life-and-death importance to people. We are throwing out lifelines to people who are floundering in the sea of life that threatens to overwhelm them. The images and illustrations must be weighty enough to bear this enormous burden. We do not want to use images or illustrations that suggest the gospel is whimsical or irrelevant.

When and How Many?

When should we use an illustration? How many should we include? Illustrations enforce an idea that we have made. When you are tempted to ask yourself what does this look like? where do I see this happening? that is when you should think about including some type of illustration, example, or figure of speech. When you find that your sermon is flying off into the intellectual strat-osphere, an illustration will help you bring it back down to earth.

We must also connect our words and our experiences. Think about the the-ological words that fill our sermons. In her book *Amazing Grace*, Kathleen Norris recalls that her Sunday school and confirmation teachers spoke with "a scary vocabulary, not an inviting one." "In my mid-thirties, however, it became necessary to begin to reclaim my faith, scary vocabulary and all" (Norris, 2). The words, she noted, "had to become real to me, in an existential sense" (Norris, 3). For many of the people to whom we are preaching, the vocabu-lary of faith is either scary or incomprehensible. Consequently, we must make sure that we not only teach people the words but connect them with experi-ences that help them understand the concepts. We must make the abstract ideas come alive through images and examples.

Illustrations and examples, like the seasoning in a stew, perk up the flavor but must be used carefully. Too much seasoning overwhelms the other flavors. Likewise, using too many illustrations and too much variety will overwhelm a sermon. You don't want your sermon to end up being a stream of stories held together by a little "sermon" glue.

Sources

Students frequently ask, where am I going to get stories and illustrations for my sermons? While we have discussed this earlier in the book, let me return to this question.

First, let me stress using stories from the Bible. You will usually have a text or texts with which you are working on a given Sunday. But you have a wealth of other biblical stories and images that are available to you for your use. Use them. The more you draw from the Scriptures, the more you educate your lis-teners about the Bible.

You can draw illustrations from history, from the stories of the saints. You can find images in fiction, poetry, motion pictures. Open your newspaper each day and you will find numerous illustrations. As a preacher you should be an avid reader of a variety of media.

Be attentive, be mindful. God is moving and acting all around you. Do you not see it? Watch, and you will.

Confidentiality

Our lives are filled with examples and illustrations we can use in our sermons. An important question, however, is, when should we not use a story? Confi-dentiality is crucial in the ministry. Never tell a story about anyone in your congregation, either current or past, without their permission. I am not saying that you may not speak about people, their questions or experiences. What is essential is that the person knows that you will be speaking about him or her in your sermon.

Do not think that you can mask an individual enough to use the person in your sermon. You cannot. You never know who will be in the congregation. If someone knows that person's story, they will know of whom you are speaking and may very well report back to that person. If you talk about people from your congregations, you run the risk of appearing to be a tattler, and people will not confide in you, for fear that they too will appear in one of your sermons.

The issue of confidentiality also applies to your family members. Children are wonderful sources of sermon material, especially when they are younger. A three-year-old is not likely to care whether you talk about her in your sermon, but if you start talking about your eleven-year-old's messy room without his permission, you will find out quickly how unpopular you can be at the dinner table. If you are going to talk about a family member in your sermon, you should also ask her or his permission. It will go a long way to maintaining good family relations.

Weakness, Fear, and Trembling: Preaching about Yourself

Paul wrote to the Christians in Corinth reminding them, "When I came to you, . . . I came to you in weakness and in fear and in much trembling" (1 Cor. 2:1, 3). He came to tell them about the Christ who had turned his life upside down, knowing that he was an unworthy spokesman. For whatever reason, God had chosen him as a servant and apostle, and therefore Paul never hesitated to tell his own story.

How is a preacher to talk about her or himself in the pulpit? How are we to use illustrations from our own life? This has frequently been a point of disagreement among homileticians. Some urge you never to speak about yourself in your sermon. Sermons are to be about God, not about you, and talking about yourself in the sermon only focuses attention in the wrong direction.

I disagree and would point to Paul to argue that Christian preaching has, from the very beginning, been incarnational, made present in the flesh of the preacher. Therefore, I would tell you that you may speak about yourself and your experiences from the pulpit. However, I would also advise you to do that very carefully, very thoughtfully, and to take your lead from Paul, doing so with fear and trembling.

Our sermons must always point toward God and toward the good news that we have been given in the life, death, and resurrection of Jesus Christ.

Our use of personal experiences and illustrations must be carefully controlled. When you use yourself as the starting point of an illustration, I would recommend very quickly moving away from yourself and turning it over to the congregation with a question: "Has the same thing happened to you?" "How have you had a similar experience?" Another way of including your listeners is by recasting your experience in the form of a question. Rather than telling them about an experience—"The other day I was inching my way through traffic . . ."—you might ask, "What goes through your mind when you are stuck in traffic and it takes you fifteen minutes to drive a mile?"

You must also be careful of "TMI"—too much information. You must not turn the sermon into an occasion of confession or a support group for you. We are preaching the gospel, not the preacher. While you might talk about experiences or personal observations, the sermon is not the place to air family problems or your personal demons. There are things that we probably do not need to know about you.

Henry Nouwen's book *The Wounded Healer* has been very popular among clergy. It helped us to move from being "Superman" to being "Clark Kent," from being persons who felt we had to show that we knew all and could do all, to being persons who could admit that we had doubts, uncertainties, and fears. As clergy we aren't always sure, aren't always certain. However, I would like to caution you against being a "wounded" preacher. If you always display those doubts and uncertainties, without balancing them with joyous faith and the certainty of the gospel, your listeners will begin to wonder why they should listen to you. Why, they will ask, should I listen to someone who doesn't seem to know more than I do? Why should I listen to someone whose faith is so shaky? We do not preach ourselves but Christ crucified and risen. Of that we can be certain.

LANGUAGE

We are the people of the word because we have been created in the image of a God who speaks. God spoke and brought us and our world to be. The Word became flesh and dwelt among us. And so we use words to speak about the God who created us. We use words to tell about the life that God would have us live. We speak to bring hope, to bring challenge, to bring visions of the life that is possible in God. But words are slippery and messy. Using words to declare the good news is like trying to juggle china plates; we can too easily fumble and send them crashing to the floor. We can be easily misunderstood, because we speak so many different languages and do not always understand one another.

Choosing words carefully, therefore, is an important part of preaching. We must think about not only what we are going to say but also how we are going to say it.

"In Our Own Language"

Think about how many different languages you speak. There is the language you use everyday, English, Spanish, or Korean. That may or may not be the first language you learned growing up. But that is not the only language you speak. If you have an opportunity to sit in a high school lunchroom, I suspect you will need a translator. Likewise, whenever I try to read the instructions for my computer or a software program, I realize that the writers speak a language entirely different from mine.

Touched by the Spirit, the disciples of Christ on Pentecost poured out into the streets of Jerusalem to proclaim the good news. But the effects of Babel were not erased with the coming of the Spirit. We did not all end up speaking the same language. Rather, everyone exclaimed in questioning amazement, "And how is it that we hear, each of us, in our own native language? . . . Cretans and Arabs—in our own languages we hear them speaking about God's deeds of power" (Acts 2:8, 11). It is the responsibility of the preacher to speak in a language, both the words used and the pronunciation of those words, that will be understandable to the congregation.

You speak not only Swedish, French, or Chinese. You also speak the "languages" of a number of other cultures that you inhabit. The same is true of your listeners. You inhabit the culture of your race, your age group, even your hobby or profession. Doctors, musicians, electricians—all have their own specialized language, and each group has to be careful when speaking to those outside of that culture, to make sure that listeners will understand what they are speaking about.

This is especially important for clergy who have learned to speak "theologese" during their time at seminary. One learns a new language and unfortunately forgets that most people do not use "eschatology" or "synoptic" in their everyday speech. While these are perfectly good words and our listeners are certainly able to learn what they mean, it can be frustrating when a preacher sprinkles the sermon with "theologese," either forgetting that others do not speak that language or trying to impress the listeners with how learned he or she is.

Likewise, different parts of a country will use words differently. For example, in New York, if you need to buy a ticket, you have to get "on line," while in the Midwest you have to get "in line." If you order black coffee in Chicago, that is what you will get: coffee with nothing in it. But if you order black coffee in Boston, it will include the sugar—and believe me, that is a shock for one who is not expecting it.

When you move into a new community, you will need to learn a new vocabulary. You may also need to modify your pronunciation. Some years ago I had a student from a very small island in Chesapeake Bay. (Don't worry, he knows that I tell his story all of the time.) Tangier Island is a fascinating place where the English that the natives speak is frequently studied by linguists. It is very close to the English spoken when Shakespeare was writing his plays. That may intrigue linguists, but it makes it difficult for those of us who are not Elizabethan. My student realized that congregations might have a difficult time understanding what he he was saying, and he was correct. He and I worked together, but not to get rid of his accent—that would have been terrible. We didn't want him to sound like a television anchor. But we did need to soften his pronunciation a bit to make him more understandable. We will return to this dimension of speech again in chapter 11.

Proper English?

Another important question for preachers is the importance of using proper grammar. As I mentioned in an earlier chapter, in *Mass Appeal* Father Farley rebukes Deacon Dolson for using grammar that is too stiff and formal.

> **Dolson:** Sermons can't be grammatically correct?
>
> **Farley:** Sermons should be understood. Proper grammar doesn't necessarily help understanding. (Davis, 18–19)

What do we need to do to make sure that our sermons are understood?

In the schools of rhetoric, the students were taught that the speaker could choose among three levels of style. The speaker had to decide which level was most appropriate for the audience and the occasion. The *grand style* was for formal occasions. The language was quite stately, and the speaker made extensive use of figures of speech, metaphors and similes. *Middle style* was the language of the legislature or the court. The speaker was to use proper grammar but did not give the impression that the speech had been carefully crafted and composed. *Plain style* was delivered in the language of the people, employing slang.

What is a preacher to do? Are you supposed to use proper grammar? I would say, as a rule of thumb, yes. But you shouldn't sound stiff and aloof. You will choose different levels of formality, depending on the formality of the occasion. Some sermons will be more informative, others more conversational. The church picnic will call for a more relaxed style of speech than the major service on Christmas Eve or a funeral. But in each case, you should use grammar that would make the English teachers in your congregation proud. (Don't worry, they will correct you if you don't.) If you do make mistakes, make sure that you are making them intentionally—better sins of commission than omission.

Inclusive Language: "Where No One Has Gone Before"

There is one final important issue about language choices: inclusive language. In the late 1960s we were introduced to the crew of the *Enterprise* and their celestial adventures. Each week the program opened with Captain Kirk's describing the ship's mission and informing us that it was to go "where no *man* has gone before." With that declaration, the ship would take off at warp speed. Decades later, when the next generation of the *Enterprise* appeared on our television screens, the program began with the voice of a new captain, Picard, describing once again the mission of the star ship, but with one significant change: the crew now went "where no *one* has gone before." What happened?

Between the 1960s and the 1990s a shift in language usage occurred. When the script writers penned the introduction to the original *Star Trek*, it was considered appropriate to use the word *man* to refer to everyone, whether male or female. But by the '90s, the cultural perceptions had changed. *Man*, as many of us know, does not always refer to everyone. Ask a woman what happens when she walks through a door marked "Men," and she will tell you that it doesn't. Over the centuries, women had to constantly evaluate. When did "men" include them, and when did it not? The church declared that women were included when it said that Christ came to save "all men." But it did not include them when it came to Christ's calling "men" for ordination. There, Christ called men and not women. What was a person to do?

At the same time the general culture was shifting its understanding of the use of *men*, the church was wrestling with the way we speak about God. While these two issues are always linked in the discussion of inclusive language, I would like to hold them apart. When we are speaking about men and women, we must absolutely, positively speak of men and women. The broader culture has changed, and so too must the church. We cannot speak of "men" and think that women will consider themselves included. That is just not possible any more. Preachers cannot use the generic term *men* for all people. It is no longer acceptable. They will not be understood. If *Star Trek* could change, so can we.

Now on to the stickier issue, how we speak about God. Over the past few decades we have been wrestling with the way we address and speak about God. Is God father or mother? Is God he, she, or it? In Exodus we were commanded to "not make for yourself an idol" (Exod. 20:4). We were not to picture God exclusively as anything that flew in the air, swam in the water, or walked on the earth. Consequently, throughout the Scriptures, God was spoken of with a multiplicity of images—rock, eagle, father, mother, shepherd, fire, wind, dove—to help us to get to know the God who has created us, who has redeemed us, and who sustains us. But we like idols. We like to focus on one thing. The church came to picture God as father, Abba, because that is how Jesus spoke of God and that is how he taught us to pray.

The challenge before the church today is to learn how to broaden our speech. Some would argue that, if we are going to use the masculine image and pronoun when speaking of God, we must combine it with the corresponding feminine image and pronoun, that is, Father/Mother God. Others argue that God is male, and that is what the Bible tells us. They claim that the members of their church are not bothered by speaking of God as father and that they couldn't get used to any other way. What is a preacher to do?

A preacher is challenged to pray, think, read, study, and grow. While I am uncompromising about the use of inclusive language when we speak of men and women, I think that we are learning new/old ways of speaking of God. Yes, the Scriptures are filled with references to God the father, God the male. But there are also images of God—the woman who sweeps the house looking for us, lost coins; holy Wisdom that pitches her tent in the midst of the teeming city, calling us to come in and learn. Your sermons will be enriched and enlivened when you expand the ways that you speak about God.

Oral Writing

Before we leave our discussion about the language that we choose, it is important to discuss the difference between written and aural/oral language. We have begun to touch on this issue in our discussion about proper grammar. Deacon Dolson had prepared his sermon using written language, the style he would use for a class paper. Father Farley was encouraging him to use what Richard Hoefler identifies as "Oral Writing." In his book *Just Say the Word*, Robert Jacks reminds us that we must write for the ear not the eye. They are different.

Writing for the ear demands a livelier, brisker, less complicated style. It requires shorter, simpler sentences. You need to take breathing into consideration. Think and write in phrases or thought units that you can deliver with one breath. When we are conversing, we never take a breath in the middle of a thought. If you do when you are preaching, it will sound as though you do not know what you are saying.

Speaking also requires simpler words. As Jacks observes, don't use a 50¢ word when a 5¢ word will do. (I suspect that shows the effects of inflation.) Oral writing demands the active rather than the passive voice. You need to use contractions—*I'll* or *we'll*, rather than *I will* or *we will*. All of this in an effort to write as we speak.

Look at the Hoefler and Jacks books. They will help you develop this skill. After years of preaching, I can hear myself delivering the words that I am writing. I have come to know how they will sound.

Finally, think about using a refrain. African American preachers have taught us the value of a phrase that reappears throughout the sermon. That phrase or refrain becomes something that your listeners will be able to repeat with you and will anchor the sermon. They will know what you are talking about because they will be able to join you as you preach the sermon. Evans Crawford's book *The Hum* will help you learn this skill.

GATHERING THE PIECES: THE PREACHER'S SCRIPT

When you are at the start of what we hope will be a very long life of preaching, sermon preparation is quite different from what it will be in ten or twenty years. Over the years you will eventually develop both your personal method of sermon preparation and the sermon "script" that works best for you. Some of you will continue to be manuscript preachers because that is what makes you most open to the movement of the Spirit in the preaching moment. Others will use some form of an outline, notes, or key words to help jog the memory. While others will decide that it is best if they take nothing at all into the pulpit.

I recommend that you begin your preaching career by writing a sermon manuscript. You may decide to turn that manuscript into an outline that you will take with you into the preaching moment, but the discipline of writing a complete manuscript will force you to think carefully about the form and structure of your sermon, the words you choose, and the images you use.

When your sermon is in a more or less complete form, it affords you the ability of reviewing what you are going to say and looking critically at it. I encourage you to write out everything you want to say. But some manuscripts are easier to preach from than others. What you take into the pulpit matters.

On July 8, 1741, when Jonathan Edwards mounted the pulpit at the church in Enfield, Connecticut, to deliver his now-famous sermon "Sinners in the Hands of an Angry God," he probably carried with him a densely packed manuscript written in his own hand that his poor eyesight made difficult to read. Consequently, it was necessary for him hold the manuscript quite close to his face. This hardly fits with the picture of the "hell and brimstone" preacher pounding the pulpit and shaking a condemnatory finger at the "sinners" gathered before him. Nevertheless, his words caused the people in the pews to writhe in spiritual agony, terrified that they, like the spider, would fall into the fiery pit of hell. Edwards's listeners expected their preachers to read their carefully crafted, lengthy sermons from a manuscript.

Today that is not the case. Delivery is culturally determined. Contrast the delivery style of a Presbyterian teaching elder with the "whoop" of an African American preacher. One is not right or wrong, better or worse, but each fulfills the expectations of his or her listeners. What has changed in general is that most listeners today are not comfortable if a preacher steps into the pulpit with a large sheaf of papers and begins to read the manuscript with little inflection or vocal variety. It is important for today's preacher to prepare a preaching script that will make her or his preaching lively and conversational. Your listeners expect you to make eye contact with them. If you don't they will grow bored and restless. We will return to this in chapter 11.

Do you remember sitting in first or second grade listening to your classmates read aloud? They, like you, labored over every word. There was no emphasis or phrasing. They punched each word equally and, like an old typewriter, stopped at the end of a line, took a breath, and moved down to the next row. While I am not suggesting that manuscript preachers are that bad, I do want to illustrate what can happen when we are held captive by a manuscript that looks like the page in this book.

Preachers easily slip into a reading tone when they have before them a page filled with words in small font. They read because they are afraid of losing their place on that crowded page. If they raise their eyes from that crammed document, how will they ever find where they were? They also tend to drop their voice when they get to the end of a line, take a breath, and pick up again at the start of the next line. Not good. What can we do?

We can go a long way to prevent "readeritis" by preparing a pulpit script. The bigger the font, the fewer words on a page, the easier it will be for you to have your words before you and still look at the people to whom you are preaching. Computers have made it immensely easy to take a complete manuscript and turn it into a script that you take into the pulpit. Your sermon should not look like a paper that you would turn in for a class. It should look more like an actor's script. Let me show you what I mean by taking part of this paragraph and turning it into a preaching script.

We can go a long way to prevent "readeritis"
                              by preparing a pulpit script.
The bigger the font, the fewer words on a page,
          the easier it will be for you to have your words before you and still
                    look at the people to whom you are preaching.

Computers have made it immensely easy
    to take a complete manuscript
        and turn it into a script that you take into the pulpit.

Play with this concept of a script, and find what is most readable for you. There are many ways of accomplishing this goal.

A few further thoughts about what we should take into the pulpit. In addition to a larger font, try not to fill the entire page. Leave the bottom third empty. If you fill the entire page, when you try to read the final lines on the page, you will have to drop your face. No only will it be more difficult to maintain eye contact; your voice will be directed at your feet, rather than at your listeners. Remember, sound goes where you point it.

Don't staple your pages. You want to be able to move them quietly and unobtrusively. You are trying to make your listeners think that you don't have a manuscript at all. If you are flipping pages, you will blow your cover. Number your pages. You will drop your notes sometimes. When you do, you will want to be able to reorder them quickly.

THE GOSPEL SQUINT: PIECE BY PIECE

We have been discussing various "ingredients," various pieces of sermon preparation. But before I end this chapter, I want to discuss a way that you can judge how those pieces are coming together. The epigraph that opens this chapter is from Stephen Sondheim's musical about the artist Georges Seurat. His painting *Sunday in the Park*, of people strolling by the edge of a lake, is perhaps the most famous example of pointillism. If we could travel to the Art Institute in Chicago and see the wonderful painting, which covers an entire wall, we would see—when we got as close to the painting as the guards would allow—that the man and woman strolling through the park, the grass and trees, the sky and water are all composed of small dots of color placed very close together. It is estimated that Seurat placed 3,456,000 dots to make the picture! When we back away from the painting and can no longer see the individual points, we see how they work together to produce the painting that pulls us into a lazy French summer afternoon.

Your sermon is made up of many—while not three million—words, images, ideas, arguments, and transitions that work together to produce a sermon that helps the people of God realize they are living in God's world and gives them a vision of God's reign. While you are putting it together piece by piece, take a cue from Monsieur Seurat and "squint" at your sermon. What do I mean by that?

Visual artists have a fascinating way of judging their works in progress: they squint. They move forward, back up, even turn the work, if possible, on its side or upside down. They do all of this in an attempt to make a critical assessment of what they are doing. They do this to see what is out of balance, what has been missed. Squinting allows them to see differently and to experience the wholeness of their project. Stephen Sondheim is correct; every detail plays a part, but when we are putting things together, we have to step back and squint in order to get a sense of the whole.

Through his teaching and parables, Jesus is inviting us to squint at life. He challenges us to get close, to immerse ourselves in the lives of those around us. He tells us to back up and get a sense of the "big picture" so that we know that our lives and our world are at this moment in time a part of God's unfolding story. Jesus tells us the stories of Samaritans who help those battered by life, of lepers who are healed, of workers who all get the same pay, in order to turn life on its head because God, through the incarnation and resurrection, has turned all of life upside down. We need not fear powers and principalities, hardship or distress, because "neither death, nor life, nor angels, nor rulers . . . will be able to separate us from the love of God in Christ Jesus our Lord" (Rom. 8:38–39). But the assaults of life make it difficult for us to remember, so we need the gospel squint.

When I was teaching art, it was easy to teach students to squint. It was easy to tell them how to take a drawing or painting and turn it upside down. We could put their painting on one side of the room and walk to the other side to see what the painting looked liked from a distance. To do that with a sermon is more complicated. I suggest a number of ways that you can "squint" at your sermon.

- When you have finished your sermon, turn it into another outline. That will make it easier for you to see the "moves" or the building blocks of your sermon and to see their arrangement, the order in which they appear.
- With highlighters of several different colors in hand, read through your sermon. Whenever a different idea or theme appears in the sermon, use a different color to highlight it. This will help you see how many different "sermons" you are preaching in one sermon.
- Using a fresh copy of your sermon, take the highlighters again, and highlight all theological language and Scripture references. Read the sermon through the eyes of a seeker or newcomer to the faith. How much do you assume on the part of the listener? Do you assume that he or she knows what you mean when you talk about love, grace, salvation, redemption? Do you assume that he or she has heard of Noah and Moses, Thomas and Barnabas? Squint at your sermon and make sure that it is hospitable, that it welcomes the person who is not well versed in the faith story or comfortable speaking the Christian language.

PUTTING IT TOGETHER

One of the challenges for an artist is knowing when to declare a work of art is finished. When does one declare that there are no more pieces to add? How does one know when to stop? Preachers are confronted with the same questions. Many preachers don't "stop" preparing the sermon, don't declare a sermon "finished" until they begin to deliver it. In a way, they are correct. Sermons are not really finished even when the preacher has finished delivering the sermon. As we begin to preach, the thoughts, ideas, and images that we are sharing with our listeners begin working in their hearts and minds, and even after we stop speaking, our listeners continue "writing" the sermon. They turn it over and over, they add their own examples and illustrations, their own experiences. They wrestle with and challenge what we have said. They continue to "put it together—piece by piece."

In an earlier chapter I stressed flexibility. As preachers, we must be open to the movement of the Spirit in the preaching moment. We must be flexible and recognize that, unlike Seurat's painting, *Sunday in the Park*, which was finally finished and which hangs on view in Chicago, our sermons are, in a way, never done. The Spirit will work on us while we are preaching, and the Spirit will work on our listeners. Our sermons become "pieces" of the much larger work of God's art.

QUESTIONS

1. Take a sermon that you have written. When you wrote the sermon, it was for a particular group of people. Your introduction was crafted for them. Imagine several different groups of people and different contexts, for example, a youth service or a service at a nursing home. Write a different introduction to the sermon, taking into consideration the differences in listeners and context.
2. Go through one of your sermons with colored highlighters. Highlight the various illustrations, examples, and images that you use. Do you have a variety of illustrations that will reach the rich variety of people who are listening to your sermon—women, men, young, old, people from different cultural backgrounds? Do you provide them with an entry point?

READ MORE ABOUT IT

Crawford, Evans. *The Hum: Call and Response in African American Preaching.* Nashville: Abingdon, 1995.

Davis, Bill. *Mass Appeal*. New York: Dramatists Play Service, 2002.

Hoefler, Richard Carl. *Creative Preaching and Oral Writing*. Lima, OH: C.S.S. Publishing, 1992.

Jacks, G. Robert. *Just Say the Word!: Writing for the Ear*. Grand Rapids: Eerdmans, 1996.

Norris, Kathleen. *Amazing Grace: A Vocabulary of Faith*. New York: Riverhead Books, 1998.

Perelman, Chaim, and L. Olbrechts-Tyteca. *The New Rhetoric: A Treatise on Argumentation*. Notre Dame: University of Notre Dame Press, 1971.

10

Seasons and Festivals:
Preaching Special Occasions

Why is one day more important than another,
when all the daylight in the year is from the sun?
By the Lord's wisdom they were distinguished,
and he appointed the different seasons and festivals.
Some days he exalted and hallowed,
and some he made ordinary days.

Sirach 33:7–9

OUT OF THE ORDINARY

A friend of my mine still grimaces when he tells of a painful experience that occurred in his first few weeks as a pastor. With newly minted degree in hand and fresh from his ordination, he set out to begin his tenure as the pastor of a small church in rural Kansas. He had learned much, but his first funeral convinced him that he still had much to learn.

A young woman with small children had died, and her husband was struggling to cope with his grief over her loss. His pain was compounded by her family's anger at him. She had grown up in a conservative branch of Christianity, and her family felt that she had abandoned her faith by marrying outside of the church she had grown up in and becoming a Methodist like her husband. In fact, they believed that her death was punishment for that action. Consequently they blamed her husband for her death and did not hesitate to tell him so.

At the end of the funeral service everyone moved to the cemetery, gathering around the freshly dug grave. My friend spoke the words of committal. As the coffin was lowered into the grave, the woman's husband out of grief and despair leapt from his seat and flung himself on top of her coffin. As everyone stared in shock, my friend looked helplessly in horror at the scene unfolding before him and thought, "They never covered this in seminary!"

Unfortunately seminary can't cover every contingency. While we will hope that you won't experience a similar moment, the ministry is filled with unique moments that will give you, like my friend, a lifetime of stories.

In this chapter we will look at some of the special moments in the pastor's preaching life. While the majority of your preaching will be the week-in, week-out Sunday morning sermon, a number of different special occasions will challenge you in a variety of ways.

"GRACE CATCHERS"

James Wallace reminds us that feeding the people is an important understanding of preaching: "The accounts of the feeding of the multitude, then, can speak to all in the ministry or preaching. . . . [W]e have been told, '*You* feed them.' And so we must" (Wallace, 8). If we think of preaching as preparing and serving a meal, there will always be the nourishing but more familiar sermons that we prepare for Sunday morning worship, like the meals which we prepare week in and week out.

But occasionally we are called upon to prepare meals that take extra work and preparation, like Thanksgiving or a special birthday dinner. The unusual ingredients and additional coordination demand much from those preparing the meal. David Schlafer observes that these special events or "meals" in the life of the church call for that same additional coordination in order to offer "a word fitly spoken." Some preachers, he observes, make the mistake of "preaching *around* a special occasion" or "homiletical avoidance" (Schlafer, 12). They either ignore the occasion or deal "with issues at the periphery of the situation" (Schlafer, 12).

If ignoring a special occasion can be a problem, so too can focusing too much on the occasion. If we preach *about* the occasion, Schlafer observes, we tend to deliver "a sermon that is a theological information package" and lose the personal focus (Schlafer, 15–16). Finally, we have a tendency to "preach *at* the occasion" in such a way that it overwhelms those involved. What does he suggest?

Schlafer encourages preachers to preach *through* the special occasion. To preach "through" means to acknowledge the history and tradition of the occasion, as well as the uniqueness of the event, in order to "catch, incorporate, and engage listeners with the plot of this out-of-the-ordinary experience (Schlafer, 18). When we do this, he argues, these special event sermons become "grace-catchers." The sermon "selects and focuses colors from the spectrum of God's grace both through and for the particular special occasion" (Schlafer, 20). In the remainder of the chapter we will examine some of these special occasions and explore the ways that we may catch the abundant grace of God that flows in and through these particular moments.

HOLY DAYS AND HOLIDAYS

Think about the number of different calendars by which you organize your year. We have a civic or secular calendar that organizes the year from January 1 to December 31. Throughout that year are a number of special days. If you live in the United States, you know that on the Fourth of July government offices will be closed and people will gather after dark to ooh and aah at the fireworks that will light up the sky.

If you are in school or have children who are, your life may also be governed by the academic calendar. That calendar dictates the beginning of the school year and the end. It prescribes when you will take a vacation: winter, spring, or summer.

You also, I trust, keep a personal or family calendar that marks the birthdays and anniversaries of those you love. You are then able, through cards, flowers, and gifts, to acknowledge those special days.

Your church family also maintains at least two calendars. First, it will probably follow the calendar that organizes the church year. For some of you, that will mark primarily Christmas and Easter. But others will follow the more complex liturgical year that begins on the First Sunday of Advent and continues through the seasons of Advent, Christmas, Epiphany, Lent, and Easter, as well as periods of Ordinary time. The seasons will shape your worship and preaching, and throughout the year will come those special days—the high holy days of the church year: Christmas, Ash Wednesday, Easter, and Pentecost—that demand, like that Thanksgiving meal, special ingredients and extra attention.

Finally, your congregation's year will also follow a program calendar. That calendar, although tied to the church year, will revolve around the events peculiar to your community. Your educational schedule will call for special observations—perhaps the Sunday you kick off the new year or honor those who teach. Your calendar will also be marked by events such as homecoming, bazaars, special dinners, and picnics. Your congregation will also participate in local community events, and they will have an impact on your worship schedule.

Each holy day and holiday calls forth special attention. Although we can't explore all that will arise, discussing a few will give you an idea of the issues and questions that arise when preparing sermons for those special occasions.

Christmas

Even before the Halloween candy and costumes have been purchased, stores and malls begin the intense preparations for Christmas. They fill their aisles with decorations, the air with Christmas music, and the shoppers with reminders of how important it is to buy that "special gift" for your "special someone." It is all but impossible to hold on to the ancient church's tradition of observing the four weeks of Advent before Christmas as a time of quiet reflection and preparation for the feast of the incarnation. Gone also are the twelve days of Christmas that followed December 25. We no longer have time for golden rings, leaping dancers, partridges, and pear trees. By December 26, the decorations are gone, the music has ceased, and the sales urge you to return all of those unwanted gifts and buy what you really want because they are putting up the red and white decorations of Valentine's Day.

How is the church able to compete with the marketing engines that drive our economy and silence competing worldviews? How are we able to compete with Santa Claus and reindeer, George Bailey's transformation, and Hallmark's visions of the perfect Christmas? How can our message of the Word made flesh contend with the message of materialism, memories, tinsel, and trees?

For many churches the four candles of the Advent wreath must compete with Christmas trees, poinsettias, and carols. They are unable to hold on to the liturgical season that reminds us that while we prepare to remember the birth of the baby in Bethlehem, we must also recognize that "Christ has died, Christ is risen, Christ will come again." Advent and Christmas are as much about our present and our future as they are about our romanticized past.

To step into the pulpit for the Christmas Eve services is to step into the middle of a beehive. The church literally buzzes with anticipation. In an earlier chapter we explored the issue of "noise" in preaching. On Christmas Eve there are both literal and internal noises. Children who are unable to sit still produce the hum that will provide a counterpoint to your sermon. But their charming noise will be drowned out by the internal noises in the hearts and minds of your listeners.

Some will walk into the church on Christmas Eve lonely and sad. This may be the first Christmas since the death of someone they loved, a spouse or a parent. Others may come to worship thinking not about the gracious message of the gospel, but focused rather on the externals—Christmas trees, twinkling lights, candles, and flowers. They view the service, not as worship of God, but a stage set for the perfect Christmas.

While we may make jokes about Christmas-and-Easter Christians, as you look out into the congregation on Christmas Eve, the reality will be that many of your listeners do attend worship only then and at Easter. The reasons for being there are numerous. Some may be there because they have come to celebrate Christmas with their churchgoing parents or siblings and have been cajoled into attending the service as part of that celebration. Others may come hoping to recover the feelings of childhood Christmases. For still others, this may be the first worship service ever attended. Many of those visitors will be anxious and uncomfortable. They do not know what to expect or what to do. They are not used to sitting beside strangers. And they are certainly not used to group singing.

Christmas Eve is therefore an important time for the church to exercise gracious hospitality. Ushers must be attentive to drawing people into the community, helping them find their way, and providing the resources they will need to make this a comfortable experience, whether it is a bulletin, service aid, or prayer book, hymnal, or Bible. You must also perform the same functions in your sermon. Your message must be one of hospitality, not scolding. Christmas Eve is not the time to berate people for missing the other fifty or fifty-one weeks in the year.

We have an amazing message to proclaim: Emmanuel, God is with us! Crafting a Christmas Eve sermon must negotiate between disparaging the outward and visible symbols of the secular celebration or becoming so caught up in those symbols that the important message we have been sent to proclaim becomes lost. We do not want to domesticate this startling announcement, but we must also realize that many people seated before us know little or nothing of our story. We cannot remind them of something they do not know.

Don't be afraid to stick with the basics. People's minds may be focused on the gifts they have purchased or are going to receive, but the stable door opens into the amazing mystery of God's great gift to us. It is the time to remind everyone of the news that we need to hear over and over again. There is a God who loves us, and that loving God has created us, become one of us, died for us, and risen for us. The Christmas sermon needs to see through the joy of the manger, through shepherds, angels, and magi, through candles, wreaths, and carols, to the gospel, the good news that in the infant Jesus, God became flesh and pitched the tent of welcome and wisdom in our midst.

We must be sensitive to people's biblical and theological ignorance. Many will have only a slight understanding of the meaning of the manger. This is not the time to overwhelm them with biblical information or doctrinal abstractions. People on a milk diet will not be able to digest meat. But it is also

not the time to take the safe route and simplify this startling news into holiday pablum. The message of the incarnation is that God came to us and
became one of us in an unexpected and surprising way. Our sermons must continue to proclaim the good news that God continues to be with us and to surprise us each day, and that ultimately all we are and all we do is in the hands
of God.

Easter

Some years ago, in the midst of a preaching class that was exploring how we
are to preach the astonishing news of the resurrection, a student raised an
important issue. We had been discussing the challenge of preaching life after
death to people schooled in the scientific method and Enlightenment. How,
he wondered, could he work with the church leaders to keep the arrival of a
man dressed as an Easter Bunny from being the centerpiece of his church's
Easter service?

In many ways, the issues that challenge the Christmas sermon also apply to
Easter. The pull of bunnies and jelly beans may not be quite as strong at Easter
as that of Santa and gifts, but one still is faced with a congregation that is either
naive or skeptical about the Easter message. This message is at the heart of the
gospel. This message is what we must proclaim. Without the message of the
death and resurrection of Jesus the Christ, we are not Christians.

We must understand that preaching the resurrection is exciting but difficult. We need to remember the reaction by those who first heard this good
news. The apostles who had followed Jesus thought that Mary's news was a
foolish, idle tale. Thomas, who was not with the others that first night, refused
to believe: "Unless I see the mark of the nails in his hands, and put my finger
in the mark of the nails and my hand in his side, I will not believe" (John
20:25b). Should we be surprised that people continue to view this as a foolish,
idle tale and refuse to believe?

As preachers of the gospel, we must continue to preach the good news that
Christ is risen. We must not try to explain away the mystery. We must not try
to recast this startling message in culture-friendly terms. Easter is not the time
to go down the safe path of butterflies and Easter eggs. Nor is Easter the time
to attempt to explain the abstract theological concepts of the resurrection and
Christology. David Schlafer argues that we must avoid "talking about the
scriptural stories or giving simple summaries." Rather, our Easter preaching
should be "a judicious selection and weaving of images, actions, or motifs from
the scripture stories . . . that can offer an experience of resurrection power
touching and transforming the tombs and prisons of human experience
(Schlafer, 102).

Mother's Day / Pentecost

In the 1600s a tradition grew up on the Fourth Sunday of Lent of visiting one's mother and taking her a cake to thank her for all she had done. England and Canada continue to observe Mothering Sunday during Lent. In the United States the tradition of Mother's Day traces its history back to Julia Ward Howe, the author of "The Battle Hymn of the Republic." In 1872 she began to encourage the observance of a Mother's Day that would promote peace. Gradually more and more states began to hold a Mother's Day observance, but we owe both the date and the national observance of the day to Ana Jarvis, a woman from Philadelphia.

Following the death of her own mother, Ana Jarvis began to militate for more intentional observance of the day. In 1907, two years after her mother died, she persuaded her mother's church in Grafton, West Virginia, to observe Mother's Day on the second Sunday in May, the anniversary of her mother's death. Spurred on by the success of that observance, she began to militate for a national observance, and in 1914 President Wilson signed a bill declaring the second Sunday in May as Mother's Day.

Because Mother's Day became a very popular day for card manufacturers, florists, the phone company, and restaurants, Miss Jarvis came to lament her success. As she witnessed the growing economic popularity of the day, she reportedly declared that she regretted ever starting the observance. But start it she did, and given the fact that Mother's Day falls on a Sunday, preachers must decide how they will address this secular holiday.

Several problems confront the preacher as he or she approaches Mother's Day. A major problem is that Mother's Day often occurs on the same Sunday as Pentecost. The preacher is faced with the challenge of observing a major festival of the church year, while at the same time honoring mothers. In many churches Mother's Day is a major festival marked by the gift of flowers and perhaps a special luncheon. Church leaders and mothers will not be happy if their place of honor is usurped by Pentecost. Nevertheless, in the life of the church, in spite of the importance of mothers in all of our lives, Pentecost should take precedence over Mother's Day.

This does not mean that the creative preacher cannot observe both days if they happen to coincide. When we preach through the story of Pentecost, lifting up the community of faithful called by God to proclaim the good news and share God's love with all people, we may turn to mothers and fathers as examples of those who nurture and form us in our life of faith. The author of the Second Letter to Timothy reminded Timothy of the importance of his mother Eunice and grandmother Lois. The strong faith that had lived in them now lived in him, and he should not forget that. That message can always be preached to strengthen the community of the faithful.

Timothy may have had a loving relationship with his mother and grand-mother. Unfortunately, that is not the case for many people in the congregation. For a variety of reasons, many do not or did not have a healthy relationship with their mother. The observance of Mother's Day, therefore, can be problematic for them. Ana Jarvis supposedly promoted Mother's Day so strongly out of guilt over her stormy relationship with her own mother. Others will be troubled because their mothers have died, while others will be bothered by the observance because they are having difficulty becoming parents.

Because some will understandably be troubled by an observance of Mother's Day does not mean that you should avoid it all together, but you must be sensitive to the wide range of feelings and emotions that will be present as you preach. You cannot assume that everyone had or has a strong and loving relationship with his or her mother.

A way to negotiate this challenging path is to broaden your discussion beyond biological mothers. Many of us, even those who have had wonderful mothers, have also had other women who were like mothers to us, who nurtured and formed us in the faith. By raising up that possibility, you extend the reach of this important day. Even those who have not been able to have their own biological children have served, are serving, or have the potential to serve, as parents in Christ.

Finally, we must be aware of the broader cultural questions and issues about motherhood, parenthood, and family that confront our listeners. Being a parent is difficult and challenging work, and those who are parents need tremendous help and support from their faith community. Our culture questions what it means to be a parent. What makes one a father or mother? How does one integrate work in and outside the home? These questions are also tied to the questions about marriage and the nature of the family. Turning to Scripture for neat, pat answers is not always easy. I suspect that most of us will not use Matthew 10:34–35 for our Mother's Day text: "Do not think that I have come to bring peace to the earth; I have not come to bring peace, but a sword. For I have come to set a man against his father, a daughter against her mother, and a daughter-in-law against her mother-in-law." That will certainly win the hearts and minds of many.

An important part of preaching is sensitive pastoral care. It is not about ignoring issues, but neither is it about confronting issues head-on. It is about being aware of the undercurrent that flows through these celebrations and navigating that current carefully, honestly, and with great sensitivity.

Thanksgiving

Each week the people of God gather to lift up their hearts in the name of the Lord and give thanks for all that God has done and is doing for them. In word, song, and prayer they praise God and remind themselves that thankfulness should be their posture every day. They gather around the table for *Eucharist*, thanksgiving, to share the bread and wine, the body and blood of the Christ who feeds them, nurtures them, and strengthens them for his service. Thanksgiving is the Christian's way of being in the world.

How can it be, therefore, that we have come to view Thanksgiving Day as a secular, civic observance? Aren't the roots of the celebration biblical? Weren't those who gathered for that first Thanksgiving meal people of God gathering to lift their hearts in the name of the Lord and giving God thanks for all that God had done for them, sustaining them in this new life?

We do not know when and where they gathered. We do not know who actually sat at the table or what they ate. What we do know is that, over the intervening centuries, Thanksgiving Day came to be a celebration more of nationalism and patriotism than of Eucharist. Preaching on Thanksgiving requires, therefore, the recovery of an understanding of faithful thanksgiving and gratitude. It means attempting to separate the grace of the occasion from the secular, patriotic overlay.

More and more, Thanksgiving services are coming to serve as an ecumenical opportunity. Rather than each church observing Thanksgiving alone, churches, synagogues, and mosques are coming together for a joint celebration. An additional challenge for the preacher is recognizing the constraints called forth by such a congregation, as well as the opportunities presented. How can we come to see that we are all children of the one God, and how do we all join together in a posture of thankfulness and gratitude? Might this be an occasion that opens conversation of understanding and fellowship and, in doing so, lives out the goal of that first Thanksgiving?

INDIVIDUALS

As preachers, we must think constantly about the congregation or audience to whom we will be preaching. Who are they? Why are they gathered before us? What are they seeking out of this occasion? Weddings and funerals pose the most challenges in this regard. These services, by their very nature, focus more on an individual or individuals than on the community of the faithful. While you stand before the people in attendance in the name of God, many of those people have little or no interest in what God has to do with the occasion. There are many, often competing, agendas. How do you as a preacher take these various agendas into consideration? How do we speak God's word in the marketplace of concerns and ideas?

Weddings

Ask clergy to talk about their experiences with weddings, and I doubt whether you will be able to get them stop. They will tell you funny stories of mishaps and missteps, painful stories of family conflicts spilling over into this joyous occasion, and just plain odd stories. My best friend is also a pastor. We have a running contest to find the most unusual experience at a wedding. She hasn't been able to top the wedding I did where the musical instrument for the service was a didgeridoo, an Australian aboriginal instrument.

Throughout this book we have been exploring the relationship between preaching and the broader culture and context in which we preach. Nowhere is this more crucial than planning and preaching at weddings. As clergy we must always think like anthropologists who are engaged in ethnographic research. What is our culture teaching young women about weddings? Go and buy several wedding magazines. (You will need a truck for getting them back to your office, they are so big.) Here brides are told that the most important aspects of the wedding are the dress and the reception—not the content of the ceremony or an understanding of marriage.

Several things are important when thinking about your role in weddings. First, you are usually not the first person that a couple calls. The first thing that they will do is arrange for the site of the reception. Since they must frequently make that reservation a year in advance, it is often the reception, not the wedding ceremony, that drives the event. This is because you will find it a rare experience to have a young couple who are members of your church. You may have a couple whose parents or parent is a member, but it will be unlikely that either the bride or the groom regularly attends worship service. This means that you will not only have to discuss the service with the couple, but it will be equally important that you take time with the couple to explore their understanding of marriage and educate them about the church's understanding. Marriage preparation classes should be a crucial part of your church's program.

The couple may also engage a wedding planner or coordinator, someone who helps them plan the ceremony and the reception and the many components that go into their big day. While we must be willing to work with that person, *we* are in charge of the ceremony and what happens during it, not the wedding planner. It is not always an easy task wresting control from that person. Likewise, be prepared to work with the mother of the bride. She will probably have very strong feelings and opinions about what should and should not take place in the wedding.

You, therefore, will need to think about what marriage is and why you, as a minister of God, are involved in the ceremony. While John tells us that the first miracle performed by Jesus was at a wedding feast, and Mark tells us that Jesus challenged the understanding that a man could divorce his wife (Mark 10:2–9), it was not until the fifteenth century that wedding ceremonies began to take place in church. The early church actually discouraged marriage. Many of the church fathers viewed celibacy as the best preparation for the *eschaton*. They understood marriage as a civil contract that was dictated by Roman law; therefore they did not want the church to become involved in those issues.

Over the centuries, however, Christians came to desire some recognition of their marriage by the church. For most of our history, there was a blessing of the marriage that took place, not in the church, but on the church steps. While the Roman Catholic church had always considered marriage one of the seven sacraments, it was only in the 1500s that we begin to see wedding ceremonies that actually took place in the church itself.

Who may marry whom, whether divorce is possible, when people may be married—these have all been subjects for lively debate throughout the history of the church they continue to be today. Therefore, for both theological and practical reasons it is important that you and your congregation make decisions about marriage preparation, marriage requirements, and where and when a wedding ceremony may take place, as well as the charges involved. If you have a nave and sanctuary that brides find particularly photogenic, you may find couples approaching you about having their ceremony at your church. Weddings potentially demand a great deal of your time; you must decide if you want to participate in all of those weddings.

The bride and groom should work with you in planning the service. When you think about the message that you will deliver during a wedding ceremony, it will help if the couple has chosen the Scripture passage or passages that will be read during the service. You may then, during your message, let those attending know that the passage was chosen by the couple.

Short. That should be the length of a wedding message or homily. Unless the wedding party can sit down while you preach, you must keep your message short. The couple is very, very nervous, and standing before you and in front of their guests makes them anxious. Always be prepared for the bride or groom to faint. (During the rehearsal you might remind them to keep their knees slightly bent while they are standing. If they lock their knees, they may pass out.) So keep your message short. A friend of mine limits her wedding messages to what she can say in two long breaths. While you might be tempted to say a little more, no one there—the bride, the groom, or the guests—is interested in a lengthy sermon. So what can we say?

A wedding sermon should not be confused with a rehearsal dinner speech. This is not a time for humor, jokes, or stories about the bride or groom. Rather, at a wedding, as at any other service, the focus of our message is God.

A wedding message reminds the couple that God is at the heart of their relationship, sustaining and empowering them, helping them to form a family that
will be a sign of God's reconciling love in a divided world.

You are speaking to two different audiences. First, you are speaking to the
bride and groom—the reason everyone has gathered. They need to be
reminded that this is not the start of their relationship. They have, we hope,
already been developing a relationship of love and respect. The wedding is,
however, an important point in that relationship, and with the help of God,
their family and friends, their newly wedded relationship will continue to
grow, deepen, and mature. They have come together before God and before
their family and friends to make their promises to live together in the covenant
of marriage.

Unfortunately, it is almost impossible for them to hear what you are saying.
They are thrilled, excited, frightened, nervous, scared, happy, and feel countless other emotions. Write out what you say and give it to the couple, along
with a copy of the service and the marriage licence. Then they will be able to
read your message when life has calmed down.

Your second audience is the family and friends of the couple. Think about
weddings as a wonderful opportunity for evangelism. Many of the people in
the wedding party and the guests may rarely, if ever, attend worship services.
Your demeanor, your posture of welcome, your sense that this is an important
and solemn moment and that God is an important part of this moment will go
a long way toward introducing people to the God we serve.

This is also an opportunity to remind those attending that weddings are not
a spectator sport. The couple has invited them to be there, not just for the celebration, but to ask for their love, help, and support as they begin their new
life together. This is an opportunity for those present to renew the promises
that they have made in their own lives.

The wedding homily or message is not the time for openly inviting them
to your worship service, but it does present you with the opportunity to be
welcoming and engaging, giving those present the experience of the Christian
community. We are children of a loving God who receives all who come, and
we bear the good news that in Christ we have been given new life. You are
there to remind the couple and their family and friends that God is a part of
their new life—day in, day out, week in, week out, in the good times and the
not so good times that lie ahead of them.

Funerals

In many ways the challenges of preaching at funerals are similar to those of
the wedding homily. Obviously the tone is quite different, but again, this is an

opportunity to proclaim the good news that through Jesus Christ, "whether we live or whether we die, we are the Lord's" (Rom. 14:8).

Unlike a wedding, for which you will have time to prepare, funerals often arise unexpectedly. You do not have much time to write the sermon. This will be more of a problem early in your ministry than later on, after you have delivered a number of funeral sermons. You will develop what are known as commonplaces. In traditional rhetoric a commonplace was a short speech on a generic topic that a student developed and had ready, should the need for a speech arise. Throughout our preaching life we essentially develop commonplaces, much like Buttrick's "moves." We develop statements about a variety of theological topics—Christ, revelation, sin, redemption, and resurrection—that we fold into various sermons. Over the years you will come to develop a number of funeral commonplaces, relatively generic funeral sermons, that you can then modify to fit the particulars of the situation.

Although it seems rather odd to state it this way, there are good funerals and bad funerals. When my grandmother died at the age of ninety-eight, hers was a good funeral. Her life had been fascinating and filled with devotion to her faith, her family, and her friends. She was a marvelous grandmother (who baked wonderful cookies). She had seen the world with my grandfather and her trusty leather train case. A few years before she died, she began to talk about her funeral and burial (teaching me how important it is to make those plans). She wanted to be ready for her journey to the heavenly city. "Lucy," she would tell me matter-of-factly, "I am going to be cremated and buried in my train case." And of course she had her way, as she usually did. When we gathered on a cold Winnipeg winter morning, the subzero temperatures outside the church were warmed by the joy of our remembrances as we all gazed at her train case that sat in front of her 1918 high school graduation portrait and a dozen yellow roses. That was a good funeral.

But you will also encounter many difficult and painful funerals, like the one at which my friend watched as the deceased's husband jumped into the open grave, or the funeral that I did of a child who had fallen off a cliff while hiking with her family in the mountains of North Carolina. There was supposed to be a fence along the path, but it had been removed for the making of a motion picture. The fence had yet to be replaced, and the young girl ran ahead of her parents, plunging off the path before they could reach her. That was a very difficult funeral.

In preparation for preaching at weddings and funerals, you need to reflect upon and develop your theology of marriage and of death. As a minister of God you will have the privilege of entering into the most joyful and the most painful moments of people's lives. You come as a representative of God and the church. But you also come with your own understanding and your own questions. If you have had a difficult relationship in your own marriage, this could be reflected, not so much in the words that you say, but in the tone of your voice and the way that you stand as your deliver your message during the wedding ceremony. Likewise, if you have unanswered questions and doubts about human suffering, death, and what happens following our deaths, your uncertainty or doubt will shape your message. Jesus proclaimed to the grieving Martha that her brother Lazarus would rise again and said further, "I am the resurrection and the life. Those who believe in me, even though they die, will live, and everyone who lives and believes in me will never die" (John 11:25–26). He then asked her a crucial question, "Do you believe this?" Before we write a funeral sermon, we must answer Jesus' question. Do we believe that "everyone who lives and believes in [him] will never die?"

Whether it is the funeral of one who has lived a long and happy life or one who has experienced an early and painful death, a funeral service is usually difficult and sad. People are struggling to understand and cope with their loss. This is not the time for simplistic assurances or admonitions not to grieve. As Qoheleth, the Preacher, reminds us, there is "a time to be born, and a time to die; . . . a time to weep, and a time to laugh; a time to mourn, and a time to dance" (Eccl. 3:2a, 4). Weeping is not a sign that we do not believe. Even Jesus wept outside the tomb of his friend Lazarus. We do grieve, and the funeral does not serve to send the deceased to heaven; that is in God's hands alone. Rather, we gather to celebrate the deceased and to support each other in this difficult time.

There will be times when you will be officiating and preaching at the funeral of one whom you have come to know well. At other times you will be asked to plan and officiate at the funeral of someone you have never met. Prepare for both funerals in the same way—by meeting with the family to plan the service, choose the lesson or lessons to be read, and offer the family a time to reminisce about the person who has died. This gives you an opportunity to learn more about a person you did know or learn about a person you did not, and gives the family a wonderful chance to begin the healing process.

But like weddings, funerals can be a time for family conflicts to arise. As you prepare the funeral, be prepared for anger, rivalry, and acrimony.

While we do want to take this time to celebrate the life of the person who has died, this is not the time to declare God's judgment. You do not want to condemn either the deceased or those attending the funeral. Nor do you want to canonize one who had lived a normal, less than perfect life. Likewise, you want to avoid explanations that second-guess God. God does, in the grand scheme of things, call all of us to participation in the heavenly banquet. Do we know exactly why this person has died at this particular time in this particular way? Can we really know that God was lonely and therefore "called our brother home"?

We do not want to forget God or the message of the resurrection. Too many funeral sermons turn into eulogies and neglect the proclamation of the gospel. Funerals, like weddings, are an opportunity to remind everyone present that we have a God who loves us and supports in times of sorrow as well as times of joy. It is the time to announce the good news of the resurrection, that through the death and resurrection of Jesus Christ we all have been given the hope of new life. It is also the time to draw people together in mutual support. All are grieving, not only the loss of the person who has died, but also the fact that, like that person, we too will die. We cannot underestimate people's sense of vulnerability as they attend a funeral. We live in a culture that has extreme avoidance of illness and death. To attend a funeral is to confront that reality, and increasingly people do not have tools for dealing with that reality. You can help provide them with those tools through scriptural references and the support of the church.

FOR EVERYTHING THERE IS A SEASON

The preaching life is one of special moments and the ordinary. It is filled with moments of joy and pain, celebrations and crises, as well as the quiet observance of the passage of time. As preachers we must be ready for everything—the highs and the lows and the in between. We are asked to preach in every season of life—the coming in and the going out, the times of laughter and the times of weeping—and we are called to help build up when life would break down. We must be prepared "for every matter under heaven," with the reassuring words of the Preacher who went before us:

> I know that whatever God does endures forever;
> nothing can be added to it, nor anything taken from it;
> God has done this, so that all should stand in awe before him.
> (Eccl. 3:14)

QUESTIONS

1. In the United States we speak of the separation of church and state. But it is not always easy to decide where faith leaves off and patriotism begins. In this chapter we discussed the challenge of preaching a Thanksgiving sermon. But that is not the only occasion with this challenge. Write a sermon to be delivered the weekend closest to the Fourth of July or Memorial Day.
2. Prepare a brochure that will be given to those who would like to hold their wedding in your church. What will you ask of them in preparation for the

wedding? How often will you need to meet with the couple? What will be allowed during the ceremony? What will not? What instructions would you give to the florist, the photographer, the videographer? What about music? What is and isn't allowed? Look at wedding planning books or magazines to give you an idea of what couples might be asking.

3. I have recently read of a new trend in funerals. People find church funerals "too sad" and impersonal. Instead, they hire funeral planners who not only help the family plan the funeral, but also prepare and deliver eulogies that are very personal, usually humorous and touching. Imagine that the elderly parent of a family in your church has just died. They are thinking about hiring a popular funeral planner rather than having the funeral in the church. How would you try to convince the family to have the funeral in the church?

READ MORE ABOUT IT

Hedahl, Susan. *Preaching the Wedding Sermon*. St. Louis: Chalice Press, 1999.

Hoffacker, Charles, *A Matter of Life and Death: Preaching at Funerals*. Cambridge, MA: Cowley Publications, 2002.

Schlafer, David. *What Makes This Day Diffferent? Preaching Grace on Special Occasions*. Cambridge, MA: Cowley Publications, 1998.

Wallace, James. *Preaching to the Hungers of the Heart*. Collegeville, MN: Liturgical Press, 2002.

11

Open My Lips

O Lord, open my lips,
and my mouth will declare your praise.
Psalm 51:15

FILLING THE SPACE

My brother-in-law loves to tell the story of a public speaking class he took in seminary at the Catholic University of America in the 1950s. The class was held in a small auditorium that was part of the music school. At one point in the class the instructor placed all of the students on the stage. He told them to read a passage from Scripture so that he could hear it. He then walked away from them, off the stage. He walked into the auditorium and up the aisle. He walked through the doors and out of the theater. He kept walking down the steps and crossed the street that ran in front of the theater. He finally sat down on the hill across from the theater. In yes, his "outdoor voice," he explained to them that he was now sitting as far away from them as he would be if he was in the back row of St. Patrick's Cathedral in New York. What, he asked, would they do if they were preaching there and the sound system went out? How would they fill the space? They needed to speak so that *everyone* could hear them, even the people in the back row.

We are astounded when we look at pictures of famous preachers such as John Wesley or George Whitefield or politicians such as Henry Clay speaking to thousands out in fields. They did not have public address systems—no microphones, no bullhorns. How did they speak so that all of those people

could hear them? They had learned that delivery, the performance of their sermon or speech, was as important as the content. They had learned that projection and phrasing were as crucial as arguments and arrangement. They had
been trained to lengthen their vowels and essentially "sing" their words so that
the sounds would carry greater distances.

Unfortunately, with the advent of the electronic amplification of the voice,
delivery became the neglected and often forgotten dimension of public speaking. Since most preachers no longer had to worry about volume, about being
heard, they assumed that delivery was taken care of. They assumed that, since
people could hear, they didn't have to bother learning public speaking. How
wrong they are! Speaking—delivery—is much more than volume. It is a complex of vibrations, body, gestures, and expressions that come together to communicate. This chapter will explore the various dimensions of delivery and
help you to understand how to give voice to the sermon that you have prepared, how to fill the space.

A WAY OF BEING

In the introduction to his work *Effective Speech Communication*, Charles Bartow challenges us with questions central to our calling:

> Worship focuses our attention on God and the difference God makes
> for those who believe that life is to be lived in fellowship with the
> divine. How does one speak in such a Presence? How does one speak
> *to* such a Presence? How does one lead others in the worship of the
> One who is present with each of us and all of us together in ways that
> go clean beyond our capacity to comprehend? (Bartow, 9–10)

Bartow argues that these questions are questions not only of theology but of
"speech communication." They are questions that must drive how we prepare
and conduct our sermons and services. He reminds us that delivery is more
than standing before a microphone that will amplify the sounds we are making. It is a way of thinking and of being before the Lord.

Fortunately we are surrounded by a great cloud of messengers who never
forgot the importance of delivery, performance, the physical act of speaking.
Charles Bartow, Robert Jacks, Jana Childers, Clayton Schmit, and Richard
Ward lead us into an exploration of that way of thinking and being. They teach
us how to stand before God and the people that God has called together and
speak, as Jana Childers challenges us, with "passion, life, authenticity, naturalness, conviction, sincerity, . . . animation . . . fire, sparks, electricity, mojo, spiritual lava, or juice" (Childers, 18).

Preaching is or ought to be, Childers reminds us, a transforming, lively event, "an off-the-page and into-the-air kind of enterprise" (Childers, 26). In order to present that passion, authenticity, naturalness, and conviction, these messengers urge us to learn who we are, why we are doing what we are doing, and the skills necessary for an "honest performance."

Unfortunately most people who stand before a congregation to lead worship and deliver or perform a sermon have little or no training in public speaking. Consequently they are unprepared for the challenges that these activities present. An "honest performance" is, according to Childers, *when the interpreter is making careful use of experience. An honest performance starts internally. The interpreter connects his or her experiences with the words of the text*" (Childers, 51).

There are definitely skills and techniques that we can learn to make us effective performers, but this way of thinking and being is much more than techniques that will help us project our sound to the back of the church. We are invited into a way of thinking and being that helps us to negotiate the tension between being important in the worship and preaching event and becoming transparent, so that the focus is not on the speaker but the God who has called the speaker and who fills the space, the moment, the event.

How we speak, how we move, how we deliver our sermon are all culturally determined. One has only to attend several different worship services—Roman Catholic, Presbyterian, African American Baptist, a megachurch praise service—to realize that the performance style of one community will not necessarily work in another. Therefore, as we learn the techniques and skills of performance, we are learning how to "be ourselves" and *not* "be ourselves."

When we stand before a congregation, we are speaking as ourselves, but we are also speaking on behalf of the congregation. That changes what we can do and what we must do. There is a large physical distance between us, the speaker, and them, the listeners. That changes what we can do and what we must do.

On a quiet afternoon, when there is no one in your church, go and sit in the back pew. Look up at the front of the church and examine the seats and the hangings. What can you tell about the details? Most of us will be able to see only general outlines. Even in the barest church or worship space we may see colors and shapes, but we will not be able to see small decorations or the weave of the material covering the chairs. No matter how good our eyes are, distance robs us of that ability. So, when you step into the pulpit or stand in front of the congregation, the distance between you and your listeners demands that you become bigger. You must speak with a larger, more powerful voice. Your inflection, phrasing, emphasis must all take into consideration the fact that people are farther away. Your listeners will not always be able to see the facial expressions with which you are accustomed to augmenting your words, and your gestures must be big enough for the people in that last pew to see you.

We cannot present a flat and lifeless sermon. We cannot mumble. Neither can we become a caricature of the preacher, one who adopts a "pulpit" or "stained-glass" voice. Our speaking must be lively, engaging, energetic, clear, and faithful. We must develop what Kristin Linklater describes as our "natural voice. . . . Everyone possesses a voice capable of expressing, through a two-to-four octave natural pitch range, whatever gamut of emotion, complexity of mood and subtlety of thought he or she experiences" (Linklater, 1). However, "the tensions acquired through living in this world, as well as defenses, inhibitions and negative reactions to environmental influences, often diminish the efficiency of the natural voice to the point of distorted communication" (Linklater, 1). We must learn how to remove those defenses and inhibitions.

We are called to learn how to speak clearly, forcefully, faithfully, and sincerely—proclaiming the good news of the gospel in ways that will be heard and understood by the people God has placed before us. In this chapter we will explore the various dimensions of your natural voice and ways that you will develop a performance style worthy of your calling.

YOUR VOICE: AN INTRODUCTION

Think about how amazing it is. Unlike the languages that you may have learned later in life, no one taught you how to speak your first language. Your parents helped and encouraged and corrected you, but you were the one who figured out how it all worked and put it all together.

As an infant you started by making sounds, all sorts of them. You babbled, cooed, and played with your voice. You made soft sounds that pleased your tired parents. You also found that you could make sounds so loud they shook the rafters. As you manipulated your lips and tongue, you found that you could shape the sounds in different ways. And you quickly noticed that when you made certain sounds, you could produce quite a reaction in the people who took care of you. They would come running if you made a sound that approximated "mother" or "father." They liked that—and you got what you wanted!

Over the years you learned not only how to form the sounds that made words, but how to put those words together in ways that could communicate your wants, needs, ideas, and thoughts. Your words became much more efficient and productive than piercing screams. You could speak softly if the occasion demanded, or you could speak loudly if you needed to call to someone across a field.

You grew up amid people who spoke a certain way—loudly or softly, with a high pitch or low pitch—and you learned to shape your voice to match theirs. In some cultures a high, soft voice is valued for women, so that is what women in that culture come to understand as the "natural" voice. In other cultures a loud, gruff voice is considered manly. So, if you are a man, you shape your voice that way without giving it a second thought. The reality is, however, that you have tremendous control over your voice. You are able to change and manipulate your pitch, your volume, the quality of your voice, your rate of speech, and many other factors that we will return to shortly.

Unfortunately, most people who are asked to engage in public speaking, whether it is preaching a sermon, delivering a speech, or reading a passage of Scripture, have had no formal training in using their voice for the task. They believe that in order to speak to a large group they have only to use a microphone or speak louder. They are unaware that there are right and wrong ways of using their voice. You cannot "just be yourself." Therefore, an introduction to your voice is in order.

Speaking begins, not with a sound, or even a breath that will produce that sound, but with a thought. You think about what you want to say, to whom you will be speaking, and the context. Different situations demand different volume and pitch. Different emotions also shape our communication. At any moment you are experiencing different emotions. You may be pleased, happy, joyful, angry, frightened, or concerned. The voice you project will be different for each emotion, and your listeners have learned to evaluate those differences. You think about what you want to communicate, and that sets in motion a series of physical impulses that put it all together.

Earlier chapters of this book included questions and exercises at the end of the chapter, but in this chapter the exercises are included throughout. As you read the following paragraphs, don't be afraid to do what we are discussing. Try preparing to speak in slow motion, and be attentive to what happens to your body. It is important to understand what is involved, so that you can identify the various points that can prove problematic for a speaker.

All vocal production, whether speaking or singing, involves your whole body. As you prepare to make a sound, you relax and open your nose and mouth so that you will be able to draw in enough air to produce the sound you need. Imagine you are going to be speaking to someone who is standing right next to you. You will draw in more air than you would if you were just taking a breath. But now imagine that you are going to shout at someone who is far away. You will draw in a much larger breath.

The lungs are large air sacks. But unlike the heart, they are passive organs. Your heart is a muscle that performs the function of pumping the blood through the lungs, where it is oxygenated and then back through the heart and through the body. Your lungs, on the other hand, must depend on another muscle, the diaphragm, for the inhalation and exhalation of air. The only time you are aware of this important muscle is when it goes into spasm and you experience the hiccups.

When it is at rest, your diaphragm is a dome just below your heart and lungs, separating the chest cavity from the abdominal cavity. When you contract the muscle fibers of the diaphragm, it flattens out, and, in doing so, pulls down and opens up the space of the chest cavity. As the space expands, it creates a vacuum, and since nature abhors a vacuum, the air outside of your body is drawn into your lungs, either through your nose or your mouth. If you are breathing without speaking, your diaphragm then relaxes, and as it does, the air gently leaves your lungs. However, if you are going to produce sound with that air, the diaphragm goes to work, contracting either abruptly, in order to produce a loud yell, or slowly, in order to manage the exhalation. The muscle of the diaphragm is aided by the abdominal muscles. Did you ever think that doing sit-ups or crunches would be helpful to your speaking voice?

We will discuss breath control in greater detail shortly. But for now, let's turn our attention to what happens to the air after it leaves your lungs. When you are inhaling and exhaling without speaking, your windpipe is unrestricted. If you wish to make a sound, however, you tighten your windpipe the same way you might close off a water pipe in order to build up the water pressure. You tighten your windpipe with your larynx, which includes your vocal folds. When you tighten them and they begin to vibrate, you are able to produce a sound. As a child discovering all of the different sounds that you could make, you were learning to manipulate your vocal folds, which are essential to the production of sound. If they are inflamed because of a cold or are damaged by misuse, you experience their importance—you become hoarse or, at the extreme, can't talk.

The vocal folds are able to produce changes in pure sound and pitch. If you open your mouth and produce a sound, you will see what they are able to do. You will also observe however, that the production of communication is not complete. While there are times when a pure sound is all you need to get your thought across, most of the time you want to use words. If you wish to communicate a thought to someone, you need to shape that pure sound with the use of your tongue, oral cavity, jaw, and lips. They produce the vowels and consonants, the articulation and pronunciation that make us understandable. When our face is tight, as we shall see shortly, we have a difficult and tiring time speaking.

Our sound is essentially complete. We have moved from thought, to breath, to vibration, to articulation, and we are now able to send our message. Before moving on, however, we need to mention one other important part of our personal "sound machine" our resonators.

The vocal folds produce a relatively small vibration. Think of the string on a violin or guitar. If you pluck a string, it makes a sound, but it makes a much larger sound if the string is attached to the body of the instrument. That large wooden structure amplifies the vibrations, and you go from a small pluck to a lovely, rich tone. Your body does the same thing for the vibrations produced by your vocal folds. We have already mentioned one structure, your mouth. But the vibrations are also magnified by your chest cavity and sinus cavities that are located throughout your head. Again, you know how your sound is affected when a cold or allergy blocks your sinuses.

FREEING YOUR VOICE

You have been using this complex system for years, but you have probably not been aware of all the intricate and crucial parts. They work well for you when you are speaking to another person or even a small group. However, making the leap to speaking to a larger group without training often proves problematic, because many people don't realize how complicated the process is. Unfortunately, trying to help someone become a better public speaker or performer through a book is a little like trying to teach someone to swim or ride a bicycle by reading a book. I can give you a heads-up about the problem areas or the ways to address those problems, but it would be much more beneficial if you sought out a speech or drama course with an instructor who would work with you to learn the best way to speak. However, I do think that it is possible in this book to give you an idea of the things you need to be working on.

Posture, Posture, Posture

Many of you probably got tired of your mother telling you to stand up straight when you were a child. Well, she was right. Most people don't realize how important your posture is to producing a big sound. Singers do. They know that you need to stand tall in order to open your chest cavity. That way, you are able to take a full breath, filling your lungs.

When you stand straight, your neck is extended and your head is up. You are then able to look out at your listeners. As we noted in an earlier chapter, many people have a problem with looking down at the Bible or at their preaching manuscript. When they do, their mouth is pointed not at their listeners but at their feet. Consequently, the sound is directed at their shoes.

You want to stand tall, but you don't want to stand like a Marine—tense and stiff. You want to have your head up and your shoulders relaxed, not scrunched up around your ears. Your spine should be in alignment, and your feet about a shoulder's width apart. Your arms should be relaxed at your side. Try to get in the habit of returning to this position when you are not moving, the same way a tennis player returns to her stance when she is not moving toward a shot.

There is an interesting and ironic dimension of performance or public speaking. Athletes, singers and actors all know that when you are using your body, you must be at the same time relaxed and ready. Whether one is preparing to run a race, pitch a game, sing an aria, or perform a soliloquy, one must warm up the body with stretching exercises. Tense muscles constrict one's movement and lead to injuries. Therefore, one must learn to relax one's arms, back, even facial and neck muscles. You then are more ready for the physically demanding work ahead of you.

Numerous warm-up exercises are available. Robert Jacks's book *Getting the Word Across*, (pages 125–48) offers numerous exercises that will help you "warm up your instrument."

Breathing

Like many other dimensions of speaking, breathing is something we take for granted. However, breath control is a dimension of speaking that proves problematic for many speakers. If you are reading a passage of Scripture and find that you run out of breath, or you get to the end of preaching a sermon and find that you are gasping, you are not in control of your breathing.

To begin to get control, we need to understand the importance of abdominal breathing. Even though our lungs are in our chest cavity, the evidence that people take a breath is in the expansion of their stomachs, not their rib cage. Remember, it is the lowering of your diaphragm into your abdominal cavity, not the expansion of your ribs, that makes inhalation possible.

Stand in front of a mirror and take a deep breath. If you see your chest expand and your shoulders rise, you are breathing incorrectly. You are chest breathing not abdominal breathing. This is not a problem if you are speaking to another person, but if you need to project your voice to a large group, you will not be able to take in enough air. Furthermore, you will not be pushing the air out with your abdominal muscles. Instead, you will be pushing the air out with your upper chest and throat muscles, which are not nearly as strong as your abdominal muscles. That means you have to work much harder. You will produce a much harsher sound, and in the long run you can do permanent damage to your vocal folds.

If by the end of a Sunday morning you are hoarse and your throat is sore and rough, it means you are not using your abdominal muscles for exhalation but are pushing the air out with the muscles around your larynx. This is known as hyperfunction. It often results in nodes on your vocal folds that are similar to blisters or calluses you build up on your hands if you are doing yard work without gloves. The body produces extra skin to protect itself from the assault. If you learn to breathe correctly and take care of your vocal folds, the nodes may heal, if you have not permanently damaged your throat.

When people have laryngitis because of a cold or allergy, they are tempted to whisper, thinking that gives their voice a rest. Don't. Not only does it not rest your voice, whispering is actually harder on your vocal folds than normal speech. Complete rest is the best cure. However, if you cannot do that, it is better to try to speak normally, even if that means your voice cracks. You might also try warm, not hot, liquids.

Shifting from chest breathing to abdominal breathing is not easy, since breathing is an automatic function. However, if you wish to experience abdominal breathing, lie down on the floor. When lying down, we all breathe abdominally. While you are on the floor, you might try a few crunches, modified sit-ups. They are very helpful in strengthening the muscles you need to be a good speaker.

For some reason, many speakers have come to believe that they should not let their listeners see them take a good breath. You need a great deal of air to produce a sound that will fill a large space. So don't be afraid to take deep breaths. Your listeners will not be surprised to see that you breathe! Pauses, which we will discuss shortly, are an excellent time for filling your lungs.

Loose Lips

During World War II a popular poster announced that "Loose Lips Sink Ships." While loose lips may have been a problem then, they are not a problem in public speaking. Although you need to be tightening your abdominal muscles, you need to be loosening up the muscles in your face and jaw.

You shape the sounds you produce with your tongue, lips, and teeth, and by moving your jaw to open and close your oral cavity. If the muscles in your face are tight and your jaw is locked, you will have to work much harder to produce understandable words.

A fun and effective exercise I call "horse lips." Try relaxing your lips, but keep your mouth closed. Now blow out your breath through your mouth. It should make your lips vibrate and tickle. If you find this difficult, begin by lightly placing your forefingers at the corners of your mouth, then blow. This exercise reduces the tension in your face muscles. (It is also a good way of reducing your overall tension when you are nervous. I love to do this when I am sitting at a stoplight. I can only imagine what the people in the other cars think I am doing!)

Another method of removing that tension is massaging the muscles in your lower face and jaw line. We are so used to keeping a smile on our face we don't realize how tense those muscles are. We will return to a discussion of the importance of your face shortly.

VOCAL INGREDIENTS

I wish I could place on the rear wall of every church a large sign that announces, SLOW DOWN / SPEAK UP. The rate at which you speak and your volume are crucial to your delivery. But they are not the only elements that make up your vocal production. With what do we communicate?

Rate

I had a voice teacher who once advised that, "if it feels as though you are speaking too slowly, you are probably getting much closer to what is appropriate." In our everyday conversation we speak very rapidly. Have you ever had to listen to someone's phone message several times in order to copy down a phone number, because they gave it so quickly? When you are reading a passage of Scripture or delivering a sermon, you *must slow down*. We are able to read more quickly than we are able to listen. You must give people time to take in and process the ideas that you are putting forth.

What happens if you try to water a plant in parched ground? If you pour a bucket of water on the plant, very little will reach the roots because most of the water runs away quickly. The ground is so hard that it cannot absorb the life-giving water. In order to nourish the plant you must pour the water very slowly, allowing the soil to become moist and therefore take in the water that it needs. Our souls are the same way. They are often hard and dry. The living water of the gospel, if delivered too quickly will run off quickly. Slow down. Deliver the living water slowly, so that we can receive the nourishment and hope that it brings.

Gauging the appropriate rate of our delivery is difficult to do alone. Practice reading before a friend. Someone listening to you will give you a much better idea of your rate. What feels terribly slow to you may actually sound like the right speed to your listeners.

Volume and Projection

As I mentioned at the opening of this chapter, the advent of sound systems that amplify the voice have lulled many speakers into thinking that all of their delivery problems are solved. That is not so. You still need to think about producing a big sound that reaches all of your listeners. That is why we need to think of not only volume, but projection.

In the musical *The Music Man*, the traveling salesman told the young people of River City that he would teach them to play their nonexistent instruments by the "think system." While it didn't help them to learn to play the trumpet or clarinet, the "think system" does work when we are speaking to a large group. Speaking begins with thought, with the recognition that you need to speak to someone who may be nearby or far away. You need to think about filling the space in which you are speaking. Your words must reach both the people in the front row and the people in the back pews.

Volume and projection require strong abdominal muscles. They require you to keep your face up and to speak up and out. You can't mumble, but you don't want to yell. Again, bring in people who will help you. Have people sit in the rear of the church. Are they able to hear you?

Pitch

While we are used to thinking about pitch when it comes to singing, we don't usually realize that our spoken language employs pitch. But it does. We tend to have a range in which our voice moves. Women in many cultures have been trained to move in the higher ranges while men move in the lower ranges. When we speak, our voice also goes up and down in a sort of melody line. If you listen to someone speaking English who was raised speaking a different language, you will observe what happens when one speaks one language with another language's melodic patterns, it doesn't sound quite right.

While we want you to sound like yourself when you are leading worship or preaching, those who have a particularly high- or low-pitched voice might want to think about pulling your pitch into a middle range. That gives you the possibility of a broader range of movement. It also carries further. Finding your middle range is actually quite easy. Hold your hand on your upper chest and make the sound "ahhh . . ." Do you feel the sound vibrating in your chest? If not, try lowering or raising the pitch until you do. That is where I would recommend your pitch your voice.

The movement of pitch is what gives our voice emotion and indicates the meaning of what we are saying. If we wish to ask a question, for example, we end our sentence with a rising inflection. While the rising inflection at the end of a sentence is appropriate when asking a question, it is not a good way to end every sentence. Unfortunately, many speakers today seem to end every sentence or even every phrase with a rising inflection. It gives their speech a hesitant, tentative quality: "Is this all right with you? Are you pleased with what I am saying? May I continue?" Record yourself in everyday conversation. You will be able to notice if you have fallen into this habit.

Another pitch problem can be lack of movement. A monotone voice, in which everything is read or spoken within a very narrow pitch range, sounds boring and not very engaging. It tends to put people to sleep, because they can't tell what is important.

One final caution about pitch. Because you are trying to fill a large space and reach people who are far away from you, be careful not to drop either your pitch or your volume at the end of a phrase—which many of us have a tendency to do. When you do, your listeners will miss what you are saying. In public speaking, unlike intimate conversation, you must keep your pitch and your volume up through the end of your phrase, so that the sound waves are sent out to the farthest reaches of the space you are trying to fill.

Quality

Most of us wish that we had a voice that sounds like a great dramatic actor— James Earl Jones or Judy Dench. Yes, they could read the phonebook, and we would all enjoy listening. Alas, most of us have to make do with the voice we have been given. But you actually have a great deal of control over your voice. It is not only nature, but nurture as well.

You want to sound like yourself when you are speaking, but you do need to have a bigger, fuller, richer voice. You do, however, want to avoid what some call a "stained-glass" or "pulpit" voice. You are not acting. You are not becoming someone else in the pulpit. You are still *you*, and you have control over the voice you project.

Remove or soften irritating habits that call attention to your voice. For example, if you have a tendency to expel air through both your mouth and your nose when you speak, your speech will have a nasal quality that most people find distracting. Learn how to close off the passage between your nose and your mouth.

Tape record yourself reading a passage of Scripture or preaching a sermon. This is a difficult thing to listen to. When you listen to your voice, it does not sound the way it does when you are speaking. You hear it from the "inside," while we hear you from the "outside." Once you overcome that disconnect, you will be able to identify a number of vocal ingredients—your rate, your pitch, and the quality of your voice. Does it sound grating or harsh? If so, work on smoothing the rough edges.

Variety

When we are speaking with people, our thoughts shape and drive our delivery. If we are excited about something, our pitch rises and we speak more quickly. We don't need to think about doing that: it just happens. Likewise, in conversation we don't speak every word at the same pitch or the same speed. We raise and lower our pitch; we speak some phrases more slowly, others more quickly. Our speech is marked, therefore, by a great deal of variety. Without that variety we sound wooden and artificial. To keep our reading and our delivery sounding natural, we must work on varying our volume, our rate of speech, our pitch, and our phrasing.

Pronunciation

The pronunciation of words is culturally and geographically determined. Ask individuals from Boston, Houston, and Minneapolis to say the word *park* and you will get very different pronunciations. This gives our speech character and distinctiveness. However, there are times when these differences in pronunciation can make it difficult, if not impossible, for one's listeners to understand what one is saying. If one is moving from one region of the country to another, one should be aware of these changes.

One should also be careful about learning the correct pronunciation of words. For example, many people mispronounce *et cetera*. Notice that it is "et," not "eck." You might also want to invest in a dictionary for pronunciation of biblical names and places. How do you pronounce *Michmash* anyway?

Articulation

Our speech is made up of vowels and consonants. Unfortunately, many speakers today have grown very sloppy and have a tendency to mumble. All of the vowels sound the same, and they seem to have given up articulating their consonants.

When it comes to articulating your vowels, think about opening up your mouth. Imagine that you have an orange in your mouth as you run through the vowel sounds "ay, ah, e, i, o, oo, u." The more you open your mouth, the more clearly people will be able to hear the difference between *day* and *die*.

Consonants also require your attention. In everyday conversation it seems rather forced to pronounce the final consonants of words. They are, however, crucial to our ability to be both heard and understood. The next time you are listening to someone preach or lead worship, listen very carefully to what you hear when he or she says the word *God*. I suspect that rather than "God," you will actually hear "gah." They will not fully articulate the "d". To get in the habit of articulating all of your consonants, pick up a passage of Scripture, or even the morning newspaper and read it out loud, making sure you articulate every consonant. That will feel odd, but this is the way you will make sure that people understand what you are saying.

Earlier I mentioned the importance of relaxing your jaw and facial muscles. Articulation is the reason this is important. If the muscles in our face are taut, we are not able to open our mouth fully, and the tension stifles the vibrations. When your muscles are tight, you have to work much harder to articulate your words, making delivery much harder.

Phrasing

When we communicate, our thoughts are delineated by phrases. In writing we use punctuation to indicate thought units. Commas, colons, periods, and question marks all signal that something is happening. When we are speaking, we use inflection, pitch, pauses, and stops to accomplish the same things. (It is important to remember that punctuation marks are attempting to mimic speech, not the other way around. You do not need to make quotation marks with your fingers when speaking. Let us know that you are quoting someone else by changing the tone of your voice and by pausing before and after the quotation.)

Communication begins with a thought. Know what you are trying to communicate, what you are trying to say, in order to decide the phrasing and pauses that will shape your speech. This is not as crucial when we are delivering our own sermon (although many people read from their own manuscripts as though it were written by someone else). When we are reading Scripture or prayers, however, we must decide where we will break and how we will make sense of what we are reading. As Robert Jacks notes, punctuation is not always helpful. In fact, we must often disregard the punctuation, because it chops up thoughts into units either too small or too large.

Pauses are also important in signaling that you have finished one idea and are going to move to another idea. You will note that I have placed an empty line between different sections of this book. When you see that space, you know a new section will be starting. When I am finished discussing *phrasing*, there will be a blank line before I move on to the discussion of *emphasis*. This is no less important in spoken language. Don't be afraid to pause. Don't be afraid of silence. It is the signal that your listeners need to prepare to listen for something different. It also gives you an opportunity to take in a large breath.

Emphasis

A companion ingredient of phrasing is emphasis. What word or words do we stress, and why? Jana Childers calls this the "art of prioritizing . . . *the word that carries the meaning of the sentence forward is emphasized*" (Childers, 84, 86). Not all words are equally important. Therefore, when we are speaking, we stress some, and move quickly over others, so that our listeners know what is important and what they should remember.

Phrasing and emphasis give shape and character to what we are saying. They make our speech understandable. Unfortunately, some preachers fall into the trap of thinking that everything they say is equally important. Stressing everything has the opposite effect. When you stress everything, nothing stands out. Likewise, if you stress nothing and speak with the rhythmic equivalent of a monotone, we will be confused and unengaged.

WORD MADE FLESH

We have already mentioned the importance of good posture. But there are other elements that are crucial to the kinesthetic or bodily dimensions of communication.

Body Language

We speak with our whole body. We "read" people's body language all of the time. We just aren't always aware that we are doing it.

Try an experiment. As you move about your day, watch the interactions of people that you can see but cannot hear. Watch people as they talk in a restaurant or on a bus. Watch people as they walk down the street together. Can you tell how they feel about one another? What can you tell about the nature of their conversation even though you can't hear what is being said?

By the way a person moves, stands, and gestures, by how close a person stands to someone else, we can tell how that person is feeling. The way someone moves her hands or head tells us if she is irritated or frustrated. In many cultures, when a person puts his hands in his pockets and shifts his weight to one leg, he is telling us that he is either relaxed or perhaps somewhat unengaged. How we stand and move when we are preaching and leading worship tells our congregation a great deal about what we are feeling and how engaged we are in what we are doing.

When we are in front of a congregation—whether we are preaching, leading prayers, singing hymns, or even sitting and listening—people are watching us. The are watching how we move, how much we are engaged. Actors will tell you that a major difference between acting on the stage and acting in motion pictures is the fact that, when one is on stage, one must be engaged all the time. The same is true for us when we are involved in a worship service. We are never "off camera."

We must be aware of what we are doing with our body. Do we look

engaged? Do we look involved with what is going on? Does our body communicate joy, excitement, and a willingness to be there? Can people tell that we
are serious about what we are saying? How we stand, how we walk, and how
we sit often communicate as much as the words we are speaking. We must also
think about what we do with our hands and the gestures we make.

In everyday conversation you probably never think about what to do with
your hands and arms. For some, the culture in which you were raised taught you
to use your hands and arms a great deal. In fact, some people say that if their
hands were tied behind their back, they wouldn't be able to speak at all. Most of
us gesture when we speak. Watch someone who is talking on the phone. Even
though the person to whom she is speaking can't see her, she will still move her
hands and arms, point, and gesture. But when we stand before a group of people, we tend to become very self-conscious of our hands and gestures.

When you are standing in front of a group of people, you don't want to
stand stiff and lifeless like a statue. You wouldn't speak that way if you weren't
in the pulpit. You shouldn't move that way when you are. However, you don't
want to go to the other extreme and move around a great deal and gesture
wildly. That will be distracting, and people will focus more on you than on
what you are saying. Your hand movements and gestures should be a little
larger and slower than your conversational manner. Distance makes a difference and demands changes in what you normally would do.

Facial Expression

Think about your facial expression. What was true for your posture and body
language is also true for the look on your face. You can't look into the face of
everyone before you, but they are looking into yours. And as they do, they are
seeking a sense of what you are thinking and feeling. Do you look engaged or
bored? Do you look at them with the spirit of Christian love? And perhaps
most importantly, do your facial expressions match what you are saying?

Many preachers have difficulty being serious in the pulpit. They want to smile
and have an encouraging look on their face. We are, after all, proclaiming *very*
good news. Unfortunately, there are some things that when we are talking about
them, we should not be smiling. When we are speaking of the passion and death
of Jesus, when we are engaging the prophetic texts, when we are being challenged
by words of judgment, we should not have a beaming look on our face.

Eye Contact

Finally, a word about making eye contact with your listeners. Get in the habit of
looking into the eyes of people all around the room. Look at people in the front

of the church and the back. Look at people on the right and on the left. If your listeners do not perceive that you are looking at everyone, they will feel excluded. If the choir sits behind you, think about turning and looking at them occasionally. However, if you have a stationary mike rather than a lapel mike, be aware that, when you turn away, the congregation will not be able to hear you.

How we stand and move, what we do with our hands and arms, the look on our face, our ability to make eye contact are crucial to our delivery. It is possible to analyze how one is doing if one has access to a video camera and records a worship service. Be aware of the potential problem of playing to the camera. If you are aware that you are being videotaped and will eventually be viewing yourself, you may have a tendency to be self-conscious during the service. Remember, we are our harshest critics. So, if you videotape yourself, in addition to critiquing your tape yourself, enlist the help of several people in the congregation.

Your listeners will give you a much more accurate picture of how you are doing. You don't have to gather a group, but one on one, ask them to give you feedback on your delivery. Can they hear and understand what you are saying? Are your physical movements appropriate or distracting? Does your manner draw them in? Do you have any repeated motions or gestures that they find distracting? They will perceive problems that you may not. Likewise, something that bothers you about yourself may not bother them at all.

PIECE, BY PIECE, BY PIECE

From our opening prayer, to our study of Scripture, to the pronunciation of our final consonant, we have been putting together our sermon. Filled with and confident in the grace of God, we step before the people of God to bring words of joy and comfort, justice and hope.

For two thousand years women and men have put together sermons, piece by piece. You are preparing to join their ranks. But where is preaching going? What should preaching look like in this new millennium? In the final chapter of this book I will invite you to reflect with me upon these crucial questions.

READ MORE ABOUT IT

Bartow, Charles. *Effective Speech Communication in Leading Worship*. Nashville: Abingdon, 1988.

Childers, Jana. *Performing the Word: Preaching as Theatre*. Nashville: Abingdon, 1998.

Jacks, Robert G. *Getting the Word Across: Speech Communication for Pastors and Lay Leaders.* Grand Rapids: Eerdmans, 1995.

Schmit, Clayton J. *Public Reading of Scripture.* Nashville: Abingdon, 2002.

Ward, Richard F. *Speaking of the Holy: The Art of Communication in Preaching.* St. Louis: Chalice Press, 2001

12

Communicating the Gospel: Looking Forward

I am about to do a new thing;
now it springs forth, do you not perceive it?
Isaiah 43:19

The wind blows where it chooses,
and you hear the sound of it,
but you do not know where it comes from or where it goes.
John 3:8

When one is beginning to learn the art of preaching, it hardly seems fair to ask you to think about doing new things when you aren't even comfortable with the "old." Nevertheless, in this final chapter I would like to invite you to dream with me. I would like to challenge you to think about where preaching is or should be going. And why do I ask you? You are the preachers who will be preaching in ten, twenty, thirty, and even forty years.

God has always been calling people to live into the new. Mary of Magdala did a new thing when she returned to the followers of Jesus locked in the upper room and announced to them that she had seen the Lord. When he was filled with the Spirit of God, Peter stepped out of that upper room and into a crowded Jerusalem street and did a new thing. Braving arrest and possible death, Peter declared to the assembled throng the great good news: "You that are Israelites, listen to what I have to say: Jesus of Nazareth, a man attested to you by God with deeds of power, wonders, and signs that God did through him among you . . . God raised him up, having freed him from death" (Acts 2:22, 24a). Struck blind on the road to Damascus, Paul journeyed throughout the Mediterranean world doing a new thing. This great good news about Jesus of Nazareth was not meant only for Israelites; it was meant for the whole world. "Through [Jesus Christ] we have received grace and apostleship to bring about the obedience of faith among all the Gentiles for the sake of his name" (Rom. 1:4b-5).

Whether they were Jew or Gentile, slave or free, male or female, the followers of Jesus Christ "broke bread at home and ate their food with glad and generous hearts, praising God and having the goodwill of all the people" (Acts 2:46–47). They did a new thing and worshiped the God who had given them new life by hearing the word proclaimed and sharing the bread and wine of the eucharistic feast. During that worship, preachers spoke to the assembly seeking to find ways that would help the assembled understand what God had done and what God would have them do. Combining exposition of a biblical text with classical rhetoric, Melito, a late second-century bishop in Asia Minor, sought to declare a new Christian Passover:

> The scripture from the Hebrew Exodus has been read
>   and the words of the mystery have been plainly stated,
>   how the sheep is sacrificed
>   and how the people is saved
>   and how Pharaoh is scourged through the mystery.
> Understand, therefore, beloved,
>   how it is new and old,
>   eternal and temporary,
>   perishable and imperishable
>   mortal and immortal, this mystery of the Pascha.
>   (Edwards, 19–20)

Throughout the centuries, following the example of Mary Magdalene, Peter, Paul, and Melito, preaching has been old and new, seeking to proclaim the eternal and imperishable with the temporary and perishable words of mortals. How are we to shape preaching as we move into the twenty-first century? How can we combine the old and the new? What must the new look like?

God is doing new things all around us. The Spirit of God is blowing in and through the lives of people and is calling us to speak to those lives, to challenge and encourage them to live into the gospel reign. How are we to speak that life-giving word in a world far different from anything our preaching ancestors ever imagined? God is always doing new things, life-giving actions all about us. How can we, in our preaching and worship, do a new thing while still holding on to the tradition that has nurtured us for so long?

The Spirit of God is continually moving over the face of the earth, renewing us, challenging us, blowing us in new directions. Preaching continues to move the hearts and minds of God's people, and like those who went before us, we are being called to shape God's message for our time and our people. We have been created in the image of a creating God. How must we respond to the challenges and opportunities that confront and call us as preachers today?

It is my hope that this chapter will challenge you and serve to begin essential and ongoing conversations among you, your preaching colleagues, and those to whom you preach. I cannot cover all of the issues and questions that we know are facing preachers. I have, however, identified and highlighted several important issues that I and others who preach have come to perceive as challenging, pressing, and engaging in contemporary preaching.

COMMUNICATING THE GOSPEL: A MULTISENSORY APPROACH

Frequently attributed to Francis of Assisi is the admonition, "Preach the gospel always. If necessary, use words." Through most of this book we have been focusing on the words that we choose to preach the gospel. Words are essential to the preaching and teaching of the church. We must not neglect them. Nevertheless, we must also be challenged by the realization that there are many ways, in addition to our words, that we are preaching the good news. We must be about tasting, touching, hearing, and seeing. We must look for all of the ways that we can sing God's praises and proclaim God's holy word.

Jesus taught us this lesson when he directed our attention to the "preaching" of the widow in the temple (Mark 12:41–44). By offering her small coins, she gave all that she had. While she spoke no words, her actions preached to the world that we are to give everything we have to the God who created and loves us, even unto death.

This is an exciting time in which to be a preacher. So many new resources are available to enliven and enrich our preaching and worship. Computers and the Internet connect the preacher and the congregation to the rest of the body of Christ in ways that those who went before us could never have dreamed possible. How might our preaching move beyond the limits of words alone? How might we draw on more of our senses—not only hearing and sight, but touch, taste, and smell as well?

The House of the Lord

"You prepare a table before me. . . . and I shall dwell in the house of the LORD my whole life long" (Ps. 23:5a, 6b). The environment in which we speak has a profound impact on what we say and how we say it. If you are trying to speak with someone in a noisy place, you must speak more loudly. Preaching and leading worship for thousands of people will necessarily be very different from a small group worshiping in an upper room. Therefore, we must think, not only about preparing our sermon, but about how we and our community will prepare and shape the space in which we worship and preach so that space will also communicate the gospel.

The early church gathered surreptitiously in the homes of the believers. Meeting around the table of the owner of the home, they shared a meal, celebrated the Lord's feast, and witnessed to the good news of what God had done in Jesus Christ. They declared to one another that, whether they had seen him or not, they did believe that he was risen and that their lives had been changed because of this. Luke joyously announces that "day by day the Lord added to their number those who were being saved" (Acts 2:47b). This was good news, but it also meant that it becomes increasingly difficult to worship in someone's dining room.

With the conversion of Constantine, the faithful were able to move out into the open and began to worship in large, public spaces. They also began to ask, what should our worship space look like? How should we design and build "the house of the Lord"? Throughout the centuries different communities have answered that question in vastly different ways, from the vast expanse of a Gothic cathedral, to the gloriously decorated baroque church, to the simplicity of the meetinghouse of the Society of Friends. Each community, in its own way sought to discover what space would best communicate the good news that God has created and redeemed us and has "spread a table before us."

We must think about the message that our worship space communicates. Does it invite us into the presence of the God who has called us together with inclusion and hospitality, as well as convey a sense of awe and mystery? Does it tell the stories of the faith and those who have gone before us through the use of images? Are we able to recognize that we are in "the house of the Lord"?

There has been a trend recently to remove all symbols of the faith, in an effort to make newcomers welcome and comfortable by creating worship spaces that are indistinguishable from theaters or concert halls. What message do we preach when "the house of the Lord" looks much like a movie theater, concert hall, or convention center?

The space around you as you preach amplifies and reinforces your message. When you speak about the table that God has spread for us in the midst of the enemies that would destroy us, is the table large and substantial? Can they see the table around which they will gather? When you preach about baptism through which we are welcomed into the body of Christ and the community of the faithful, can they see the font or pool? Is it a major visual symbol that proclaims the good news that "all of us who have been baptized into Christ

Jesus were baptized into his death? Therefore we have been buried with him by baptism into death, so that, just as Christ was raised from the death by the glory of the Father, so we too might walk in the newness of life" (Rom. 6:3–4).

It is God who spreads the table, God, in whom "there is no longer Jew or Greek . . . slave or free . . . male or female" (Gal. 3:28). From beginning to end, through our preaching and our worship, we must think about how we welcome friends and strangers alike. How can we preach about all being welcome in Christ if a person in a wheelchair is not able to enter our worship space? Do we have multiple ways that people are able to find out what time we worship? Do they know how to enter the buildings and how to find the space in which the community will be gathering? Do people greet them and draw them into the worshiping community? Through each moment and each action, our thoughtfulness and hospitality preach our message on many different layers.

Touching All the Senses

"O taste and see that the LORD is good" (Ps. 34:8a). Another layer on which the gospel message can be apprehended is that of our senses. Our worship, our preaching must be savory and mouthwatering. Too often today the preaching and worship of the church has "lost its taste" (Matt. 5:13a). We do not want to be "thrown out and trampled under foot" (Matt. 5:13b). What must we do to retain our saltiness, to be the salt of the earth? A challenge for preachers today is to refine and cultivate, not only on the words that they use, but all of the other ways they and their community communicate the gospel.

Does our worship touch all of the senses? People will hear our prayers and preaching, the sound of the choir or musical group. What do people see? How have we adorned the space in which we gather? What do people touch—the chair on which they sit, the floors on which they walk or kneel, the hands of sisters and brothers in the faith extended in greeting? Do they taste the Lord in the finest wine/juice and bread? I have often thought that we should have a small oven just off our worship space. Then, when people enter the church to celebrate the supper of the Lord, they will be able to smell fresh bread baking.

If we are attentive, people will hear, see, touch, taste, and smell the goodness of God. They will hear the gospel message in different ways through different paths.

The New Stained Glass

The greatest challenges and opportunities to engage the senses today lie in the use of visual media and presentational technology. We are living through a technological revolution. How can we use these resources creatively and responsibly? The technological advances that allow us to project words and images during our preaching and our worship are not neutral. They reorganize our senses and our ways of thinking. We must reflect upon these changes as we think about incorporating them into our preaching and our worship.

Again, think about the space in which you will preach. What will it look like? Will it look like a traditional church? Will it be filled with paintings, sculptures, and stained glass, or will the windows be clear and the walls plain? Will you be preaching in a space that even fits anyone's traditional definition of church? Will you be preaching in a theater or an open space with flexible seating?

As we think about the use of images and film clips in our preaching, we need to step back and think about why some churches are highly decorated and others profoundly plain. Why do communities choose the worship space they do? We need to examine the theological differences that led to these differences. The theological understandings that gave rise to the Gothic cathedral or the Quaker meetinghouse are still with us. They will have a significant affect on your congregation's reception as you think about using images and film clips in your preaching, because the acceptance of images has always been controversial in church history, and the rejection of images is not easily overcome. Setting up a screen and video projector in the worship space will not necessarily guarantee acceptance by your listeners.

The early church began incorporating images into its worship spaces as soon as they could claim spaces of their own. Drawing on Greek, Roman, and Jewish images, the early Christians began to develop their own iconography. They filled their churches, like Solomon's temple before them, with flowers and vines: "[Solomon] carved the walls of the house all around about with carved engravings of cherubim, palm tress, and open flowers" (1 Kgs. 6:29). They used fish to signify the Christian community and lambs to remind them Jesus was the lamb of God who took away the sins of the world. They produced paintings and mosaics that depicted the biblical stories and the saints of the church. And they developed a sophisticated christological iconography portraying the nativity, the passion, the resurrection, ascension, and enthronement of Christ. Images helped them to proclaim that this Jesus was the Son of the living God.

Over the centuries the church grew. More and more Christians meant that they must have larger and larger spaces in which to worship. Larger and larger churches meant more and more space to decorate. In the eighth century a controversy arose over the appropriate use of images, in particular, images of Christ. There was, after all, the Mosaic injunction against images: "You shall not make for yourself an idol, whether in the form of anything that is in heaven above, or that is on the earth beneath, or that is in the water under the earth. You shall not bow down to them or worship them" (Exod. 20:4–5a).

Some believed that visual images were yet another way that we came to know Jesus: "Blessed are the eyes that see what you see!" (Luke 10:23). "The Word became flesh and lived among us, and we have seen his glory" (John 1:14). Others believed that icons and images were detrimental to the faith, because "faith comes from what is heard, and what is heard comes through the word of Christ" (Rom. 10:17).

The iconoclastic controversy was suppressed in 787, when the Second Council of Nicaea reaffirmed the use of icons. But the debate was far from silenced. The same issues arose once again during the Reformation, when a new group began, once again, to disparage the use of images. Statues were removed and destroyed, stained-glass windows were broken and replaced with clear glass, and images on the walls of churches were covered with whitewash. Hearing the word of God proclaimed in Scripture and sermon, they argued, is the only way to "preach" the faith. With this iconoclastic assault there was no Council's response to counteract their arguments, and the controversy has continued through the intervening centuries. Therefore, the ornateness of baroque ornamentation has stood alongside the simplicity of a Protestant chapel.

Only now are we beginning to see those churches that rejected the use of images in worship explore their possible return. Some do this through the use of banners. Others are filling their worship spaces with projected images in both their worship and preaching.

Why Images?

If you are driving down any highway today, the sight of twin yellow arches that form a stylized M instantly communicates a message to you. You know that if you enter the building that sits at the bottom of that sign, you will be able to buy a certain kind of food. You also know that whether that building is in California, or Idaho, or Maine, the food will be virtually identical. You have seen no word or name, but that sign communicates.

Earlier we explored the use of illustrations in our preaching—stories, metaphors, analogies that enrich and expand our message. Preachers today are beginning to experiment with the addition of visual images in their preaching. Through the use of visual media they are projecting not only key words but images during their sermon. While this may not exactly be new—preachers throughout the centuries often preached in the midst of painting, sculptures, and stained glass—the medium is new and offers the preacher a wider selection of images.

Why might we employ the use of those images or film clips in our preaching? We use images because they are more than simple illustration. Images are another way of learning and communicating. In his work *Visual Thinking*, Rudolf Arnheim examined the split between rational and perceptual thinking. We privilege words and numbers, he argued, because we think that they involve a higher level of reasoning, while the arts—painting, sculpture, dance, and composing—because they are based on perception, "strengthen man's dependence on illusory images" (Arnheim, 2) and are therefore inferior. "The arts are neglected because they are based on perception, and perception is disdained because it is not assumed to involve thought" (Arnheim, 3). Arnheim's project was to demonstrate that the arts are in fact not inferior but, rather, another way of thinking:

> My contention is that the cognitive operations called thinking are not the privilege of mental processes above and beyond perception but the essential ingredients of perception itself. I am referring to such operations as active exploration, selection, grasping of essentials, simplification, abstraction, analysis and synthesis, completion, correction, comparison, problem solving, as well as combining, separating, putting in context. These operations are not the prerogative of any one mental function; they are the manner in which the minds of both man and animal treat cognitive material at any level. There is no basic difference in this respect between what happens when a person looks at the world directly and when he sits with his eyes closed and "thinks." (Arnheim, 13)

Therefore, according to Arnheim and his understanding of "visual thinking," whether we are listening to a sermon about Luke 1:26–39 or viewing Giotto's *Annunciation*, we are grasping, analyzing, comparing, and exploring. The painting challenges us to understand this pivotal moment—about God's presence in the world and Mary's faithful response—as much as an expositional sermon.

Verbal illustrations in preaching are more than mere ornamentation; illustrations, examples, and metaphors are alternate ways of thinking. Likewise, visual images in our preaching—photos and paintings—are more than simple ornamentation; they invite us into a different way of thinking and understanding. We relate differently to an image, processing it and relating to it in a different way. By making use of visual media in our preaching, we are able to expand our vocabulary. When using both words and images, we are able reach people in more ways. That is the crucial concept as we move forward. We must employ words and images together. The images are there to expand and deepen our perception, not to entertain and amuse. Images can do things that words cannot. Likewise, words can communicate information that images cannot.

Challenges arise, therefore, for both the preacher who begins to make use of visual media in his or her preaching and those who are now asked to both listen and watch those sermons. I could devote an entire book to the use of visual images in preaching. I will not do that, but I will introduce you to some of the questions one must begin to explore when thinking about employing this new approach to preaching.

Beginning Questions

Many of you reading this book have already grown accustomed to the use of visual media in preaching and would think it odd to consider preaching without them. For you, my challenge is to think critically about how you do it and what images you employ.

Others of you are worshiping in churches that have not yet begun to incorporate computer generated text and images. The concept of projecting film clips and images may be foreign and somewhat objectionable. I challenge you to consider the possibility. Most of us live in cultures that are growing more and more dependent on images. Whether we are a post literate culture is up for debate. What we know is that many people now spend more time with television/movies/video games than with books/magazines/newspapers. Visual media has become a way to communicate with those for whom this is a major mode of communication, and how we reach them becomes an important challenge for us as we preach. Visual images, as was just noted, also expand our vocabulary. How often do preachers attempt to describe a picture or a place? Why not show rather than tell? This becomes a way to incorporate art into our preaching and worship.

This may be a new dimension of preaching, but many preachers have been incorporating visual media in their sermons for some time. They have been experimenting with the possibilities and have begun to share the fruits of their labors through books, DVDs, and conferences. Take advantage of their insights and recommendations. They will help you to understand that this can greatly enhance your preaching, but it comes at a cost of both money and time. They have also discovered that some things work and some things you should avoid. They will also tell you that you will find that your preaching will become more of a cooperative venture, because this is something that you cannot do alone.

For the last fifty or sixty years preachers have used technology in their preaching. Most of us have grown used to and dependent on electrical amplification of our voice. Now we will have to learn how to work with another form of technology—software programs and projectors that enable us to integrate visual media, whether text or image, into our preaching. We will, therefore, have to think about what projector and screen works best in our worship space and become familiar with the software packages that are available. I will not mention any projectors or software because, as we all know, they change and/or become obsolete altogether too quickly. Instead, I encourage you to cultivate those in your congregation who can help you with these new technological opportunities.

Cost becomes an issue. Can you afford the hardware and software needed to project an image that will be visible to all in your congregation? This is not like trying to show slides in your living room. You need a projector and a screen or screens for a very large space.

Most of you will find people in your congregation who will know how to buy and run the hardware and software that you will need, as well as people who are artistically and liturgically knowledgeable, who will be able to help you identify the images you will use. The use of technology in worship takes more time than the traditional mode of preaching. You cannot write your sermon at the last minute (which of course you wouldn't be doing anyway!). If you are going to use both words and images, you or someone with whom you are working must search for and find the appropriate images, insert them into the program, and work with you to know when to run the film clip or move to the next image.

You will also have to think about the legal dimensions of what you can and cannot show. Many of the film clips and images are covered by copyright law. You must become familiar with and abide by their constraints, the same way you do for quoting the written work of others in your sermons.

You cannot begin to use visual media in worship and in preaching without also understanding that many in your congregation will need to be educated about how to read, interpret, and understand images. As we prepare to use a film clip or image, we will need to ask many of the same questions we ask as we prepare to employ a verbal illustration or example. Can people connect with the image we are projecting? Do they know or understand what it is and why we are using it? We need to think about what images to use and how many, how often. We need to think about what is appropriate to show, and what is not. Is it appropriate to show an image of violence or destruction? Will the image overwhelm what we are trying to say? Think about how people will respond and what they will carry away. We also need to think about the sources of our images. Do we use only the work of European or North American artists? What are the ethnic backgrounds of the people whose pictures we use? Will our listeners/watchers be able to connect with the images we use? As preachers we must learn to incorporate theological, communication, and aesthetic analysis and decision making into our use of images.

There may be people in your congregation whose eyesight is failing, who will not be able to see what you project on the screen. How will you preach your sermon in such a way that they will not be missing a significant dimension of your message?

How do we reshape our worship so that we involve more of the senses? That is a significant challenge to preachers and worship leaders, but it is not the only one. In the remainder of this chapter I will introduce several other issues that I believe are challenging and will challenge preachers.

YESTERDAY, TODAY, AND TOMORROW

As preachers we are called to tell the old, old story. We turn to Scripture to hear the word of God, to proclaim the good news, to teach about what God has done for God's people yesterday. But God's grace continues to fill the lives of people. God continues to do new things, to redeem and deliver. Another challenge for preaching today is to maintain a balance between what God did in the past, what God is doing today, and what lies in God's future.

Increasingly, preachers are finding that those listening to their sermons are not familiar with the Bible or with the church's story. How we incorporate teaching about the Bible and about our faith story must become a crucial dimension of our preaching as we move forward. People need to hear the "old, old story" because it provides them with the foundation, the footing of stone, upon which they will build their life of faith and discipleship.

Those who are preaching to younger congregations report that they are searching for more, not less, Scripture in the preaching of the church. But they are also finding that an in-depth exploration of Scripture must be connected to one's faith life and not an abstract, academic approach. How to incorporate Scripture in such a way that you both educate and connect will continue to be a challenge. Our preaching must include Bible study, but it is not *just* a Bible study.

Likewise, our sermons must include life lessons. Our preaching must connect with where people are and the questions and concerns they bring to our sermon. But we must make sure that our sermons are more than "life-coaching." We raise our family, work, make decisions as Christians, not because the life of faith will make us healthier and wealthier, but because it helps us to love God with all our heart, and all our soul, and all our strength, and all our mind. What we preach must grow out of Scripture and our faith tradition, not only the insights of psychology and economists.

Finally, we must remember that not only is God part of our past and present; God is leading us into the future. As preachers we are called to be prophetic. Our preaching must challenge all of us to live into God's future. We must not limit our focus to what we are doing in the here and now.

THE FLEXIBLE PREACHER

I teach with a pastor who serves a large suburban congregation. On Sunday morning they have four services, each of which is different. The services range from a traditional service with traditional hymns and music, to a blended worship, to a casual contemporary service with contemporary music, visual media, and a more relaxed tone. His congregation began to understand that the people have different expectations and different understandings about how to worship God. Some wanted a connection with the way their community had been worshiping for a long time; they preferred a more quiet atmosphere. Others had come to appreciate new songs and new ways of doing things; they looked for a worship service that was livelier and where they would not feel that they had to "dress up."

Four different services means planning four different worship events, as well as writing and shaping four different sermons. The sermon crafted for the congregation that attends the traditional service early on Sunday morning will not meet the expectations or needs of those who attend the casual, contemporary praise service. While the pastor will develop one theme for the day, he will have to approach that theme from four different ways.

His experience is an example of a major challenge facing all preachers today, the need to be flexible. All preachers need to learn to prepare for a wide range of service types, from the formal and traditional to the casual and contemporary. They will also need to be ready to communicate to a wide variety of people, different ethnic backgrounds, different age groups, and so on. You cannot think that you can develop one kind of sermon for one kind of worship service. Those days are long past. Flexibility is a skill and attitude all preachers need to develop.

THE BODY OF CHRIST

Finally, think about the ways that your preaching nurtures and develops an understanding of what it means to be the body of Christ. More and more people have not grown up within a Christian community. Not only do they not know what it means to be a follower of Christ; they do not know what it means to be part of a faith community. Through our preaching we pass on the tradition of the faith, we help people come to understand what it means to live a life of faith, but we also help to weave the connections between people.

Hospitality, therefore, must be a hallmark of our worship and our preaching. We cannot assume that people know the stories and the traditions of the faith. In our preaching we must always be teaching and expanding their knowledge. We must also reach out to all people, no matter who they are or where they have come from. Christ welcomes all to the table, and we can do no less.

Perhaps our preaching might live into the vision of the body of Christ by drawing more into the conversation. John McClure, in his book *The Round-table Pulpit*, challenges preachers to involve members of the congregation in the sermon preparation process: "Collaborative preaching is a method that involves members of a congregation in sermon brainstorming. Preaching becomes a 'rhetoric of listening' through which the biblical interpretations and theological insights of the congregation find a voice in the pulpit" (McClure, 7). While the preacher will provide the single voice for the group, more members of the body will have been involved in planning and developing the message.

What if we wish to explore the possibility of more voices in the sermon itself? Lucy Rose begins an exploration of conversational preaching in her book *Sharing the Word: Preaching in the Roundtable Church*. Can we live into a concept of preaching, she writes, that is "nonhierarchical, heuristic, and communal . . . rooted in a relationship of connectedness and mutuality between preacher and worshipers" (Rose, 3)? Can we "invite everyone to participate in the life-giving conversation" that is the preaching of the church? What happens to the preaching and the worship of the church if all are challenged to "accept responsibility for being interpreters of life and faith, accountable in these areas to God, one another, and the larger household of faith"? (Rose, 89)

I have preached with a worshiping community that sat at round tables all throughout the worship service. Although mine was the only voice as I preached the sermon, following my message they explored and discussed my sermon. I would encourage you to experiment with this or a similar format.

The preaching of the entire community and mutual faith sharing might be a wonderful vision. Unfortunately, logistics and reality often challenge that vision. If one is preaching to a relatively small group of people who both know each other and are comfortable sharing with one another, as was my experience in the community that regularly "preached" that way, you may be able to engage in a more conversational style of preaching. That becomes difficult, however, when you have a much larger group. Space makes sharing more difficult, as does the hesitance of people to speak before a crowd. The preacher must also be prepared, when opening up the conversation, for people who love to monopolize the conversation or who have rather odd ideas that might not be such a good idea to share with the wider congregation. How one is to manage a conversational sermon becomes an important concern.

DOING A NEW THING

It would be most helpful for preachers if they, like H. G. Wells's time traveler, could go into the future and see which "new things" worked and which didn't. What should we be adopting, and what should we ignore?

As you move forward in your preaching life, you will constantly be asking yourself these questions. There will be trends and fads that, although they seem fascinating at the time, will go out of style as quickly as they come in. It is important for you as a preacher to look both ways, to the past as well as the future. Firmly ground yourself in the traditional preaching skills, but be open to new ways of communicating and new ways of sharing the good news. God is doing new things. We should be ready to do new things as well.

READ MORE ABOUT IT

Arnheim, Rudolf. *Visual Thinking*. Berkeley: University of California Press, 1969.

Jensen, Richard. *Envisioning the Word: The Use of Visual Images in Preaching*. Minneapolis: Fortress Press, 2005.

McClure, John. *The Round-table Pulpit: Where Leadership and Preaching Meet*. Nashville: Abingdon, 1995.

Rose, Lucy. *Sharing the Word: Preaching in the Roundtable Church*. Louisville, KY: Westminster John Knox Press, 1997.

Epilogue

Workers in the Field

"The harvest is plentiful, but the laborers are few; therefore ask the Lord of the harvest to send out laborers into his harvest.

Luke 10:2

The ability not only to plant crops but to harvest them is an image of peace and prosperity that occurs frequently in the Old Testament. A wandering people, sent into exile, knew the frustration of building houses and planting crops, only to discover that others would enjoy the fruits of their labors. Others, not they themselves, would gather at the table under the sturdy roof that they had constructed, eating the fruits and grains that they had planted. All too often this echos a dimension of the preaching life—we do not always see the fruition of our labors.

Therefore, in closing, I offer you one final challenge. We, as preachers, must learn to live with this reality of the preaching life. We have been called and sent out to proclaim the good news. We are asked to join in the preparation of the soil and the planting of the gospel seeds, but, because we or our listeners move on, we are not always able to see the plants that flourish and bear fruit from those efforts. In the end, preaching is an exercise in hope and trust. We must hope that our words will make a difference, and we must trust in God's oversight.

While some might find this frustrating, I would remind you that we must take the long view of our work. We should not expect to see results immediately because, while we are an important part of God's work, we provide, nonetheless, a tiny fraction of that ongoing work. The work of the Holy Spirit has been going on long before we became a part of the effort and will continue after we move on to other fields. Our preparing, planting, and watering are only moments in God's ongoing process, and this understanding should be freeing and liberating.

We are called to do our best in the moment. Our efforts at preparing, at planting, at watering, and at building are crucial, but it is not all up to us. We are to preach the good news of God's love, but all that we are, all that we do, and all that will be are always in the hands of the one who gave us life and gave it abundantly. Ultimately, we must always remember that our ministry and our preaching are not up to us; they are up to God.

You have been created and called by a God of grace and love. May you answer your call as worker, minister, and prophet with faithfulness and love, allowing God's grace to enter and do the rest.

> I trust in the steadfast love of God
>   forever and ever.
> I will thank you forever,
>   because of what you have done.
> In the presence of the faithful
>   I will proclaim your name, for it is good.
>   Psalm 52:8b-9

Works Cited

Allen, Ronald J., ed. *Patterns of Preaching: A Sermon Sampler*. St. Louis: Chalice Press, 1998.

Allen, Ronald, Barbara Shires Blaisdell, and Scott Black Johnston. *Theology for Preaching: Authority, Truth and Knowledge of God in a Postmodern Ethos*. Nashville: Abingdon, 1997.

Aristotle. *On Rhetoric: A Theory of Civic Discourse*. Trans. George A. Kennedy. New York: Oxford University Press, 1991.

Arnheim, Rudolf. *Visual Thinking*. Berkeley: University of California Press, 1969.

Augustine. *On Christian Doctrine*. Trans. D. W. Robertson Jr. Upper Saddle River, NJ: Prentice Hall, 1958.

Bartow, Charles. *Effective Speech Communication in Leading Worship*. Nashville: Abingdon, 1988.

Buber, Martin. *I and Thou*. New York: Charles Scribner's Sons, 1958.

Burke, Kenneth. "Psychology and Form." In *Counter-Statement*. Berkeley: University of California Press, 1968.

Buttrick, David. *Homiletic: Moves and Structures*. Philadelphia: Fortress Press, 1987.

Campbell, Karlyn Kohrs. *The Rhetorical Act*. Belmont, CA: Wadsworth Publishing, 1996.

Childers, Jana. *Performing the Word: Preaching as Theatre*. Nashville: Abingdon, 1998.

Childers, Jana, ed. *Birthing the Sermon: Women Preachers on the Creative Process*. St. Louis: Chalice Press, 2001.

Chrysostom. *Treatise concerning the Priesthood*. Book V, 1–6. Trans. W. R. W. Stephens. In *A Select Library of the Nicene and Post-Nicene Fathers of The Christian Church*, ed. Philip Schaff, vol. ix. New York: Christian Literature Co., 1889.

Cicero. *De inventione, De optimo genere, Oratorum topica*. Trans. H. M. Hubbell. Loeb Classical Library. Cambridge: Harvard University Press, 1976.

Clader, Linda L. *Voicing the Vision: Imagination and Prophetic Preaching*. Harrisburg, PA: Morehouse Publishing, 2003.

Corbett, Edward. *Classical Rhetoric for the Modern Student*. New York: Oxford University Press, 1990.

Craddock, Fred B. *As One without Authority*. Nashville: Abingdon, 1986.

Crawford, Evans. *The Hum: Call and Response in African American Preaching*. Nashville: Abingdon, 1995.

Cunningham, David S. *These Three Are One: The Practice of Trinitarian Theology*. Malden, MA: Blackwell, 1999.

Davis, Bill. *Mass Appeal*. New York: Dramatists Play Service, 2002.

Dulles, Avery. *Models of Revelation*. Maryknoll, NY: Orbis Press, 1996.

Edwards, O. C., Jr. *A History of Preaching*. Nashville: Abingdon, 2004.

Elliot, Mark Barger. *Creative Styles of Preaching*. Louisville, KY: Westminster John Knox Press, 2000.

Fahnestock, Jeanne. "Modern Arrangement." In *Encyclopedia of Rhetoric*, ed. Thomas Sloane, 44–50. Oxford: Oxford University Press, 2001.

Gadamer, Hans-Georg. *Truth and Method*. Trans. Joel Weinsheimer and Donald G. Marshall. New York: Continuum, 1994.

Geertz, Clifford. *The Interpretation of Cultures: Selected Essays*. New York: Basic Books, 1973.

Geest, Hans van der. *Presence in the Pulpit*. Trans. Douglas W. Stott. Atlanta: John Knox Press, 1981.

Hedahl, Susan K. *Listening Ministry: Rethinking Pastoral Leadership*. Minneapolis: Fortress Press, 2001.

Hilkert, Mary Catherine. *Naming Grace: Preaching and the Sacramental Imagination*. New York: Continuum, 1997.

Hoefler, Richard Carl. *Creative Preaching and Oral Writing*. Lima, OH: C.S.S. Publishing, 1992.

Hogan, Lucy, and Robert Reid. *Connecting with the Congregation: Rhetoric and the Art of Preaching*. Nashville: Abingdon, 1999.

hooks, bell. *remembered rapture: the writer at work*. New York: Henry Holt and Co., 1999.

Jacks, G. Robert. *Getting the Word Across: Speech Communication for Pastors and Lay Leaders*. Grand Rapids: Eerdmans, 1995.

———. *Just Say the Word! Writing for the Ear*. Grand Rapids: Eerdmans, 1996.

Jasper, David. *A Short Introduction to Hermeneutics*. Louisville, KY: Westminster John Knox Press, 2004.

Jensen, Richard. *Envisioning the Word: The Use of Visual Images in Preaching*. Minneapolis: Fortress Press, 2005,

Jeter, Joseph R., Jr., and Ronald J. Allen. *One Gospel, Many Ears: Preaching for Different Listeners in the Congregation*. St. Louis: Chalice Press, 2002.

Johnson, Elizabeth. *She Who Is: The Mystery of God in Feminist Theological Discourse*. New York: Crossroad, 1996.

Kennedy, George A. *Classical Rhetoric and Its Christian and Secular Tradition: From Ancient to Modern Times*. Chapel Hill: University of North Carolina Press, 1980.

LaCugna, Catherine Mowry. *God for Us: The Trinity and Christian Life*. San Francisco: Harper San Francisco, 1991.

———. "God in Communion with Us." In *Freeing Theology: The Essentials of Theology in Feminist Perspective*, ed. Catherine Mowry LaCugna. San Francisco: HarperCollins, 1993.

———. "The Trinitarian Mystery of God." In *Systematic Theology: Roman Catholic Perspectives, Vol. I*, ed. Francis Schüssler Fiorenza and John P. Galvin, 152–92. Minneapolis: Fortress Press, 1991.

Linklater, Kristin. *Freeing the Natural Voice*. New York: Drama Book, 1976.

Long, Thomas. "And How Shall They Hear? The Listener in Contemporary Preaching." In Gail R. O'Day and Thomas G. Long, ed. *Listening to the Word: Studies in Honor of Fred B. Craddock*. Nashville: Abingdon, 1993.

Lowry, Eugene L. *The Homiletical Plot*. Atlanta: John Knox Press, 1980.

Lucas, Stephen. *The Art of Public Speaking*. Boston: McGraw Hill, 2004.

McClure, John S. *The Round-table Pulpit: Where Leadership and Preaching Meet*. Nashville: Abingdon, 1995.

Moltmann, Jürgen. *The Trinity and the Kingdom: The Doctrine of God*. Minneapolis: Fortress Press, 1993.

Nieman, James R., and Thomas G. Rogers. *Preaching to Every Pew: Cross-Cultural Strangers*. Minneapolis: Fortress Press, 2001.

Norris, Kathleen. *Amazing Grace: A Vocabulary of Faith*. New York: Riverhead Books, 1998.

Perelman, Chaim, and L. Olbrechts-Tyteca. *The New Rhetoric: A Treatise on Argumentation*. Notre Dame: University of Notre Dame Press, 1971.

Peters, Ted. *God as Trinity: Relationality and Temporality in Divine Life*. Louisville, KY: Westminster/John Knox Press, 1993.

Placher, William, ed. *Essentials of Christian Theology*. Louisville, KY: Westminster John Knox Press, 2003.

Resner, André. *Preacher and Cross: Person and Message in Theology and Rhetoric*. Grand Rapids: Eerdmans, 1999.

Rose, Lucy. *Sharing the Word: Preaching in the Roundtable Church*. Louisville, KY: Westminster John Knox Press, 1997.

Sayers, Dorothy. "The Dogma Is the Drama." In *The Whimsical Christian*. New York: Macmillan Publishing, 1978.

———. *The Man Born to Be King*. Grand Rapids: Eerdmans, 1979.

Schlafer, David. *What Makes This Day Different? Preaching Grace on Special Occasions*. Cambridge, MA: Cowley Publications, 1998.

Tanner, Kathryn. *Theories of Culture: A New Agenda for Theology*. Minneapolis: Fortress Press, 1997.

Taylor, Barbara Brown. *The Preaching Life*. Cambridge: Cowley Publications, 1993.

Tiffany, Frederick, and Sharon Ringe. *Biblical Interpretation: A Road Map*. Nashville: Abingdon, 1996.

Tisdale, Leonora Tubbs. *Preaching as Local Theology and Folk Art*. Minneapolis: Fortress Press, 1997.

Toulmin, Stephen. *The Uses of Argument*. Cambridge: Cambridge University Press, 1986.

Troeger, Thomas. *Imagining a Sermon*. Nashville: Abingdon, 1990.

Viorst, Judith. *Alexander and the Terrible, Horrible, No Good, Very Bad Day*. New York: Aladdin Books, 1972.

Wallace, James. *Preaching to the Hungers of the Heart*. Collegeville, MN: Liturgical Press, 2002.

Ward, Richard F. *Speaking of the Holy: The Art of Communication in Preaching*. St. Louis: Chalice Press, 2001.

Waznak, Robert. *An Introduction to the Homily*. Collegeville, MN: Liturgical Press, 1998.

Weber, Max. *The Theory of Social and Economic Organization*. Trans. A. M. Henderson and Talcott Parsons. New York: Free Press, 1947.

Wiles, M. F. "Origen as Biblical Scholar." In *The Cambridge History of the Bible: From the Beginnings to Jerome*, ed. P. R. Ackroyd and C. F. Evans. Cambridge: Cambridge University Press, 1978.

Willimon, William. *Calling and Character: Virtues of the Ordained Life*. Nashville: Abingdon, 2000.